ALL
IN A
LIFETIME

"ENGAGING . . . further testimony to
the human capacity for survival,
growth and transformation. It doesn't
happen often these days, but with Dr.
Ruth it is true: Behind the veneer of
celebrity is a real person."

—Washington Post Book World

■   ■

"A FULL-SCALE REVELATION . . . Dr.
Ruth is nothing if not lovable, and one
can hear her bubbling German-Jewish
accent behind every paragraph."

—Kirkus Reviews

■   ■

more . . .

"Dr. Ruth writes with honesty and humor, and comes across as a gutsy lady who deserves the happiness she enjoys."

—*Chattanooga Times*

■ ■

"JAM-PACKED WITH FASCINATING DETAILS ABOUT HER REMARKABLE LIFE, both before and after she became America's most popular sex therapist . . . Dr. Ruth is as open about her own life as she is in giving advice to others . . . in this engaging book."

—*Publishers Weekly*

■ ■

"Her characteristic sense of humor shines through, providing amusement and insight."

—*Houston Post*

■ ■

"Probably the leading psychosexual therapist of our time, the cheerful Dr. Ruth Westheimer has looked into her own past . . . and produced a moving look at what it meant to be a Jewish child in Europe at the time of the Holocaust."

—*Dayton Daily*

■   ■

"HIP! HIP! HOORAY! FOR THIS BOOK ABOUT THE HUMAN SPIRIT ENDURES. What *All in a Lifetime* manages to do is make you enjoy [her] success just as much as she does. You practically want to stand up and cheer her glee as she collects the perks and financial rewards that have come to her."

—*West Chester Sunday Local News*

■   ■

"FASCINATING, SURPRISING, AND INTERESTING."

—*Wilmington Sunday News Journal*

Also by Dr. Ruth Westheimer

Dr. Ruth's Guide to Good Sex

First Love:
A Young People's Guide to Sexual Information

Dr. Ruth's Guide for Married Lovers

Published by
WARNER BOOKS

ALL IN A LIFETIME

An Autobiography by

Dr. Ruth K. Westheimer

with Ben Yagoda

WARNER BOOKS

A Warner Communications Company

WARNER BOOKS EDITION

Grateful acknowledgement is given to *The New York Times* to
quote from "A Voice of 'Sexual Literacy'" by George Dullea,
© 1981 by The New York Times Company.
Reprinted by permission.

Cover design by Paul Gamarello
Cover photo by Ken Nahoum
Book design by H. Roberts

Warner Books, Inc.
666 Fifth Avenue
New York, N.Y. 10103

 A Warner Communications Company

Printed in the United States of America

This book was originally published in hardcover by Warner Books.

First Printed in Paperback: November, 1988

10 9 8 7 6 5 4 3 2 1

I dedicate this autobiography to my beloved parents and grandparents, who in an indescribable sacrifice sent me, their only child and grandchild, to safety and who perished in concentration camps.

The set of values, the joie de vivre, and the positive outlook they instilled in me live on in my life and the new family I have created to carry on their traditions.

Acknowledgments

In addition to the individuals mentioned in this autobiography, I have a long list of friends, relatives, colleagues, clients, listeners, readers, and viewers to thank for their encouragement and constructive criticism. They all have helped me in my endeavors. I wish I could thank all of you by name.

I am grateful to the terrific professional and technical staff of the television and newspaper syndication King Features-Hearst Corporation under the leadership of Frank Bennack, Bruce Paisner, and Joe D'Angelo; the Lifetime Cable Network and its president Tom Burchill; the NBC radio network under the stewardship of its president Randy Bongarten.

I'd also like to thank: Marga and Michael Miller, Ezra Nothman (Putz) from Israel, Ilse Wyler-Weil, Pierre Lehu, Susan Brown, John Lollos, Larry Angelo, Al Kaplan, Dale Ordes, Gigi Simeone, Lou Lieberman, and John A. Silberman, who all helped significantly in the writing of this book;

Helen Singer Kaplan, M.D., Ph.D., who has given her best in training me as a sex therapist;

Rabbi Robert Lehman, Rabbi Leonard Kravitz, Rabbi Selig Salkowitz, Frederick C. Herman, Julius and Marguerite Westheimer, Evelyn and Nathan Kravetz, Ph.D., Arthur Snyder, M.D., William Sweeney, M.D., Else Katz, Vincent Facchino, Nicole Harris, Avi Feinglass, Harvey Gardner, Hirsch Cohen, Dean Gordon, Martin Herman, Fred Zeller, Lieselotte Hilb, Fred Moser, Marcella and Tullio DiGiorgi, and Alfred A. Häsler, who all have an important part in my life.

And Mike Glaser, Cliff Rubin, Olena Smulka, Mary Cuadrado, Marga and Bill Kunreuther, who helped organize my time and space during this special time of writing this book.

This is my fourth book with Warner Books and as always the Warner staff, Bernard Shir-Cliff, Harvey-Jane Kowal, Margery Schwartz, Steve Boldt, chairman of the board William Sarnoff, and president Larry Kirshbaum, were superb.

Dr. Mark J. Blechner, therapist *extraordinaire*, helped me shine a light on my early years, which I had always kept hidden in darkness.

Ben Yagoda not only made this difficult task as much a pleasure as was possible with his writing skills, patience, and understanding, but has become a close friend.

Those who sow in tears will reap in joy.

Psalm 126:5

prologue

1939

My name was Karola Siegel. I was ten years old. The day was January 5, 1939, and I was at the railroad station in Frankfurt, Germany, saying good-bye to my family.

I didn't know when I would see them next, nor did I know that I would one day have a new country, a new family, and a new name—Ruth Westheimer. All I knew was that six weeks before, early in the morning after a night when I had slept between my parents in their bed, my father was taken away from our apartment in Frankfurt. There was a knocking at the door, and into the apartment walked several big men wearing shiny boots. My mother cried, but said nothing. I was terribly frightened and started to cry, too. They told me to be still. The men were polite—there was no hitting, nothing brutal—but they insisted that my father come with them. And so he did. My grandmother was wearing a long skirt that went all the way to the floor; she took out some money from the seam of the skirt and gave it to the men, telling them to take care of my father. I saw him walk out of the house, slightly bent, bespectacled, mustachioed, short, slender. From behind their drawn curtains, our neighbors peeked out and watched him. At the curb was a big truck holding some other men. I remember that the truck's engine made a lot of noise as it idled. Before climbing in, my father turned around and waved; he tried to smile, but he couldn't manage it. There was too much pain in his face.

My mother, my grandmother (my father's mother), and I (I had no brothers or sisters) each went into separate rooms. It was deathly silent in the apartment—after the initial outburst, we had all stopped crying. That was not only because we were all still in shock, but also because we were all good German Jews—more German than the Germans, as the saying goes, and certainly not ones to make an excessive display of emotion.

It was the same in the days that followed. I remember making a decision not to talk about my father, so as not to upset my mother and grandmother. Before, the two of them had many little disagreements and arguments. Now, with this shared worry, I noticed that they got along much better.

Chanukah came a couple of weeks later. This had always been one of my favorite Jewish holidays—I especially loved the potato pancakes we would eat. But this year, for the first time in my life, my father wasn't home to light the candles on the menorah on each of the eight nights. I had to do it myself, which made me very sad.

Every night before going to bed I used to say the Shema, the most important prayer in the Jewish religion—"Hear, O Israel, The Lord Our God, The Lord Is One." After my father was taken away I would end the prayer by saying, "Dear God, watch over my dear sweet daddy and send him home." Even before my father was gone, my mother used to lie with me in my bed, which was in a sleeping alcove off my parents' room, until I fell asleep. She still did so, but I missed seeing my father in his bed, reading or praying. Some nights I climbed into bed with my mother to be comforted.

One night, about five weeks after my father was taken away, my mother and grandmother came into my room and sat down on the bed. They told me I was to join a "Kinder transport," a group of German Jewish children going to Switzerland. I knew that some bad things were happening to the Jews in Germany, and not only because of my father's arrest. We didn't go to synagogue anymore because it had been burned to the ground, and about a week before my father had been taken away, classes at my school had stopped. But I didn't want to leave home, and I said so. I started crying and put my hands over my ears so that I wouldn't hear what they were saying. I had only been away from home once, to a children's camp during one summer, and I hadn't liked it at all, mostly because I was a very bad eater and they forced me to eat more than I wanted to.

My mother and grandmother said that if I went to Switzerland, then my father could get out of the detention camp where he was being held and come back home to Frankfurt. They told me that Mathilde, my best friend, would be going on the train. And then they told me—and I remember this very clearly—how much good chocolate there was in Switzerland, and that I would be well taken care of, and that they would all come and pick me up soon. I still didn't want to go. But a few days later they showed me a letter my father had written, from a place that I later found out was called Buchenwald. He said, "It would make me feel much better if Karola would go to Switzerland." And I said I would go.

One night less than a week later, my mother and grandmother took me by streetcar to the orphanage in Frankfurt where I would spend the night with all the other children going to Switzerland. I don't remember anything about that night. The next day, very early in the morning when it was barely light, all of us, about a hundred children, walked the few blocks to the railroad station. My mother and grandmother had taken the streetcar there to see me off. I had one suitcase with me, with my clothing, some chocolates, a doll, and one item from our house, a washcloth, which I still have today. Later, I was to wish so hard that I had brought more from that house—the Sabbath candlesticks, a dish, anything. But I didn't, because I thought I would be back soon.

At the station it was drizzling and gray. The trains made a lot of noise, the big steam engines hissing and bellowing. Everything looked enormous to me. On the platform the children got ready to board the train to Switzerland—not a special train, but a regularly scheduled route. The youngest were a few years younger than I, the oldest a few years older. They all were making their farewells to their mothers (there were no fathers at the station) as I said good-bye to my mother and grandmother. My mother lifted me up into her arms—even though I was ten years old, I was very small—and said, "Be good. Study hard. It will be nice in Switzerland. And we will see each other again." My grandmother, who was very religious, said, "Trust in the Almighty God."

And then I was on the train. I looked through the window as it pulled out, and I saw my mother and grandmother running after it, waving good-bye, as the train crossed a side street. It was something for my grandmother to be running, because she seemed to me to be very old. I remember that I was very sad, but I didn't cry. I smiled, so that *they* should not be sad.

chapter

1

Considering that I was to become famous as an advocate of contraception, it's somewhat ironic that my parents didn't use it at precisely the point when they should have. My mother, whose name was Irma Hanauer, was from a village in Germany called Wiesenfeld, where her father was a cattle dealer. In 1927, she came to Frankfurt, fifty or sixty miles away, to be a household helper in my father's family's house. And she got pregnant.

I can only imagine the reaction to this news. For an Orthodox Jewish household, it must have been devastating. Abortion was not an option—for which I thank God, because if it had been, I would not be here. (This does not, I should point out, mean that my commitment to a woman's right to choose is any less strong.) So marriage was the only course of action.

But the decision to legalize the love affair could not have resolved all of my parents' problems. My grandmother Selma, a strong-willed, intelligent woman, must have had high hopes for my father, Julius Siegel, who was her only child, and here he was marrying a household worker. (I don't know much about my father's father, because he died the year before I was born.) I once heard that my grandmother didn't even go to the wedding, but I'm not sure if this is true. In any case, it was clear that my father was marrying down. My mother was from the country rather than cosmopolitan Frankfurt, her parents had no money, and she didn't have anything more than a grade-school education—I don't ever remember her reading books. She and my grandmother never really got along, and I'm sure that part of the reason why was Selma's resentment of what my father had done.

In any case, I was born and named Karola Ruth Siegel. Karola is an unusual name in Germany (Karoline is much more common), and I'm not sure whom I was named after —probably a great-grandmother or great-aunt. The biblical Ruth was probably included to make sure I had a Jewish name in addition to the German one.

The tension between my mother and grandmother may have been the reason my mother went back to Wiesenfeld to give birth to me and stayed there for the first year of my life. My father came from Frankfurt on weekends. I don't remember anything about that year, but we went back to Wiesenfeld every vacation after that until I was ten, traveling part of the way by bicycle and part of the way by train. I loved it there. My mother's father, Moses Hanauer, was a good, religious person, but he was not a particularly successful businessman. I remember he once suffered a loss when some people took advantage of him by having him feed their cattle and then not paying him. He was a short, squat man, and he had a big welt on the back of his head from a wound he had suffered in World War I. My grandmother, Pauline, was cheerful, pretty, and short. She came from Berlin, from what was referred to as a "good family." I remember that the men in the village liked to flirt with her.

I always had a good time in Wiesenfeld. Part of the reason why was that I was my grandparents' first grandchild (my mother was the oldest of six brothers and sisters), and so I was a little bit spoiled. I loved being with my mother's siblings, especially her brother Benno, who worked with his father on the farm and loved me dearly, and her youngest sister, Ida, who was only a few years older than I. I looked on her as an unofficial big sister. One day, she was going with a horse and buggy to see some friends in a meadow near the forest, and my grandparents insisted that she take me along. She was upset about this intrusion, and she hit me. She must have felt bad later, because she gave me a necklace of pearls that glowed in the dark.

I also liked being on a farm, with cows and chickens and geese. The geese were particularly important because they figured in one of the great crimes of my life. One summer —I must have been five or six—I suddenly decided that the geese should not be cooped up. So I let them out of their pen into the village. There was a great commotion as everyone had to go gather them back, but I don't think I was punished as much as I might have been had I not been such a favored granddaughter.

Back in Frankfurt, we lived in a ground-floor apartment on Brahmsstrasse, in the northern part of the city. Frankfurt, referred to in Germany as Frankfurt am Main (the city is on the Main River, about nineteen miles east of the Rhine), had a population of more than half a million. It was a major commercial center, the home of the Rothschild banking empire, as well as the birthplace of Goethe. The city was very aware of its cultural heritage. For example, although our neighborhood was lower-middle-class, all of the streets were named after composers.

Unlike the streets in Wiesenfeld, Brahmsstrasse was paved and had sidewalks. It was lined with four-story red brick row houses, with shutters on the windows (and it is unchanged today). Farther north of us was a Jewish cemetery, across the street was a Catholic hospital, and at the end of the block was a small park with swings, a slide, a sandbox, and benches. It was covered with old, old chestnut trees. My fond memories of that park may be why I love chestnuts today, especially marrons glacés.

The park and the chestnut trees were also instrumental in one of the major projects of my childhood. In the park I collected june bugs, which I took home and kept in a shoe box. I gave them lettuce to eat and fallen leaves from the chestnut trees as their bed. I must have collected about ten of them, and I remember being very sad when one of them died; it was lying on its back with its feet up in the air. Now, why I accepted this arrangement but balked at the geese being kept in a pen, I can't tell you.

At the far corner of the park was a little store, which was also a significant place in my world. We'd buy our household necessities there, but what I really liked were the candies—especially the tiny ones of all colors that would come out of a little walking stick, and *Gummibärchen*, little teddy bears made out of candy. They also had a wonderful chocolate-covered pastry with whipped cream inside, *Mohrenkopf*.

Our apartment consisted of four rooms—my parents' bedroom (with a sleeping alcove for me), a room crammed with the notions that my father sold for a living, my grandmother's bedroom, which we also used as a living room, and a kitchen. The apartment was my grandparents' before my parents were married, and with four people it was a little crowded. The furniture was old-fashioned and not at all elegant. There was a long hallway, down which I used to roller-skate and ride my wooden scooter. The backyard had grass and flowers and long lines where all the people in the building hung up their wash—they were each allowed to use a common laundry room on certain days.

I tended to be spoiled in Frankfurt as well as in Wiesenfeld. After initially being upset that my father had married the household worker and not someone from Frankfurt society, my grandmother made her peace with the marriage, and I suspect that I was the reason why. Being the only child, I was given a lot of love. I had my thirteen dolls. My uncle Lothar, my mother's brother, brought me my roller skates. I had chocolates often.

I couldn't subsist on sweets alone, of course. At home we ate very little meat because kosher meat was so expensive, and the kosher butcher was a long streetcar ride away; we had a lot of chicken and fish. At meals, I remember that my mother would sit with only half her bottom on the chair, so as to be able to jump up and get something as soon as it was needed. (I find myself doing the same thing today.) My favorite beverage was *Himbeersaft*, a raspberry syrup mixed with water. We didn't have an oven, so my mother would knead dough, then send me with it to the baker, who would bake it for us. Every Friday afternoon she would send me with two loaves of challah, plus a little one for me. She also made cakes with streusel on top, little sweet crumbs, and I used to pick some of them off on the way home, carefully choosing pieces that would not be missed. One food I didn't particularly care for was my daily dose of fish oil, which people then believed was something a child ought to have. But my dose was especially big—two spoonfuls a day—because I was so small. As I write this I can still taste the awful flavor. At one point, thankfully, there was a new, improved version—white instead of oily yellow, and much less offensive.

Yes, even as a child I was short. And taking fish oil or any other medicine wasn't going to do anything about it. It's true that I didn't eat very much when I was a little girl—I remember that my father used to cut bread into long strips and dip them into a soft-boiled egg to get me to eat. But I doubt that I would have grown any taller if I had eaten five meals a day. It was a question of heredity. My mother and father were both short, and so were my grandparents; and as I later realized when, as an adult, I met them in London and San Francisco and Israel, so were my aunts and uncles.

I think I was undersized from birth. One of my earliest memories is watching my mother putting laundry on the line in our backyard in Frankfurt. Being on the ground floor, our apartment was dark, so she would take me out with her to get some sun. I was so small she would put me in the laundry basket for safekeeping. I was still small by the time I was five years old and ready to go to school. I was so excited about starting first grade at the Samson Raphael Hirsch School in Frankfurt that for weeks before the term began I would prance around the house carrying my satchel, my box of chalk, my little blackboard, and my sponge. On the first day of school, I wore black patent leather shoes, knee socks, and a dress that was intended for a much taller girl—my mother had to shorten the sleeves and the body.

Six weeks into the term, a doctor came into our class to examine the children. He wanted to send me back to kindergarten because I wasn't big enough. I desperately wanted to stay, so to try to convince him that I should, I started reciting my multiplication tables, which my father had already taught me. It worked. What that story proves is not that I'm a mathematical genius—having to pass a statistics course for my master's degree in sociology was one of the hardest things I've ever had to do in my life. No, it's that, long before I had to answer delicate questions on radio or television or in a lecture hall, I was able to think on my feet.

For a long time I wasn't even tall enough to ride a bicycle, which was a problem since this was the primary mode of transportation in my family—we weren't wealthy enough to have a car. At first, my father carried me around on a special seat, with a back and handlebars, on the bar of his bike. As we were riding he used to teach me the multiplication tables—and a good thing, too! He took me to school by bike until I was nine and finally got my own bicycle. They had to lower the seat so far that it was actually touching the diagonal bar; otherwise, I wouldn't have been able to reach the pedals. I loved being able to ride home from school on my own, because I could stop at the house of an aunt who gave me delicious cookies.

Some people made fun of me because of my height, but for the most part the kidding was gentle. When I was in the first grade, the older kids would have me jump from the steps of the school, giving me candies according to the height I had jumped from. For the first years of school, we had the same teacher, Miss Spiro, whom I remember as old and very kind; she called me the dot on the *i*. In the fifth grade I graduated to a new nickname—the comma. The worst incident I can remember happened one day during recess, when the other children put me in a garbage can—with the cover on, so no one could hear my cries and sobs. Then they promptly forgot all about me, only remembering when the teacher asked where I was.

In the evenings we would sit in the living room, my mother and grandmother sewing, my father and I reading. My parents must have read the Grimm brothers' fairy tales to me as a very little girl, and by the time I knew how to read I loved books. I had all the books a girl could want, which must have been a financial sacrifice for my parents; I don't remember there being lending libraries, and there certainly weren't paperbacks. My favorites were *Nesthäkchen* ("The Youngest of the Family") by Else Uri, the thirteen-volume story of a little girl from the time she was a baby until she was a grandmother; *Der Struwelpeter* ("Wild Peter"), about a mischievous little boy so wild that he wouldn't let anybody cut his fingernails; *Max und Moritz*; and *Rumpelstiltskin*, who in the version I had was short, pulled his own foot out, and disappeared into a hole in the ground. All of these stories were late nineteenth-century children's classics, and I thought they were magnificent; I knew them by heart. When I was in Frankfurt recently, I bought copies of all of them, and they were just as I had remembered them.

I think I was a happy child; I know I always had friends. One of them was Mathilde, the girl who later went with me to Switzerland. As girls, we were literally inseparable. Once we were roller-skating together, and it was time to go home. I skated with her to her house, but we couldn't bear to say good-bye, so we roller-skated together to *my* house. We still couldn't leave each other, so it was back to her house. Finally, one of us—I don't remember which—let the other go home alone. (I still have trouble today taking leave of my friends—sometimes the good-bye takes longer than the visit.) I once got into big trouble at Mathilde's house when I tried to play a prank by pulling her chair out from under her as she was about to sit down at the table. Her father, who was a teacher, was not amused: he smacked me. My other friend in the neighborhood was a boy—not a boyfriend, more of a play companion. His name was Justin and he lived in our building. His was the only other Jewish family in the apartment building. When I was in Switzerland, my parents used to write that he sent his regards.

Going to school was definitely the biggest event of the first ten years of my life. I loved it. I know that I did well, because in the fifth grade—which started just months before I went to Switzerland—I was selected to enter the "sexta," the first part of the gymnasium, or high school. This was the first time that I had more than one teacher, which was a little daunting; I was especially intimidated by our English teacher, Miss Birnbaum, who was tall, very thin, and strict. But I still managed to get good grades.

Besides classes, I also loved school for the recesses. We used to trade pictures of dolls, the way American boys trade baseball cards, and we played hopscotch and jump rope. My favorite game was one in which the girls held hands and walked in a circle around another girl, who acted out the story of a little princess who at first was sad and cried, but then met Prince Charming. All the while everybody else sang songs about her story.

I am an incorrigible collector, and one of the things that I've somehow managed to save from those days is a photograph of my first-grade class at school. Everyone seems very happy—two pairs of girls are hugging each other. For some reason, I'm right smack in the middle of the picture, instead of the front, where the shortest person in the class usually is, and right next to me is Mathilde. In the picture I'm making a gesture with my hands, touching my forefingers to each other. I realized recently that I still do the same thing on television.

When I look at that picture, my overwhelming feeling is sadness, because more than half of these girls were not able to live out their lives.

I'm sure that some of the readers of this book will want to know the answer to a very specific question: What did I know about sex and when did I know it? When I was very young, not surprisingly, I was pretty unsophisticated. I thought that babies were brought by the stork, and I believed the German wives' tale that if you put a piece of sugar outside the window, he would bring a baby. I very badly wanted an older brother, so I (very logically, I thought) put out two lumps. In the morning they were gone, but no older brother arrived. I never really knew why my parents never had any more children, whether it was choice or necessity, or even what contraceptives they used after their marriage, if any. My mother was certainly young enough—she was twenty-five when I was born—and we weren't poor. It may have been because, in Germany in the 1930s, my parents realized that there were hard times ahead for Jews and didn't want to bring any more children into the world. But ultimately it will always be a mystery to me.

My ignorance about sex didn't prevent me from being curious about it, and I found out a little more from a book my parents had, called *Ideal Marriage*. This, I later discovered when I became a sex therapist, was written by a man named Van de Velde and was the classic "marriage manual" of the period. It was high up in a closet, behind a locked glass door. I knew where the key was, and one day I put a chair on top of a chair, crawled up, and took out the book and furtively read a few pages before I heard someone coming and put it away. I got some more practical knowledge one day behind some shrubs, when an older girl showed me a sanitary napkin and told me what it was for. Thus, when I was about ten and about to leave for Switzerland, and my grandmother sat me down on the bed and said she wanted to explain some things, I said, "You don't have to say anything. I know it already"—even though I still didn't know very much. She must have been relieved, because I don't remember that conversation going any further.

I have no doubt that my mother loved me. But looking back, I sometimes wonder how happy she was. What was it like for her, coming from the country to the city, with not much education, getting into this household, and having to live with such a forceful mother-in-law? It couldn't have been easy.

I loved my mother, but I think I realized at a young age that she couldn't fulfill all my needs. Being talkative is no new thing for me—I have *always* needed people to talk to and be with—and she, like everyone else on her side of the family, was very tight-lipped. In German, the word is *wortkarg*. Actually, my father didn't talk very much either. The only one who did was my grandmother Selma. She was heavy—as opposed to my mother and father, who were both thin—she had thin white hair worn in a bun on top of her head, and she wore long skirts. I think she must have had a tremendous effect on me. One of my best memories from childhood is that every Sunday she would take me to the

Palmengarten, a park in Frankfurt. She met with her sister Regina and her friends, who had brought their own grandchildren, and we played. We would always eat *Baiser mit Schlagsahne*, a delicious white pastry. When I visited Frankfurt recently, I couldn't go to the Palmengarten without a grandmother, so I took one along, a friend of my mother-in-law's (my mother-in-law now lives in Frankfurt in a residence for the elderly).

My grandmother's worst quality was a touch of snobbery. German Jews have the reputation of being a little haughty toward other Jews. This attitude apparently came from the leaders of the German Jewish community after Napoleon opened the ghettos of Eastern Europe. The German Jews saw it as their mission to bring "enlightenment" to the "backward" Eastern European Jews (the Haskalah movement). In particular they wanted to bring German culture to the Eastern Jews, often seeming more German than Jewish, thinking of Goethe as the greatest poet ever—and my grandmother had this quality. As a matter of fact, she wouldn't even let me play with Polish-speaking children.

It was my father, I think, who had the biggest influence on me. When his father died, my father inherited the family business, which was the wholesaling of all kinds of notions—handkerchiefs, buttons, everything. Every morning he would pack them up and go from store to store on his bicycle, taking with him a kind of triple-decker thermos in which my mother had packed his lunch. He wore gray knickers, a sweater, a shirt and tie, a jacket, and as an Orthodox Jew, always a hat. On weekdays it was a cap like a cabdriver's; on Saturdays it was a more formal black fedora.

One whole room of our apartment was filled with his things, and the rest of the place was very cluttered. I suppose that's why I have always loved to have little knickknacks around me. Today, one of the joys of my life is my big box of "freebies," promotional giveaways—T-shirts, radios, tote bags—that I've accumulated for the sole purpose of giving them away to *other* people. Even the fact that I'm an accumulator—that I take everything with me when I move (and I've moved quite a bit)—may be an unwitting imitation of my father, traveling around the city bundled down with his wares.

I only realized it much later, but my father gave me a wonderful gift: a love of and joy in learning. At the time, I didn't understand how unusual it was that he would take me, a girl, to synagogue and spend so much time teaching me things. In the Orthodox Jewish culture, this is how you normally behave toward a boy, so maybe my father knew I was the only child he would have, that I would have to serve as both boy and girl. In any case, he never said, "Be a good little girl and play with dolls." I remember that once, practicing my multiplication while on his bicycle, I made a mistake, and he slapped me. The only other time I can remember his hitting me was one day when I was in the park across the street from our apartment, and I was sitting on the lap of a stranger. I don't think the man molested me, because I would have remembered it, but my father was very angry. He spanked me and told me never to go with anybody, even if they promised me candy or dolls.

My father was a good, gentle man who loved me very much. And until recently the pain of losing him was too great for me to permit myself to think about him very much. But now I can say that I miss him. It would be nice if he were sitting next to me right now.

The Frankfurt Jewish community had a lengthy and distinguished history. Jews lived in the town from its medieval beginnings. Long before the Nazi era they had a role, larger than in any other German city, in its business, intellectual, scientific, political, and cultural life. They even had an influence on the language—the Frankfurt dialect included many Yiddish and Hebrew expressions. The "Minhag Frankfurt" was a code of prayer that Jews all over Germany adhered to, and the prayer books printed in the Rödelheim printing house were used by Jews throughout Europe. (To this day, when I see a prayer book with the Rödelheim imprint, I get very sad. I own a number of them, but for reasons I do not remember have none from my family. I cannot imagine that I would have left Frankfurt without a prayer book from home—no self-respecting Orthodox Jew travels without one.)

Frankfurt Jewry produced an amazing number of scholars—people like Moses Mendelssohn, who translated the Bible into German; Samson Raphael Hirsch, who was instrumental in modernizing the way of life of Orthodox Jews; the philosopher Theodor Adorno; and Max Wertheimer, the founder of Gestalt psychology. (Wertheimer left Germany in the thirties and went on to teach at the New School for Social Research in New York, where I later studied.) This distinguished intellectual heritage may have something to do with the fact that I've always wanted so badly to study—maybe I absorbed it from the Frankfurt air.

My family was quite religious. They were Orthodox Jews who closely observed the kashruth (kosher) dietary laws and the Sabbath. I think both sets of grandparents were equally religious, although I remember once thinking that my mother's parents were more so because they put salt on soft-boiled eggs. But my paternal grandmother was devout, too, and she had pride in her heritage. I remember her going frequently to the Jewish cemetery in Frankfurt to visit not only her husband's grave, but also those of Samson Raphael Hirsch and Paul Ehrlich, a German Jewish biologist who had won the Nobel Prize. My grandmother paid tribute to Ehrlich because once, when told that he would receive a big promotion if he would renounce his Judaism, he had refused. He was also a Zionist, which wouldn't have impressed her much. When I was in Switzerland, I asked her in a letter if she knew of a book by Herzl, the founder of Zionism. She wrote back that she didn't and what's more, she had "never been interested in Herzl or the Zionists."

Every morning my father would put on phylacteries, the small black cubes containing Torah texts that men wear at the morning service, and every Friday night he would bless me. Also on Friday evening, he would take me to the synagogue. Jews are not permitted to carry money on the Sabbath, but he always made sure there was just enough change in his vest pocket to buy me an ice cream cone on the way there, before the sun had gone down. My mother rarely went on Friday evenings—the tradition for Friday evening is for the men to go to synagogue and the women to stay home and prepare for the dinner. Indeed, it is unusual that my father should have taken me, a little girl. The synagogue was on a street called Börnestrasse. It was, to me, enormous and very beautiful, and I loved to go there. As in all Orthodox synagogues, the men sat downstairs and the women upstairs, but kids were allowed to go back and forth between both places. After the Saturday morning services, I remember the sight of hundreds of people streaming out of the synagogue. The striking thing about the scene was that virtually all of the men strolled with their hands clasped behind their backs. I'm not sure why they walked that way. Maybe it was because they had bellies and it helped to keep their balance, maybe it suggested the freedom of not working and going for a leisurely walk. Or maybe it was a way of making sure that they did not talk with their hands—something a self-controlled German Jew would never consciously do.

After services, we would go visit my father's relatives, who were better off than we were. I loved to go there because every time we visited the same joke was pulled on me. Herring was served, and my uncle would always ask me if I wanted the head. I'd giggle and say absolutely not, and then I got a very nice piece.

Sometimes, instead of going to our regular synagogue we would go to a small shul in the Jewish hospital near our house. They needed a minyan there, the minimum of ten men that's necessary to pray, and my father helped fill it.

On holidays we went to the big synagogue. On Simchas Torah, when one of the customs is that children get candy, a big group of us went from one synagogue to another, collecting candies at each one. It's interesting that so many of my early memories should be related to food, because, as I say, I didn't eat very much. Still, on Chanukah I remember my grandmother's wonderful potato pancakes, and on Purim I remember the Haman we used to eat—not the *Hamantaschen* of Eastern European Jews, but little gingerbread men, supposedly Haman, the villain of the Purim story, with raisins for their shirt buttons. My mother would bake a little one for me, and I always regretted eating it because it looked so good.

On Passover, we used to have long, long seders, because that was a mark of honor among Frankfurt Jews, stemming from a passage in the Haggadah saying that the rabbis stayed up until morning, when they could say the Shema. The next day, people wouldn't ask what you ate, but how long your seder lasted. My favorite part, of course, was looking for the afikomen, the hidden piece of matzo. When I found it, as I always did, I got a prize.

Religion was also the reason why I was sent to the Samson Raphael Hirsch School, a girls' school (Orthodox Jewish schools in Germany were never coed). It was a long-established school that in 1928 had taken the name of the translator of the Bible, and it had the most students of any Jewish school in Germany. (It also had the "right" students, according to my grandmother—one of my classmates was a Rothschild. I didn't know her well, but I do remember her house, which looked like a château, and I remember that nannies used to bring her to school.) Another school, called the Philanthropin, was closer to home, but my grandmother decided I shouldn't go there because it wasn't Orthodox enough—God forbid another child should give me a sandwich with butter and sausage in it! It must have been quite a financial sacrifice for my parents to send me there. Interestingly enough, the Samson Raphael Hirsch School moved to my neighborhood in New York City. It wasn't because of me. Ever since I've been in this country, I've lived in Washington Heights, in northern Manhattan, which has been a haven for German Jews since the 1930s. Today, the school's just a few blocks from my apartment building. I don't have any direct contact with it, but every year they send me an envelope asking for money, and every time I see that name I immediately write out a check.

As you can probably gather, I lived in a very protective Jewish environment—my school, my synagogue, my relatives. It's largely because of this insulation, I think, that I never directly experienced any anti-Semitism in Frankfurt. I don't even think that I was ever called a Jew. True, our neighborhood was largely gentile (we probably couldn't have afforded to live in the more expensive Jewish neighborhood), but as far as my eyes saw it, there was never any discrimination or prejudice. We had a very nice next-door neighbor, a Mrs. Luft, who had only one arm. She would come in on Saturdays and light the stove and turn the lights on and off because we were observant Jews and this was not permitted on the Sabbath.

But, of course, anti-Semitism existed all the same. In the elections of 1932, the Nazis, who had been around for about a decade, were voted the largest party in the Reichstag. I remember going with my mother to vote, in a big schoolyard. She probably voted for Hindenburg. In 1933, Hitler was named chancellor, and the next year he assumed the presidency as well. I don't remember hearing very much about him when I was a girl, only that he was a man who didn't like Jews.

What I didn't know was that his feelings about the Jews went far beyond mere dislike. In *Mein Kampf*, published in 1925, he described the Jew as the greatest enemy of all, the very incarnation of evil. When he came to power he started to put his theories into effect. In April 1933, Jews were forced out of government service and universities and barred from entering the professions. The Nürnberg laws of September 1935 deprived Jews of virtually all civil rights—including the right to marry persons of German blood.

As a little girl, I didn't feel the direct effect of these policies. My father's business did poorly, but I don't know whether this had to do only with anti-Semitism, or also with the poor economic situation in Germany. I do know that Jews were not allowed to have radios. My father, though, surreptitiously put one together himself, and I remember his listening to it in the evening—maybe even to the BBC from England.

It wasn't just that I was too young to know what was going on—I'm convinced that very few people did. Certainly no one knew this early that there was going to be such a thing as concentration camps. There was a great sense of national loyalty and pride among German Jews, which carried with it a confidence that they would be treated fairly. After all, they had fought for Germany in World War I.

Such illusions became harder to sustain after the events of 1938. In October—the month after the signing of the Munich agreement, which Neville Chamberlain hailed as "peace in our time"—seven thousand German Jews of Polish origin were driven across the German-Polish border into Poland, from which the Poles drove them back. Despite the snobbism of the German Jews, when the Polish Jews were taken to the border, everybody was very concerned. There were collections of clothing and a lot of charitable activity.

Then, on November 9, 1938, came Kristallnacht. This occurred after a seventeen-year-old Polish Jew whose family had been deported fatally shot a secretary of the German embassy in Paris. After Kristallnacht there were horrible excesses against Jews all over Germany. Many Jews were murdered; synagogues were burned; businesses were destroyed; and the Jews of Germany were forced to pay a fine of a billion marks to make restitution for the murder. Jews were no longer allowed to enter certain streets, any public parks, and any public buildings.

And finally, I began to experience the effects of Nazism directly. Our synagogue was burned down. Classes stopped at my school. Even though these events hit so close to home, I still didn't grasp the full import of what was happening. Just a few months before, my school had been closed for six weeks because of a polio outbreak, and I assumed that something similar was happening this time—a temporary crisis that would eventually be resolved. Even so, in the days after Kristallnacht, I did have such a sense of anxiety that I slept in my parents' bed every night.

On November 15, I was walking in the street with my father. Someone told him that terrible things were going to happen, that he should get out. My father said, "Nothing's going to happen tomorrow. It's a Catholic holiday." That's the morning the SS came to pick him up.

He was taken to a detention camp. After Kristallnacht, many Jews were rounded up and taken to places like Dachau and Buchenwald, which at this point were not concentration camps, but detention camps, where they were forced to stay as punishment for the sins of their religion. After being held there for a period of time, the Jews were frequently permitted to leave.

A few months before Kristallnacht, in August of 1938, a conference was held among the allied nations in the French city of Évian. There were representatives from thirty-two countries, including the U.S. and the League of Nations. The topic was what to do to save the Jews of Germany. The answer, essentially, was nothing. *The New York Times* wrote in an editorial, "If thirty-two nations that call themselves democracies cannot unite on a plan for the needs of a few hundred thousand refugees, then all hope vanishes that they will ever be able to reach agreement on anything at all." *The Daily Herald* of London wrote, "Responsibility has been abdicated."

One of the few tangible results that did come out of the conference was a resolve that Switzerland, Britain, the Netherlands, Belgium, and France would each accept three hundred Jewish children from Germany, not very much out of a total German Jewish population of 550,000. The idea was that they would stay for six months, during which time their parents or relatives would arrange for emigration from Germany.

I was one of the three hundred selected to go to Switzerland. It was really a stroke of luck that I could go. My parents must have gotten a call from someone in the Jewish organization, saying there was a place for me. One hundred children were to be sent from Frankfurt, and they all had to be German Jews, under sixteen, and either orphans or with a father in a camp—all qualifications that I met. If my father had still been at home, I would not have been on that train, and I would not be alive today.

Before I was permitted to leave, I had to have a physical examination. I have a document dated December 2, 1938, signed by Dr. Arnold Merzbach, a physician "licensed to take care of the medical needs of Jews exclusively," attesting that I was not afflicted with any "physical or psychological illness."

A month later I was gone. I never saw my parents again.

chapter

2

I sat in the corner of the train with tears streaming down my cheeks and not saying a word, which was very unusual for me.

I had two things to comfort me. One was a doll. Of the thirteen dolls I had at home, I had brought my favorite—a celluloid doll, of a brand called Schildkröte, with an unusual trademark on the back that looked like a toad.

The other comfort was my friend Mathilde, who sat next to me. Everyone else was a complete stranger.

Eventually, I cheered up a little bit. I later studied to be a kindergarten teacher and worked as one, but even when I was ten I liked being with younger children—probably for the same reason that I liked dolls. I got everyone on the train to start singing Hebrew songs. We needed something to do because it was a long train ride—about ten hours in all. We rode through Germany and at about noon reached the Swiss border at Basel. The older children got off there; the rest of us were given cocoa and a snack. I had a hard time understanding the German spoken by the Swiss—it sounded so harsh.

At a town called Rorschach we changed trains. It was still raining. Late in the afternoon we finally arrived at our destination, the village of Heiden. We all got off, and carrying our bags, walked through town. It was a picturesque Swiss village, with chalets and evergreens, everything covered with snow—the kind of thing you see on picture postcards, but like nothing we had seen before. In the distance, a big lake was visible. I later learned this was Lake Constance (Bodensee). As we walked through the town, the church bells started to ring, not to welcome us, but to mark the hour. I remember seeing the townspeople looking through their windows at us with curiosity, fifty frightened children from another country.

We walked down a gentle slope for about half a mile and came to a pair of buildings, a large, rather elegant one and a smaller, simpler annex. We were led into the annex.

When I got inside I put down my bag and saw that a woman was standing there. I was a well-brought-up German Jewish girl, and so I said to her, in a rush of words, "Guten Tag, guten Tag, ich heisse Karola Siegel und komme aus Frankfurt am Main." (Good day. My name is Karola Siegel and I come from Frankfurt am Main.) My parents must have told me that's how you introduce yourself.

∞∞∞∞∞∞∞

My day during the school year. I get up at six-thirty in the morning. I get dressed. We wake up the children at seven, and then I'm busy until seven-thirty, when I have coffee. After that, I set the tables with Max. Then, if the weather is bad, I arrange games for the children. Then I help Grete to clean. Then I go to school. When school is over, I clean the dining room and comb the children's hair. After lunch I put the little girls to bed for their nap. Then I have school again until five. At five-thirty I sweep, help bathe the children, or do some mending. After dinner I put the children to bed, and at seven-thirty I too go to bed.

My day during vacation. At six-fifteen Hannelore comes to wake us up. All together we walk over to the colony. First we line up the benches in the dining room, then we go to the dormitories and help make the beds. When we're through with this, we go to the washrooms and help to comb the children's hair. Then we have coffee. After I've had my coffee I get a pail of water from the kitchen and a broom and sweep the floors of the hallways and the toilets. Then I wipe everything on the outside, and then I clean the toilets. When all this is done, I mop the floor with a wet mop. On Fridays everything is done more thoroughly. When I'm through with my chores, I join Hannelore upstairs and together we do the bedrooms. By then it is eleven-thirty and time to eat. After we've eaten, I go swimming if the weather is nice. At three I come home and do mending. In the evening, I help bathe the children, and after dinner I clean their shoes. I like all my chores very much.

—diary of Karola Siegel

It's very hard for me to write or even to talk about these years. In all the hundreds of interviews I've given since I've been Dr. Ruth, I've never really discussed them. And not only because they were so difficult and painful. No, it's mostly because of the message that was so successfully drummed into our heads during all those six years in Switzerland: Never complain. You're lucky to be alive. Since I have a daughter who just turned thirty and a son in his twenties, I know how natural it is for teenagers to get angry, to slam doors or stomp their feet. Those are things we never did. And now, almost fifty years later, I still am reluctant to complain; my impulse, always, is to look on the bright side, never to make too much of a fuss about myself. The whole country now knows what my friends have always known—that I like to talk a lot. But they've often complained that, of all the words coming out of my mouth, very few of them are about myself and my feelings. That all started in Switzerland.

You can see how well I absorbed this message in the above passage from the diary I began keeping about two years after arriving in Heiden (which is located in the province of Appenzell, about fifty miles from Zurich). First I detail a daily schedule that would make Cinderella's life look leisurely. (It's no coincidence that the Cinderella story was one of my favorites, along with a German song based on the story, about a girl who has to get up very early, before anyone else is up, before the stars disappear, and has to stand at the stove and clean.) But then I write, "I like all my chores very much." I wasn't being sarcastic or even insincere. I just understood that the most important thing, no matter how hard your lot, was to be grateful. I understood it so well that I didn't even have to pretend.

Even when I couldn't control the urge to complain, I suppressed it as soon as possible. In my diaries, two pages are cut out, and in the margin I wrote, "On these pages I wrote bad things." I don't remember what horrible thing I said, but it must have been something critical about Switzerland or the home.

From the beginning I knew that things were going to be hard. The first day we arrived, in January of 1939, they led the fifty of us into a large second-story room of a plain building that had formerly been a barn. This was where we would sleep. The first night, as we were getting ready to go to bed, we discovered an opening in the floor designed for heat from the wood-burning stove downstairs to come up into the room. Of course we looked through it. We saw the people who were responsible for us opening up and examining our suitcases. They made fun of our clothing for being unfashionable and worn-out. When they got to mine, they took out for themselves the chocolate that my mother and grandmother had given me! So much for the picture they had painted to me of Switzerland as a place of beautiful lakes and mountains, where chocolate would be in abundance. I didn't complain. For one thing, there was no one to complain *to*—the people in authority were the ones who had wronged me. But even then, I intuitively sensed that I mustn't make waves. I should be happy for what I had and adapt to what I didn't. That night I literally cried myself to sleep.

The place where we stayed was a children's home for Swiss Jewish children who for some reason couldn't be with their parents—because the parents were divorced or dead or merely traveling. In the summer it became a camp where children would come to spend their vacations. Physically, it was really a lovely place: my living standard went up immediately when I got there. I had been living in a row house on a city street with little sunlight; now I was in a converted barn in beautiful natural surroundings.

In the winter, the season when we arrived, the four or five acres of grounds were covered with snow. It was lovely and quiet, but in the summer the place was really spectacular. There were lawns, lots of flowers, and a big vegetable garden with raspberries and strawberries. Next door was a farm with cows, which I loved because it reminded me of my grandparents' place in Wiesenfeld—the smell of the freshly cut hay made me nostalgic, and so did the smell of cow manure! I grew very fond of the sound of cowbells, and also of the echo you hear in the mountains. All around were wonderful Swiss meadows covered with wildflowers; I grew to love them, and now, every time I go back to Switzerland, the first thing I do is take a deep breath.

On the grounds was a playground with a slide and a sandbox, which was nice for me because it reminded me of the park in Frankfurt. There were tables and benches, where we would eat when the weather was warm. And there was a pretty little gazebo, which you couldn't see from the house—convenient for us when we wanted to play in private.

The building we stayed in at first was a former barn that had been converted into an annex of the children's home. Until we arrived, it had only been used in the summer. There was a tremendous hall downstairs where we ate and played; off it was another hall with toilets and showers. Upstairs were four dormitories—for the older girls, younger girls, younger boys, and older boys—and two private rooms for adults who worked at the home.

After three years, when some of the older children among us had taken jobs and gone off on their own, the rest of us moved into the main house. Even before then, we knew it very well—after all, we had to clean it. It was an old wooden house, three stories tall, in the style of Appenzell. There was one entrance to a big kitchen, and another to a first floor that had showers, bathrooms, and bedrooms, where children slept two or three to a room. On the second story were more bedrooms and two little living rooms, one with books and lots of toys. There were no toys or books in the annex. On the third floor were private rooms for the teachers and administrators.

The place was called Wartheim, which in German means to wait. It was an appropriate and ultimately ironic name, because that's exactly what we were doing. Originally, the idea was that we would all stay in the home for six months and then be picked up by our parents to go on—to the United States or Palestine or wherever. After six months we were still there, so we went to the police station to renew our permits. This went on until the end of the war. No one was ever denied renewal of a permit, but that terrible possibility, of being sent back to Germany, where we knew such horrible things were happening, was always in the back of our minds. Yet another reason not to complain.

Four days after we arrived, we were all given dossiers at the Heiden police station. I still have mine—as I said, I save everything I possibly can. It says that my number is 855,555; that, aside from the children's identity card, I have no documents; that I entered Switzerland for a limited stay, until further emigration can be arranged. I am of Jewish parentage; an uncle, Lothar Hanauer, lives in Palestine. The Swiss Aid Committee for Refugee Children will take care of all my expenses and has earmarked seventy-six Swiss francs a month for me.

There was occasionally talk of our going to live with foster parents in Switzerland, but in my case at least, nothing ever came of it. The problem was not that there weren't people offering foster care, but that they weren't Jewish or, if Jewish, weren't Orthodox. All of us in the home came from Orthodox families, and we lived that way there—we observed all the holidays, kept kosher, did nothing on the Sabbath. I said a prayer every night before going to bed, and if somehow I accidentally fell asleep too early, I would somehow manage to wake myself up and say it.

At the home we were often told a little story about the Swiss flag—a white cross in a sea of red—that made a big impression on me. Switzerland was a haven in Europe;

everything around it was blood red. And that was how things seemed. Heiden is up in the mountains, next to Lake Constance. It overlooks Germany. Every single day I could see Germany—where my parents were, where my friends were, where my home was—and I knew I couldn't get there. Later in the war I could see how the Allies bombarded Friedrichshafen, which was on the other side of the lake. And there I was in Switzerland, safe but abandoned. Of course it didn't matter whether or not I liked it. There was no place else to go.

∞∞∞∞∞∞

> Yesterday I was thirteen. I woke up very early in the morning. All the children congratulated me. When I later came back to the dormitory, presents were spread out on my bed: a lovely embroidered apron from Grete and a writing case from the Kapps. From Edith a picture; remnants of lovely materials from Rachele. Later I went to clean the boys' washrooms. They all came to wish me well. Fräulein Hanna said she hoped I would grow up tall and slender. Frau Berendt said I should stay as decent and nice as I now was. When I came into the dining room, I found a lovely dress on my table, a blouse, and other pretty things. Mathilde, Hannelore, and Klaerli together gave me a pin cushion with lots of pins in it, and Mathilde also gave me a book of gummed paper. Frau Neufeld said she wished I would become as good a Jew as my grandmother was. It was a lovely day.
>
> —*Diary of Karola Siegel,*
> *June 5, 1941*

Long after I had left Heiden, when I was studying for a master's degree in sociology at the New School for Social Research in New York City, I decided to write my thesis on the children who were at the home with me. I had observed from those with whom I was still in touch—and this was confirmed when I began researching the rest of them—that they had, on the whole, turned out remarkably well. They lived all over the world, but none were criminals, none had committed suicide, and a remarkably high percentage had achieved a substantial degree of professional success.

When you considered what difficult, parentless lives we had in the home, for as many as six years, this adjustment may come as something of a surprise. What explains it, I think, is the crucial importance of early upbringing: we had all come from good, solid, middle-class German Jewish homes, and the values and love we had gotten there transcended the unhappiness and loneliness we suffered at Heiden.

But there was something else, too. At the home we functioned as our *own* support system. We had no one to turn to besides each other, and we rarely let each other down. We were as close as brothers and sisters, and in some cases closer, because there was no question of sibling rivalry over parental preferences: we all got exactly the same treatment, and we knew it. The one thing we didn't do, even to each other, was to complain about our plight or show how truly sad we were. I think this was for understandable psychological reasons: we each knew that the others had their own sorrows, and we didn't want to burden them with ours.

Even so, we were a comfort to each other. I recently spoke with Marga Miller, one of several people from the home I've stayed close with over the years. She remembered, "There was no jealousy. We had a very hard time and we were all in the same situation. Before I came to the home, I was in a foster family in Switzerland, and even though psychology says that it's better to be in a family, I felt better off in the home. In a family, I was only with myself, but when I came to the home, all of the kids were in the same boat."

We needed all the comfort we could get. I still don't know how it was decided that we, the German Jewish refugees, would act as the servants for the Swiss kids at the home, but we did, and we worked very hard. We did their laundry, we served their food, we cleaned their toilets. The worst chore was having to go outside in freezing temperatures and hang sheets out to dry. By some standards we weren't treated badly—we ate well (although we only ate meat once a week because of the difficulty and expense of getting kosher meat), we got some schooling, and above all, we were safe. But there was no question that we were second-class citizens. Who decided this policy, I don't know. But there it was, and when I think of it today, it makes my hair stand on end.

There was an incredible emphasis put on cleanliness. We went to school a couple of hours a day, but the rest of the time we did housework. There wasn't that much house to clean, and as a result it was immaculate—you could have eaten off those floors. Part of the reason was that the people who ran the home wanted to show the villagers, some of whom were anti-Semitic, that Jews can be like the Swiss—in other words, superclean petite bourgeoisie.

After three years, as I said, we moved from the annex into the main building with the Swiss children, but the initial impression remained—almost as though we were in quarantine, as if we refugees might pollute the rest of that little society. I think they missed a terrific opportunity. What if they had told the Swiss kids, "Take care of those German children—look what happened to them. They had to leave their homes, they don't have parents." It would have been a comfort for us, and a beneficial experience for the Swiss. Instead, *we*, the needy ones, had to take care of *them*, who seemed to us to have everything.

It was stupid, but that wasn't surprising given the caliber of some of the people in charge of the home. The worst was a woman named Fräulein Riesenfeld. She was a Jewish refugee from Germany herself, with no children or husband, and she was absolutely unqualified for the job of taking care of us. Today, I know what her problem was—she was insecure and had no male partner—but then, she just seemed like a witch. She read all the letters we wrote to or received from our parents, and she used to beat me with a sneaker when I misbehaved. But the worst thing she did was to tell us that our parents were horrible people, that they couldn't really have loved us or else they wouldn't have abandoned us. I've recently checked with others, so I know this wasn't a figment of my imagination. She said our parents, in allowing us to go away, were *Schlangeneltern*, or snakes, animals that eat their young. Of course we never complained about Fräulein Riesenfeld to our parents (shortly after I left Frankfurt, my father had come home from the detention camp) or to the people in Zurich who were responsible for the home. As always, we knew we were objects of charity and had better be quiet and thankful. But I did have one moment of glee at her expense. She slipped and fell on the ice. I laughed uproariously and was spanked for my troubles.

Fräulein Riesenfeld and the others made a very stupid rule. We all slept upstairs in an enormous hall, and they told us that once you're upstairs in bed, you can't go downstairs anymore. Now, downstairs was where the bathrooms were, and as soon as I was upstairs and knew I wouldn't be able to go again, I suddenly became anxious and had to go. And I ended up wetting the bed. The same thing happened to another child, a boy. (He now lives in San Diego—I recently checked with him and he remembers the incident the same way I do.) Fräulein Riesenfeld not only made us wash the sheets the next morning—so everybody knew what we had done—but we had to write to our parents telling them about it.

I know how terrible this made me feel, but I can only imagine my parents' reaction—here was their well-brought-up daughter, unable to control herself. Of course when they wrote back to me, all they said was, "Be a good girl" and "We are so happy that you are there in safety." The message was clear. They didn't dare say, "What a horrible place." No, no matter how badly I was treated, I should be grateful that I was in Switzerland.

A girl named Ruth Hess, who also has been my good friend for all these years, did complain to her parents. Ruth secretly sent off a letter saying how bad things were. Naturally, Fräulein Riesenfeld read the response and figured out what Ruth had told them. As punishment, she was beaten in front of all the other children, who were forbidden to talk to her, and she was forced to sleep alone in the annex.

〰〰〰〰

My dear Karola,

Your nice letter of December 15 reached us today. We are very happy with it. Did you do your ski tour? There's snow here, too. Dear Karola, remember that the word *vielleicht* is written with a _v_ [I had spelled it with an *f*]. By this time, your Chanukah party is probably over. Was it nice? In the Philanthropin [the other Jewish school in Frankfurt] there was an exhibition of handiwork. There were some very nice things. . . . Here it's vacation, too. I am enclosing a coupon to exchange for a stamp and a sheet of paper. We haven't heard from Uncle Max for a while, and we hope to get some news soon. Does Mathilde hear anything from her brother Mathias? In your place, there must be lots of Chanukah lights. I send you regards from acquaintances. Now I wish you, my darling, the heartiest greeting and loving kisses from your loving mommy.

Dear Karola,

Skiing is a pleasure
When the sun is bright and shining.
The snow must be high and iceless.
The skis are put on the feet very fast.
You walk up the mountain short of breath.
When you call yoo-hoo, there is an echo,
And you go downhill very fast.
And when there is a turn around a sharp corner,
Sometimes it's ordained that you fall in the dirt.
And then you are very happy
If your skis are still in one piece.
Black-and-blue marks may heal,
But not a broken ski.

> With best regards and lots of kisses,
> your loving father.

My dear Karola,

As always, we were so happy with your happy lines. Now you can enjoy your vacation. Skiing is such a wonderful healthy pleasure. And it's part of the beauty of Switzerland, like sleigh riding. We also have a little snow here. It is magnificent, a beautiful white. Snow is so clean when it falls from the sky—it only loses its heavenly cleanliness from us people. In my daily walks through the park, I often have philosophical medita-

tions. . . . How was your Chanukah celebration? I can
just see you with your apron and wooden house shoes.
Do you remember how you always sang?—"When there
is a cooking pot with beans, I dance with my Marie."
Always remain healthy and in a good mood, a good girl,
and thoughtful. With regards and kisses, your loving
grandma.

—letter to Karola Siegel
December 22, 1940

The holidays are coming up, so we're cleaning the
whole house, we baked a cake, and we cooked good
things. Then we arranged our clothing and put on
nice clothes and went to synagogue. . . . When we
came home from synagogue, the mother has lit the
candle and set the table. But if she went with us to
synagogue, then she did it before. Then the father
makes kiddush and we eat. . . . There's always a holiday feeling when we sit around the Shabbat table
with the lights. After we eat, we talk about how this
Shabbat came to be and why it is so sacred, and why
people are so pleased with it. And the next day we
visit relatives or they come to us, and in the afternoon
we go for a walk. This is the way it is on almost all
the holidays.

—diary of Karola Siegel
October 1, 1940

If you read this diary entry closely, it sounds as though
I were still at home. That's no accident. At Heiden, I missed
my parents so much that whenever I could, I pretended that
I had never gone away. The holidays were when I felt the
sense of loss most sharply. All my years at Heiden, I had up
on the wall next to my bed a picture of a father holding a
little girl in his arms, lighting the Chanukah candles.

My father came home not long after I left. This was not
an unusual occurrence, since many of the Jews put into detention camps after Kristallnacht were subsequently re-

leased. But there was no possibility that my family could visit me or I them: Jews were forbidden to travel out of the country. So we corresponded; I still have all their letters. They wrote on the delicate, ornate stationery of my grandfather's wholesale-goods firm, which was printed up when he was still alive and had his name on the top. They invariably covered the front and back of the paper, nothing more, nothing less. When there wasn't that much to say, they would send a postcard. When I look at these letters today, I notice two interesting things. The first is that they are stamped with a swastika seal. The second is that next to the word "Sender," my grandmother wrote her name as "Selma (Sara) Siegel." The Nazis had decreed that all Jewish women had to use Sara as their middle name.

Looking back over the letters today, it is striking—almost a little frightening—how resolutely cheery they are. My parents talk pleasantly of relatives, acquaintances, the weather. You would think they were written in the midst of prosperity, not from a country that was about to commit genocide against the Jewish people. But I know that they wrote in the way they felt they had to—to preserve not only my peace of mind, but theirs.

I don't have copies of my letters to them, of course, but I know that they were full of good cheer, too. What I couldn't tell my parents I put in my diary—how unhappy I was, how desperately I missed them. I thought that one day, when we were reunited, I would show them the diary, and they would see how things really were.

But would we be reunited? I was supposedly in the home to wait for my parents to arrange for their emigration out of Germany, at which time I would join them. But that proved to be more difficult than it seemed. In February of 1939, shortly after his release from the detention camp, my father went to the U.S. consulate to apply for permission to emigrate. But it wasn't easy for German Jews to come to America. In order to get permission to come here, you needed to know someone here who would be willing to give you an affidavit stating that, if you didn't find work, you would be taken care of. My father knew no one. So all he got was a quota number—49,280—which was too high, since the annual quota was less than 30,000. In retrospect, I'm surprised that he even got that.

Needless to say, the prospects for emigration was the main topic in my mind and in my letters. I know I must have mentioned it in virtually every letter, because virtually every letter from *them* reported that no progress had been made. Eventually, I started to wonder whether progress would ever be made. And from the tone of their letters, I started to worry about whether my parents really wanted to leave at all.

In a letter dated April 10, 1941—more than two years after I entered the home—my mother writes, "Nothing new about our emigration. We'll let you know as soon as everything is ready. Look, Mathilde's parents left so long ago, and she still cannot join them. One has to be patient." The parents of Mathilde—the girl I had ridden with on the train from Frankfurt—were in England. She couldn't join them because the war had started.

My mother, father, and grandmother all wrote separately in every single letter, and in this one my grandmother especially said her piece. First she congratulated me on my report card, especially the good marks in deportment. "And now enjoy your vacation and keep on doing your very best, then everything will give you pleasure. Work is the best medicine." After this Calvinistic advice, she got to the real subject: "Why do you keep asking all the time about the emigration? Thank God you are well taken care of, and the sky and the sun are over us here as everywhere, just as rains and storms are everywhere. Enjoy your carefree youth and gather strength for the serious life ahead. Stay healthy and happy. All your relatives send their best wishes for happy holidays. With all my best wishes for you, I am your loving grandma."

Then it was my father's turn. My father's part of the letter was always quite extraordinary, for one reason: he always wrote it in poetry. Today, he had this to say:

Dear Karola:

A good report card is great fun.
It is a pleasure to show it to everyone.

It is the reward
For working hard.
But one has to keep working
To get rid of all one's faults
And never go slack
Or your marks will slide back.

In a letter in February 1941, he explained why he wrote in verse:

Although verses take time
And you should know how to rhyme.
Perhaps someone will teach it to you.
So you will know how to do it too.
It is possible to say in verses
What in prose is too hard to express
To speak of happy events
So the censor will strike nothing out.

The censor was often on my father's mind. He once wrote that the distance between him and me was like the great Chinese wall, so long that news couldn't get across— but if he wrote in verse, more could be communicated than in prose. He used the same image another time. Usually his letters were very cheerful, with only good news, but once he confessed that the family hadn't had any meat for a long time, longer than the Jewish fast of Tisha b'Av, longer even than the Great Wall of China. I had forgotten about that poem for years. I remembered it again in 1986, when I was *in* China with Robin Leach's television program, *Lifestyles of the Rich and Famous*, and actually saw the Great Wall.

When my father got back from the detention camp he no longer had a business. He was able to get a job as a gardener at the Jewish cemetery, the one up the street from our apartment, where my grandmother used to visit the graves of her husband and eminent Jews. I marvel when I think of my father, unaccustomed to physical labor, putting in a full day's work as a gardener, then coming home at night and writing me poems. He even did it when he was uninspired:

Today I have nothing to write.
That's why I have to give up.
If you were here at home
You wouldn't get a single verse.

Another time he painstakingly copied out an entire poem in Swiss German, which he didn't understand—"Schweizerland" by Goethe.

For my thirteenth birthday in 1941 my mother wrote, "I am looking forward to the day when I can read your diary. . . . All my best wishes and blessings for your coming birthday. May you grow up to be a good, capable young woman, always healthy and content. Your birthday present will follow later. It may take quite a while."

Then my father followed with his poem. This time it was a special birthday effort: an acrostic, in which the first letter of each line spelled out my name, Karola:

Dem lieben Geburtstagskinde!

Kannst du dich doch noch entsinnen,
Als du das Leben tatst beginnen?
Recht schwierig hast du oft gedacht,
O, vielen Leuten hast du Freude gemacht.
Lebe wohl und sei zufrieden.
Auch viel Glück sei dir beschieden.

(For the dear birthday child!

Can you still remember
in your early days
when you had such deep thoughts?
You brought joy to many people.
Be well and with peace of mind
and much luck shall fall upon you!)

One time he apologized for a spot on the letter. He said I shouldn't think it was oil or butter, because they had none to cook with. When I told a friend about this not long ago, he wondered if it was a tear. Until then, the thought had never occurred to me.

The last letter I got from my parents was dated September 14, 1941, around the time of the Jewish New Year. This is what it said:

My dear Karola,

This is an afternoon to write letters. Dear Rola [my mother's pet name for me], do you remember how I told you to add your greetings to all the New Year's letters we sent? But now you're a big girl and you do that all by yourself. On Friday we received with great pleasure your sweet letter from the seventh of September, with that vivid description of your wonderful excursion, and we were very happy. . . . Dear Karola, to the year-end I send you my very hearty greetings and wishes. I hope all of our wishes will be fulfilled, and may you only have luck, wealth, and contentment. Also for all of your girlfriends, lots of congratulations. Happy holidays. I hope you fast [for Yom Kippur] well. With lots of hugs and kisses, your loving mother.

My dear Karola,

As always we were very happy with your happy and well-described report. Your excursion must have been wonderful, and you even went in an express train! School also makes you happy, and the good grades! Now it is constantly raining here. . . . My dear Karola, for the New Year I send you my deepest regards and wishes. May you continue to develop physically and psychologically to all our and all your caretakers' pleasure, and may you remain our sunshine. A happy disposition, health, and satisfaction—these things should be your steady accompaniments. All the wishes of your heart should be fulfilled in a good way. Have a good holiday and fast well on Yom Kippur. Be very well greeted and kissed from your loving grandma.

Dear Karola!

On the New Year I congratulate you.
May you remain hearty.
Many of your wishes should be fulfilled
To be a good girl.
And mainly I wish that you should continue
To write in a happy mood.
And always have good will.
Then you are going to be content on this earth.

Regards and kisses from your loving father.

ooooooooo

I'm sitting at a window in our room, and next to me
is a picture, and in that picture is my friend Putz, and
he laughs at me all the time. In my dream last night,
he was with me. I have to write down my favorite
song in the diary, because that's the song he used to
sing to me every evening:

"You are my sunshine, my only sunshine. You
make me happy, when skies are gray."

—*diary of Karola Siegel,
June 13, 1943*

As I said, we children in the home were very close. From
the beginning we were supposed to take care of each other.
I was part of the younger group, and an older girl named
Grete was supposed to be responsible for me. But she disappointed me terribly. In May of 1940 it looked as though
Hitler might invade Switzerland. If that happened, we were
supposed to go off into the mountains in groups of two, an
older child with a younger child. At the very last moment
Grete said she would not go with me; she had chosen somebody else. I was very upset.

It so happened that the older children were all girls, and
it was very hard for them. They didn't have any boys to talk
to. And nobody trained them or told them how to be older

sisters to the rest of us. They were tough on us—almost like little dictators. I remember one of them, who now lives in California, who was just awful—she didn't let us talk in the room.

I've said that I liked being with younger children, and from the start I was helping out kids even younger than I. When I was ten, I was responsible for a boy who was six— he's now a professor in Haifa. Another little girl was upset about something one day, and to console her I gave her a necklace and my only doll, the one I had taken with me on the train from Frankfurt. What a sacrifice! (The real reason I did it was that her big brother asked me to look after her— I often did things just to please boys.) Later I was put in charge of a group of little boy scouts; I'd take them hiking and swimming. Imagine me, thirteen years old, a scout leader! Within a couple of years after arriving in Heiden, I came to the decision that I should use this interest professionally and become a kindergarten teacher, an ambition in which my grandmother encouraged me. I didn't tell her, but part of my motivation was that by teaching the little ones, I would get to play with the toys in the main building.

There *were* boys our age, which was a stroke of luck. Because it was Orthodox, you would have expected the home to be a single-sex institution, but there wasn't enough money for two sets of facilities, and therefore it was coed. From the beginning I was interested in boys. Once, when I was ten, I went out on a rooftop on a snowy night and banged against the boys' window with a pitcher, just to frighten them. They tried to open the window, and it broke. Somebody squealed to Fräulein Riesenfeld about what I had done, and I got in big trouble. That was the time she hit me on my behind with a sneaker.

My first crush was on a boy called Max, whom I used to help with his homework. The first mention of him in my diary comes on September 17, 1941, when I was thirteen. I casually wrote, "I am knitting a headband for Max." By the following March things had gotten more serious: "I've come to like Max very much. But you've got to pull yourself together, Karola." On May 12 I wrote, "As for Max, we understand each other very well," and on May 25, "In Max I really have a good friend and comrade." After he went away for a few days on a hike with a few girls and a counselor, I wrote, "I feel terrible when Max is away. Oh, well, he'll be back tomorrow. I really do have to pull myself together." In October came a major event: "Inge, Mira, Erwin, Max, and I played in Grete's room. I would never have dreamt that Max could play so well! [The word "well" is underlined three times.] We played hospital." I was so infatuated that I had to discuss Max with other people: "The other day I talked to Ignatz [Mandel, the teacher at the home] about Max, and Ignatz said that Max could be the best in his class if he would only apply himself."

But trouble was already on the horizon. In October I observed, "I can't understand Ruth L. Every time Max and I have a disagreement, she interferes!!! But strangely enough she always takes his part!!! Above all, I must promise myself never, never to be jealous." This proved to be an impossible promise to keep, especially after I caught Max and Ruth kissing. I dealt with this disappointment philosophically in my diary: "I understand why it happened that way with Max. I gave him as much love as I could. He, however, took everything and gave nothing back. Oh, well, 'Everything passes. And after every December comes May.' " This was a quotation from a popular poem.

I could afford to be so judicious because May had already come in the form of a boy named Putz. If you speak Yiddish, you know that the word "putz" means something vulgar in that language, but we didn't know that. His real name was Walter, and he was short. Maybe that's what brought us together.

He was a year younger than I was, and came to the home a year after I did, having first lived with two foster families in Zurich. I liked him right away. He was handsome and very intelligent and very good with his hands—he went on to become an engineer in Israel. In the same diary passage where I explained what had gone wrong between Max and me, in February 1943, I wrote, "Putz and I understand each other fabulously well. It's not just a superficial friendship, it's a marvelous comradeship."

It soon blossomed into more. I copied into my diary a

quotation from a book that described, in appropriately flowery terms, the way I felt: "How beautiful it was. Can something be a sin if it was so wonderful? We kissed for the first time, and then both did not know how it happened. It was a wonderful secret and will remain that way for a lifetime. And when we look at each other we think about what nobody except us knows."

When I think about Putz and me, what strikes me most was how ingenious we were in figuring out how to get time together. When we went to lectures, I always used to bring sewing or a big coat to put on my lap; underneath we would touch.

After about a year Fräulein Riesenfeld was joined by a woman named Frau Berendt. She wasn't perfect, but she was a big improvement. She was divorced, with a child who lived in the Swiss home, and she had a lot more feeling for children. She wasn't Orthodox, and one of the things she did every Friday night, when the rest of us couldn't read because of the Sabbath, was to read a chapter from the novel *How Green Was My Valley*. (I wrote in my diary, "That is the most fabulous thing I read or was read to in my whole life.") At a certain time all the younger kids had to leave to go to bed. But I didn't go to bed. I went hiding under the stairway, next to the plumbing pipes. Putz met me there and we hugged and kissed.

Boys and girls weren't allowed to go on walks together. To get around that, on Saturday mornings my friend Marga and I would go to the office and say we were going for a walk. Then Putz and Klaus, who was Marga's boyfriend, did the same thing. We'd meet at the caves in the woods, separate, and then go off necking. To this day, I could take you right to those caves. But as Putz pointed out when I saw him recently, we never went as far in the caves as we did in the home. There we had our own special nooks and crannies that nobody knew about; on the outside, we could always be caught. (If any of you are wondering if Dr. Ruth lost her virginity as an adolescent, the answer is no! Putz was an excellent kisser—he still is—but that was as far as we went.)

In my diary I gave quite a coy account of this excursion: "I would like to describe the happenings of yesterday after-

noon so that I can think about it as often as I would like to.
Marga and I went for a walk and . . . . . ."

After Putz started to go to high school in the village,
we came up with another plan. I used to have to make all
the beds every day in one of the dorms in the annex called
the blue room, for the color it was painted. I always arranged
it so that, at the very moment he was coming home from
school, I would have gotten to a certain bed in the corner,
next to a chimney, so that if anyone walked in they wouldn't
see us.

Putz—the future engineer—even invented an ingenious
communication device. He lived upstairs from me, and he
came up with a way of sending notes back and forth with
little pieces of paper and two strings. When I saw Putz in
New York last year, he told me about another project of his
that I didn't know about at the time. When I got my first
period, he started to keep a diary to figure out when I would
have my next one—why, I don't know. One day I found it
and asked him what it was. He had written it in code, but
the dates were marked, and that made me suspicious. From
then on he wrote the whole thing in code.

Putz used to tease me a lot. I see that I once wrote in
my diary, "Once again, he got me to promise not to make
the others explain dirty jokes to me." But I didn't mind,
because he was romantic, too. My favorite keepsake he made
for me was a little heart made out of two pieces of leather,
one side red, the other blue. Inside was a safety pin. I wore
it day and night—I never went to sleep without taking it off
my clothes and pinning it onto my pajamas. I remember a
friend of mine wrote a little poem about it, about how I would
look into the mirror and put on the little heart that Putz gave
me and then go to meet him. It amazes me how romantic
we were. We used to read love poetry all the time. One time
when he was away from the home, he wrote me a letter. I
was so afraid of losing it that I copied the whole thing into
my diary:

"Dear Karola, baby, you know very well that I don't
know how to write, and now you demand that I write
you a nice letter. I don't know anything but that I like

you very much. Forgive me that I'm not writing more, but you know. . . . And kisses, hearty kisses. I also like you very much and I will always want to be with you."

We had all kinds of plans. Along with Klaus and Marga, we decided that if the Germans invaded, we wouldn't go with the other kids. No, we would escape through Spain to Palestine. We planned every detail—where we would escape to, how we would feed ourselves, where we would stop and collect stragglers. There were even contingency plans: If one of us didn't show up, then we would go to a certain place and wait for him the next day. This was four kids! But we took it all very seriously. I always had my knapsack packed underneath my bed with dry food in it.

Putz and I also made plans for what we would do after the war. In a notebook he drew a scale model of the house we would build, with all the rooms and all the furnishings. The most important detail was a children's room. We so ached for family life that it was at the forefront of our fantasies.

At one point an untrue rumor—started by the same girl who had taken Max away from me—went around saying that I had undressed in front of Putz. I was crushed, and even when Putz consoled me and caressed my hair, I didn't feel any better. I went to Frau Berendt and asked if I had been bad. She said no, that I should continue my friendship with Putz, but that I should keep it clean. That helped, but what *really* made me feel better was that my archrival left the home a few days afterward.

Eventually, the romance between Putz and me ended— if it hadn't, we'd be married today. But we probably had too intense a relationship at too young an age, in too unsettled an atmosphere, for it to last. In any case, after we were together about three years, I started to be jealous of all the attention Putz had started paying to an older woman, one of the caretakers at the home. He tried to assuage me, as I wrote in my diary: "But he promised me he will always like me better. . . . The main thing is that he understands me and likes me. But does he really?" My tendency was always to think that things were my fault. "I talk too much," I wrote. "I'll have to change. . . . I've got to be more reserved."

But ultimately it couldn't last. The final break came, as these things often do, over an incredibly minor issue: I wanted him to comb his hair straight back, and he wanted to comb it sideways. After that momentous battle, I wrote in my diary, "Enough. That's it. It's over."

My relationship with Putz was incalculably important to me. We were both very lonely. And I thought that I was short and ugly and stupid, and that no man would be interested in me. When I look back on pictures of myself as a girl, I see that I wasn't bad looking. But nobody, not even my family, ever told me that I was pretty. German Jewish parents just didn't say things like that. And the people at the home wouldn't even think of it—their attitude was always, "You're a nuisance because we have to take care of you." Putz proved to me that somebody could find me desirable.

Many years later, on my annual trips to Israel, I'd see him every year, and last year when he was in New York he came to see me. Sitting in my son Joel's room, overlooking the Hudson River, I said to him, "When I think of you and those years, I always have a smile on my face."

He said, "I'm glad to say that it's mutual. I always think of you with a smile on my face."

That made me feel good.

Considering my later occupation, I'm sure people would be interested in the sex education *I* received while I was at Heiden—a period that covered my life from the age of ten to seventeen. My diaries are very interesting on that score. The first sign of puberty comes in the very first entry—on May 19, 1941, written when I was almost thirteen. My summer clothes had been in storage from the year before, and I wrote that when they were unpacked "almost everything was too small." I didn't say why.

A month or so later, I wrote that I was allowed to go hay-gathering instead of swimming. This doesn't sound like a great bargain, until you read the next line: "It was wonderful, especially that I didn't have to go to Mr. Mandel and tell him I couldn't go swimming." This meant that I was having my period, which was unpleasant not only because talking about it to men was embarrassing. We had to wash our sanitary napkins ourselves, which was a horrible, messy chore.

At this point in my life I was clearly more interested in learning about these matters than I had been two years earlier, when I dismissed my grandmother's attempts at instruction. And I found a sympathetic instructress in, of all people, Fräulein Riesenfeld, who by this time had gotten married to a man named Neufeld and had actually become nice. On July 20, I wrote: "Nine days ago I went for a walk with Frau Neufeld. I asked her all kinds of questions. She explained to me how a child develops in the mother's womb. Yesterday evening she also explained to me more things. I now wear a bra." On August 10: "Frau Neufeld again explained to me more things."

By October, the seeds of Dr. Ruth were already sown: "Yesterday I heard that Edith was told everything wrong about menstruation, that Else told her that one needs sanitary napkins when one is pregnant. I rectified it all because I know how bad it is when one is given wrong information about these things by a child."

And by the next April I was even philosophical about the subject: "I read a book called *Letters for Young Girls*. It was written by a physician for sex education. There were some things I didn't understand. I went to Frau Berendt, and she explained it all so wonderfully to me that one can't possibly think that anything about it is dirty. Everything in nature is so fantastically well organized!"

◦◦◦◦◦◦◦◦◦

I was promoted to a different group to study Bible. It pleases me very much. We study much more than in the other course.

—*diary of Karola Siegel,*
June 19, 1941

Lately I read two good books. Both by Pearl S. Buck. One is *East Wind: West Wind*, and the other is *The*

Good Earth. I learned a great deal from these books, but I can't write about all of this. . . . There is somebody here who studies with me every day an hour of French. I like to learn this language. We study!!!

—*diary of Karola Siegel,*
May 25, 1943

If only I could get the education of a kindergarten teacher, then I could manage life alone and without foreign help. That is a big wish of mine, not to be dependent on other people, the way I am right now.

—*diary of Karola Siegel,*
June 24, 1943

Always learning! When I read back over my diaries, I realize that that's the one thing I am obsessed with. Even the diary itself was a tool for knowledge. Here is what I wrote once after I had come to the end of one book: "Now this notebook is filled also. It has helped me more than all the past ones, and I hope that the next one I will like even better and that I'm going to learn a great deal through writing these diaries."

But I wasn't given the chance to learn. And that's the one thing that makes me the angriest when I think back on how the home was run. Here I was, a girl with a thirst for knowledge, and I wasn't given the chance to satisfy it.

There was a school in the home—although it took them four months, from January to May 1939, to get it under way. And when it finally did go into session, it wasn't of much use. There were forty students, ranging in age from six to fourteen, of all different levels of intelligence and education in one classroom. We met for just a few hours a day—the rest of the time we had to work.

There was only one teacher. His name was Ignatz Mandel, and he was in appearance a bit of a nebbish. He was somewhat ineffectual, he walked with a limp, and the women at the home made fun of him. That was partly, I think, because he was a Polish Jew. He conducted the school a bit like an open classroom—not teaching everybody at once, but going from group to group. He was a gentle man who did the best he could with limited resources, and I came to like him a lot. Part of the reason why, I suppose, was that he was the only adult male in the entire home. Once I wrote in my diary, "There is one man at Wartheim whom I like and admire more each day. That man is our teacher, Ignatz Mandel. One day I would like to be as nearly perfect as he is." Another time I said of him: "I can talk with him about many things. . . . Last night we discussed whether God determines our fate before we are born. Oh, well, the subject of God . . ."

We sometimes tried to get Ignatz angry, but it was very hard to do. Once, when he was talking to somebody, I kept pulling on his jacket from the back. He sent me out of the room, but he wouldn't get mad. In my diary I speculated that he didn't even want to send me out, but only did it as an example to the other children. So even at that young age, I was interested in "teachable moments," which I still talk about today in my lectures.

He liked me, too. I know this because I have *his* diary in my possession. I'm not sure how I got it—I may have stolen it in the home, or he may have given it to me years later in Israel, where he lived, when I told him I was doing a study of the children of Wartheim. About me he writes: "Her general conduct is good. She is vivacious, has a good character. Very diligent. She has a good mind, which is sometimes impaired by too much impulsiveness. Very short, below average in height, but physical development is completely normal."

There was another entry in his diary that impressed me very much: "My way as a teacher must be the way of love. God help me if I ever want only to rule. Better to have a little less discipline but more understanding, more trust."

Ignatz settled in Israel after the war. He had a house near Haifa with an orchard, and I visited him several times. I remember especially how happy he was when I showed him my two children, Miriam and Joel.

When school ended in the spring of 1943, I would be too old for Ignatz's school. On January 22, 1943, I wrote an essay for class about my education up to that point. After describing my schooling in Frankfurt I wrote, "Then came that horrible tenth of November. I don't want to discuss that day. . . . On May 1, 1939, our school here in Wartheim started. We have a very nice teacher, but he gives us too much homework. Most of what I know I learned here in this school in the children's home. I am now in the eighth grade, and next spring I should finish school. I would like much better to continue being in school. It is very sad that I cannot go to high school, because for my later profession it would be very helpful to attend a high school."

But it wasn't to be. Putz and another boy were permitted to go to the high school in the village—because they had relatives who would pay for them to go, and because they were boys. In the old Orthodox Jewish way of looking at things, a boy has to learn, while education is a luxury for girls. But I was determined to learn, and Putz and I extended our skill at surreptitious behavior to education. At night he would come down to my room, give me his books, and go to sleep in my bed. Meanwhile I'd go out in the hallway and read them—no lights were permitted in the rooms. The reason I told my diary that I liked studying French so much was that I was using Putz's book!

Somehow, we were never caught at this. The stairway creaked badly, so Putz developed a method of sliding down the stairs without making the slightest noise. Still, the supervisor's room was next door to my bed, and one night she heard Putz come in. He hid under the bed, and I pretended I was asleep, and she never discovered what was going on.

But of course I didn't complain about not being allowed to go to school. If I had known then what I know now, I would have gone to Zurich myself and raised money to go to that school. I remember walking to the village and looking into that high school with such longing. I would walk around it, look in the windows, and think, "Why can't I be in that school?" It looked to me like a palace.

But my last day in Ignatz Mandel's class would be my last formal education for a long time. As I wrote in my diary on April 7, 1943, just before the last day of school: "I have a very funny feeling, as if the gate of my childhood is closing faster and faster. It must be an enormous, giant gate—once it's closed, you can't open it anymore. What I'd like to do is put a giant rock in front of it so the gate doesn't close completely, and from time to time I can go back behind the gate again."

Every day I am less sure that I will ever see my parents again. I know that I must not lose hope, but it is not easy to keep believing in it.

—*diary of Karola Siegel*

ᴏᴏᴏᴏᴏᴏᴏᴏ

To this day I don't know why my parents seemed so reluctant to take steps toward emigrating. But I think it had to do with my grandmother, who was an important influence on my father, her only child. She didn't want to leave. In one letter from the fall of 1941, she wrote—as usual—"There's nothing new about our emigration." Then she went on to say, "As for myself, I will leave only with the last transport." Transport where? East or west? I had no idea what she meant. Another time she wrote, "Emigration is for young people only." For my grandmother, Germany was home; I think she could not conceive of willingly going anywhere else. And my parents wouldn't leave her behind.

As I said, the last letter I got from them was written in September of 1941. On October 29, I reported in my diary some momentous news: "I got mail from the Steins, who live on Röderbergweg. [These were the relatives at whose house I used to eat herring.] They wrote that my dear parents and my grandma emigrated. I don't know where to. I hope they weren't deported. I hope that they are well. All I can do now is hope."

But they were deported. I eventually learned they had been shipped to Lodz, where their address was Lodz (ghetto), Rembrandtstrasse 10. I/Zm.4. This was a city in Poland, which the Germans called Litzmannstadt. There, as in other cities, ghettos had been created for Jews—cramped quarters where they awaited shipment to the concentration camps.

I wrote to them at the address I had been given, but I never received any reply. Here is how I recorded my feelings in my diary:

November 12, 1941. I still don't have any news from my dear sweet parents and Grandma.

November 25. It is almost seven weeks that I don't have mail from my parents and Grandma.

December 14. Tonight is Chanukah, the first candle has been lit. I hope that next year we will all be reunited with our loved ones when we light the candles.

December 17. On the first night of Chanukah I was so terribly homesick.

December 18. Today it is nine weeks and one day that I have no mail from my parents.

January 5, 1942. Today it is three years that I am here. . . . I was supposed to move to Geneva to be a housemaid for a family there. But I'd rather not, because they do not keep kosher. I wouldn't mind going to Geneva, but I'm sure my parents would not want me to.

April 5. Now I must go to bed. Good night Mama, Papa, Grandma, and all, all my relatives.

On April 30 a letter arrived unexpectedly from my mother's youngest sister, Ida. It came from Izhica, a labor camp near Lublin to which she had been sent. It said, "I am always hungry." This was my first definite indication that terrible suffering was going on.

In May I wrote, "Only a few days until my fourteenth birthday. I'm glad, but this is the first birthday in my life in which I'm not getting congratulations from my dear, sweet, unique parents and Grandma. I hope they are in good health, which would be the main thing."

In September I got a letter from my grandparents in Wiesenfeld saying that my parents and grandmother were safe. I wrote in my diary, "Thank God, I know that my dear ones in Poland are all right."

But I never heard anything more about them—or about my Wiesenfeld grandparents, either. The next June, shortly before my fifteenth birthday, I wrote: "Every day I am less sure that I will ever see my parents again. I know that I must not lose hope, but it is not easy to keep believing in it." After another three months with no news—at which time I had been in Heiden for almost five years—I wrote, "I would so much like to relive the days with my parents. I did not know what my parents meant to me. But now, and especially today, I do realize it so well. I would so very much like to make up to them for all they did for me, all that I never appreciated." It seems that I had given up hope.

chapter

3

June 26, 1941. Sunday the older girls were permitted to go swimming. I was standing in the entrance to the kitchen and Frau Neufeld said, "Ach, we can send Karola along. She always helps with the household work!" And I was permitted to accompany them to the swimming pool in the village. It was wonderful. Tuesday I was also permitted to go swimming. I already can jump from the three-meter board.

July 20. Now I have a lot to write. First, we have vacation. Second, the Swiss children leave next Friday. There are some very nice girls among them. Every day we go swimming. . . . Lately, I have gone very often for walks with the little ones. Once, I was in the park in the village with sixteen children. I had been given some dried fruit to give to them, and it looked very comical when all of them were sitting down and I was handing out the fruit.

August 10. Last week we took a trip to the village of Trogen. It was very nice. Also, all the ones who help in the household went with Frau Neufeld to Rorschach. Seventeen of us went, and we even got to go to a coffeehouse. It was very nice. I quarrel almost every day with Hannelore. I got a package from home. Sweets, and also a pocketknife. Soon we have school again. I have to control myself better, not only in my behavior but in what I achieve. Today I have horrible homesickness. Now I have to prepare my things for school. Fräulein Hannah is sweet with me.

September 26. I cleaned the bookcase. I organized the books beautifully. Frau Berendt, who is so nice, praised me and made me responsible for keeping the books in order. Great! I'm very happy.

October 16. Yoo-hoo. I'm now permitted to help Lotte [the kindergarten teacher] with the little boys. That is so great of Frau Berendt to permit me. I'm so happy.

November 17. Everybody is awful with me because they're jealous that Frau Berendt is nice with me.

December 8. Today I'm going to have my hair washed by Frau Berendt. I have to be at her place at five. My essay in geography was good, and in arithmetic I got an A.

—*diary of Karola Siegel*

I was in Heiden for more than six years; I celebrated my eleventh birthday there and my seventeenth. So, as you can imagine, most of my time there was not taken up by the dramatic events and concerns I've been talking about, but by the dull—and not-so-dull—events of daily life. Things like . . .

. . . friendship. I made many friends at Heiden. Some are people like Marga and Ilse Wyler-Weil, with whom I'm still great friends to this day. Then there was Mathilde, the girl I knew from Frankfurt and rode with on the train to Switzerland. I was close to her until she died a couple of years ago. (Mathilde lived in London after the war, and once she came unexpectedly to visit me in New York, when I was to leave for Europe that night. I asked my friend Rudi— unmarried, like Mathilde—to do me a favor: "A friend of mine is here. If you like her, fine. If you don't like her, you did me a favor by showing her New York." They ended up getting married—I am the godmother of their two children. I've also made four other matches, of which I'm very proud, because as anyone who reads the Talmud knows, in the Jewish tradition making a match, or a *shiddach*, is a very good deed.)

I also made friends with someone outside the home, a Swiss girl named Erika. We weren't supposed to eat outside the home because of the possibility of eating unkosher food, but I got to visit my friend a couple of times at her house, which was wonderful for me. She used to call me Rugele because I was small and round, like a little pastry, and she once wrote a whole diary for me. Naturally, I still have it.

Probably the friend that meant the most to me then was a non-Jewish woman named Helen Haumesser, who worked as a counselor-teacher at the home. She took a liking to me, and at night, after the others had fallen asleep, she would sit on my bed and talk about what was happening in the world—at least as much as a thirteen- or fourteen-year-old could understand. She was very important in giving me this kind of affection and intellectual stimulation at the very moment in life when I was most in need of a mother figure. Even my private nickname for her, Helli, was significant, because it sounded like *hell*, the German word for light. When she was about to leave Wartheim I wrote in my diary a long, emotional "letter" to her, as only an adolescent can:

> You know, Helli, I miss you already, and you haven't even left yet. Though I address you more formally when I talk to you, I think of you as Helli. I am very proud that you have such faith in me . . . but do I deserve it? So much was going through my head when I talked to you the other day. I'm afraid I won't be able

to go on. You are religious, intelligent, educated. . . .
You are the first person I have trusted completely.
You understand me with all my faults. You were the
only one who believed in me, when I told you what I
have never told anyone before. I love you almost as if
you were my mother. And all this has to come to an
end—and so soon. . . . I feel as if something dark,
mysterious, inescapable, were coming. Helli, I really
must not think such things, but . . . You have helped
me so much, in so many ways. And you had to go
through so much, and I could do nothing to help
you, all I could do was think of you and feel for you.
Sometimes I feel I'm going to burst, it is the end of
the world, and yet nothing changes, nothing at all.
Day follows night without pity. Morning, noon,
evening—only at night it is different. But then I'm
so tired, I fall asleep whether I want to or not. . . .
I really should not call you Helli, not even in my
thoughts, but I really cannot think of you by any
other name. . . . I don't know what I would have
done if you had not come to Wartheim. And yet, I do
not have a "crush" on you, like a teenager. One cannot have a "crush" on one's mother.

. . . movies. Every once in a while we were taken to the
movie theater in the village of Heiden. This didn't happen
often, but I remember well all the films we saw. On June 27,
1943, I wrote in my diary, "Yesterday evening we were permitted to see *Mrs. Miniver*. It was beautiful, but very, very
sad. One witnesses the entrance of England into the war and
some attacks. In between, a real 'family' is shown. I cried
very bitterly, but despite that, this film is going to remain
forever in my memory." And so it has. I could identify with
the story of England under siege because, in a way, I was
living it. Greer Garson was wonderful as Mrs. Miniver, so
brave and responsible. I remember the scene where she and
her husband take the children into the cellar when bombs
are dropped on their neighborhood. I understood then that
there is an obligation to keep making small talk, to keep
going, even when horrible things are happening around you.

We also saw *How Green Was My Valley*. That was a strange experience, because Frau Berendt had read the book to us. Now, all of a sudden, the poor Welsh family and all the miners suddenly appeared on the screen. I had no idea how they did that. I cried big, big tears when I saw *Waterloo Bridge*, and the officer's returning home had a tremendous psychological meaning for me, because I was so far away from home. The woman forced to become a prostitute was so touching. I thought that having to live like that was the worst thing that could happen to you.

I also loved Vivien Leigh in *Gone with the Wind*—her tiny waist, and all those lovely crinoline dresses, and the magnificent ball where she dances with Rhett Butler. That movie was so beautiful to look at, so different from the life that I was living.

But my favorite movie star was Shirley Temple. To me, she was a princess surrounded by wealth and beauty. She had those lovely curls, and those dimples, she was so spirited and alive in those films—she made others happy, and I loved that. I had straight hair, and I always thought that I was short and unattractive. I used to think, If only I could look like that!

. . . scouting. In 1943, a man named Moise Fuks came to Heiden to start a boy scout division. Klaus and Putz were in charge of the boy scouts, and I organized a troop of eleven cub scouts. Their nickname was the weasels, and I was called magpie—"because," I wrote in my diary, "I talk so very little, as always." I also wrote that my motto was "to give my best," my watchword was "to be obedient," and my goal was "to give these boys, who have so little intellectual stimulation at Wartheim, everything they should have under normal conditions. And more than that: I would like to see true understanding and trust develop between me and my troop. I know that this can be accomplished only with great patience and much love. And with strict discipline."

Obviously, I took all this very seriously. One of the best things about it was my relationship with the scout leader of Heiden, Leni Rohner, who became a good friend, and Moise Fuks, known as the buffalo, with whom I used to have long conversations about all kinds of things. When he left Wartheim I wrote in my diary, "For me he was a true scout, in every sense of the word."

. . . my diary. My diary, which I wrote into little blue paper notebooks, the kind you would take an exam in, was probably my best friend of all—it was certainly my best confidant. I wrote in it almost every day, and I told it things I wouldn't dream of telling anybody else. I kept track of my pennies and copied poems and songs and practiced my English. I wrote down these lines—

> Write to me very often, write to me very soon.
> Letters from my dearest are like the loveliest flowers
> of June.

—and these—

> Should auld acquaintance be forgot
> And never brought to mine.

As you can see from the misconstrued last word, I hadn't quite mastered the language.

I was always worried that someone might find and read my diary. What I was afraid of was that, if they did, they would see how sad I was. Once I wrote, "I wish I had a real diary, with a key, so that I could write without having to worry that someone else would read it. The reason I don't trust others not to read it is that I myself am so nosy."

Another time I wrote: "The only other person who is permitted to look into these things is Putz. . . . I hope, with God's help, I will be able to show it to my parents one day. Ah, but sometimes I don't have a ray of hope that it will ever happen. But one can never know. . . ."

. . . crushes. What teenage girl doesn't have them? I remember one in particular I had on a Red Cross official who would occasionally come to visit the home. I wrote in my diary that he was "fabulous" (in German, *fabelhaft*, which on the evidence of my diary was my favorite word—there was no German word for "terrific"), and that I was delighted that he was coming in August. I followed the sentence with eight exclamation points.

. . . excursions. Maybe the best thing I took from Wartheim was an appreciation for nature. We'd take a lot of hikes and long walks. The reason for this, probably, was that it was a cheap activity, but I loved it—I found out what comfort you can get from mountains and meadows covered with flowers. We also did a lot of sleigh riding and ice-skating and skiing. It wasn't skiing as people do here—we had some old skis, and we walked up a little hill, and skied down. But it came in handy later when I was invited to celebrity international ski races at Sun Valley and Banff, with people like Brooke Shields, George Hamilton, and Cliff Robertson.

Occasionally we'd have breakfast at a local inn, and once in a while we'd take an excursion to the town of Rorschach, which was, of course, fabulous. But the best interlude of my years at Heiden came in 1942, when I was sent to Zurich for ten days. I was supposed to see a doctor about the fact that I was so short and possibly get hormone shots to make me grow.

I stayed at the home of a family called Guggenheim, whose daughter, Susie, had worked at Wartheim as an intern, and I was incredibly excited about going. "Dear God," I wrote in anticipation, "I'm so happy." Here are some highlights from the trip, as recorded in my diary: "Friday evening was wonderful! In the evening in bed, Susie brought me a little doll made out of marzipan!!!!!! It tasted delicious!!!!!! Then I read a long time in bed. . . . We went to the theater with Susie's boyfriend, Rudi, a nice guy. In the evening I put my shoes outside the door. The next morning they were shined. [Usually, cleaning the shoes was my job.] . . . On Tuesday they took me to a concert. Fabulous. . . . On Shabbat morning I went to synagogue [the first time I had done this in four years]. It was beautiful. In the afternoon I went to a youth study group, and I did very well. Sunday evening, to the theater. Paganini. Fabulous." For ten days I felt as if I had come back to a strange, almost forgotten world. (I wasn't given the hormone shots, a fact for which I'm now grateful—I shudder to think of the side effects they might have had.)

. . . studies. When I graduated from Ignatz Mandel's school, having completed the eighth grade, I was faced with the choice of what to do. At some point in Switzerland I had acquired the dream of becoming a medical doctor—and a dream was exactly what it was, because there was absolutely no chance in the world of its ever coming true. So I had to fall back on the plan of becoming a kindergarten teacher.

Now, Switzerland had a strange rule. In order to teach kindergarten, you first had to get a household diploma—a certificate stating that you knew how to be a maid! I suppose this was because they felt that you might be working for a wealthy family, and you should know how to clean. In any case, for the next two years I continued my housework at the home and in addition went into the village to take theoretical courses in household management. As a result, to this day I know how to mend a sweater so that you would never see the stitch, how to iron shirts in no time at all, how to air beds, how to clean in any corner, how to prepare a good Swiss meal. But I don't do any of those things now. I can't stand it when people are too neat—I had enough of neatness in those years in Switzerland.

At the end of two years I had to go to the town of Herisau to take an exam to show what I had learned. I passed my theoretical tests with flying colors and got a passing grade in sewing. But then there was a cooking test, for which we all stood behind our own stoves and made a dish. I burned some carrots. Then I had a stroke of genius, similar to the time I talked my way back into the first grade in Frankfurt by demonstrating that I knew that two times two equals four. While I engaged the supervisor in a fascinating conversation, I signaled to my friend Marga to quickly pour some water on the carrots so they would be salvaged. I passed the test.

. . . holidays and birthdays. These were the major events in our world. We got gifts once a year, on Chanukah. Every year the women from the committee in Zurich that ran the home came with a package for each child. Inside the packages was old clothing, never new. When you opened your present, you had to go to the ladies and say, "Thank you, it's wonderful," even if you didn't like it or it didn't fit. And for months, or even years, they would say, "Remember when I gave you that sweater?" And you had to say, "Yes, it was wonderful."

We put on little plays on all the holidays. One year I wrote a play for Tu B'shvat, the holiday of the trees. It was about how there was one little tree who wasn't accepted by all the others—which shows you how my imagination worked.

Birthdays were big days, always noted in my diary. Shortly before my fifteenth birthday I wrote down a list of what I wanted: a watch, a fountain pen, a little package of pins, sewing needles, darning needles, a pair of scissors, white and black yarn. As you can see, my fantasies were not extravagant—I knew not to wish for what I had no chance of getting. If I got anything on the list, I would put a little check mark next to it; I eventually got everything except the pen and scissors.

I wrote, "Soon I will be fifteen years old, and I don't want to be sixteen in this home." But I was, and seventeen, too. That year I wrote, "Seventeen. A strange feeling. I must learn to know myself better, to educate myself, and . . . more self-discipline! Everything is boiling and bubbling up inside me, and nothing happens. I seek and seek and don't quite know what. . . . No one must ever read this, or I'll be thrown out of the home."

ooooooooo

The War Is Over

It was Friday evening. The table was festively laid. Just as we were about to start the dessert, the phone rang. It was so still in the room you could hear a pin drop. Then we heard Frau Berendt's voice say: "But how wonderful!" . . . Some of us tried to guess what the wonderful news could be. . . . Suddenly she stood in the door. She had big tears in her eyes. "Dear children, I have just received some very important news. The war is over. The Allies have won!" One might have expected enormous shouting and yelling to break out, but no, there was complete silence. Each one thought of perhaps seeing parents and relatives after all these years. . . . Frau Berendt said we should pack our things on Sunday. . . . Waking up on Saturday morning, the Sabbath, was the most beautiful awakening of my whole life. My first thought was "The horrible war is over!" . . . Sunday morning we all began to pack our things. What a confusion there was! "Oh, I'm so happy!" "What are my parents going to say when I suddenly rush up to them!" "When I see my parents again, I won't know what to say to them!"—such phrases were called back and forth across the room. . . .

Saying good-bye was very moving. We had been together for four years, and we had gotten accustomed to each other. . . . Then we were standing at the station in Geneva. This was the big moment we had been waiting for: we were here to meet our relatives who were arriving from Poland. There was quite a to-do until everybody was sorted out. Our loved ones did not look very well. . . .

Eight days later we arrived in Tel Aviv. . . . My grandparents on my mother's side and my grandmother on my father's side are staying with relatives in Tel Aviv. My parents and I and an uncle who has been here for two years are going to a neighboring kibbutz. Mama and her brothers and sisters are getting used to farm work again. Papa, too, has found a pleasant job, and I will teach in the kindergarten of the children's house of the kibbutz. . . . We have a little house all to ourselves.

—*"After the War," essay by Karola Siegel
September 16, 1942*

∞∞∞∞∞∞∞

Note the date. That essay was not a report on reality, but wishful thinking written nearly three years before the fact, about what it would be like when the war was over.

While the war was going on, we heard surprisingly little about it. We didn't have a radio, we didn't see newspapers, and for some reason the adults who supervised us didn't see fit to inform us on happenings from the front. What news we did get was curiously filtered and detached. In my diary entry of December 8, 1941, right after I discussed my grades,

I noted, almost casually, "America is now in the war against Japan. Bread will probably be rationed now."

One thing we did have was a map with pins showing where the Allies were. We also occasionally saw some American soldiers—they must have been sent to Switzerland for recuperation or recreation. I think some of the older girls from the home went out with them, but I never talked to any of them. I remember thinking that they were like angels, descended from heaven to save Europe. Years later, when I was teaching at Lehman College in New York, I had some students who had fought in Vietnam. Even though I opposed that war, it made me so sad that they were ashamed of having been soldiers.

For most of the war I didn't know that concentration camps existed. But I knew that terrible things were happening. In 1942 some French children came to Wartheim from Camp Gurs, a labor camp in France, and what they reported made a big impression on me. I wrote in my diary, "Last night, Ruth, Max, and I helped pick up twelve children who entered Switzerland illegally. These children have all suffered a great deal. . . . One of the girls told me that in the morning they got some *Wasserkaffee* [water with a little bit of coffee mixed in], and noon and evening they got *Wassersuppe* [water with a little soup mixed in] with a carrot. For lunch they got a small piece of bread. Now we know better than ever how incredibly lucky we are to be here."

In 1945 some people came temporarily to the home from the Bergen-Belsen concentration camp. They were the fortunate ones; they survived. I wrote, "So many things and situations are happening that one can't even think clearly about them anymore. Up until a moment ago, Frau Mandel from Hungary was telling us of all the suffering she saw: mass murders, gas chambers, and other horrible things. It is really a wonder that these people are still alive. And then one has to ask oneself, 'And you, a tiny little grain of sand among all that horror, you are so occupied with yourself. Stop making such a to-do about yourself.' "

I began to wonder, too, if I really wanted to be a Jew. Being one seemed to mean so much suffering—did I really want to expose myself to that? Once I wrote, "What are you?

What does it mean to be a Jew? Am I a German? Am I a Jew? . . . How is it going to be in the future? . . . Look at the others, what they have been through. Will they ever again be able to laugh? To be happy? I think not. And why all this? Because they have a different faith?"

At one point, I see by my diary, I temporarily lapsed into atheism. I was worried about my household exam, and I wrote, "Dear God, please help me. . . . But how can I demand that He help me when I don't believe in His existence?"

You can imagine my emotional state. Here I was, faced with the loss of my parents, the persecution of my people—plus the normal dislocations and turbulence of being a teenager. Looking back on my diary for these years, it reads like the journal of a tortured romantic poet. Some sample entries:

I yearn for I don't know what! I am searching for something unknown—I no longer know myself.

I am ugly, I am stupid. What will become of me? Who am I? What right do I have to be alive? What duty? . . . I am a hollow, empty, very superficial thing. What is going to happen? What is my purpose in life? I'll never amount to anything.

Will I be able to stick it out? I don't know. Suddenly everything boils and bubbles inside me, and I lose all self-control. Afterwards I'm sorry if I have hurt or offended someone. I keep seeking and not finding, and I have no patience. I don't know what I want. And I don't know what I ought to do. Sometimes everything is calm inside me, and I find myself again. But then something comes creeping up again and pulls me to pieces. Everybody is so superficial—and those who aren't are far away. One word keeps coming back: alone, one is so alone in this world. One has to keep on struggling—but: alone, always alone. I do miss my parents terribly. No friend can take their

place. Oh, how I long for them, how homesick I am!
—Now I have to go back. And make a fresh start.

Whew. How did I deal with all of this turmoil? In the usual ways, I suppose. I used to go for long walks to a little church above Heiden, where I'd sit and write in my diary or talk to myself. Once, in the middle of a party at the home, I ran off to a little mountain inn and sat writing by myself in the restaurant. ("I did not really," I admitted, "behave so terribly well.") And I took great comfort from sentimental stories and songs. I've already mentioned the song about the Cinderella figure; there was another one, by Heine, that I also used to sing over and over to myself. It was about a boy who fell in love with a girl, only to see the girl fall in love with and marry another fellow. I also liked sentimental poetry. I remember I had a calendar with a quotation from a writer named Spitteler: "What if one asks you what is the most difficult, the deepest hurt on earth? To be disappointed in the one you love the most." All of this expressed deep, unfocused longing and yearning; it was very romantic, to the point of kitsch. And I liked it.

I didn't cry much, however. I didn't think I could allow myself to.

There was one other, more significant, outlet for my emotions: Zionism. You'll notice that in the fantasy I wrote in 1942 about the end of the war, I say that we are going to Tel Aviv. So I must have realized by that time that Palestine was the place where most of us would end up when the war finally was over. Switzerland clearly did not want us, and to go back to Germany was unthinkable. In order to go to another Western European country, you had to have a relative already there, which I didn't. And the United States—to me the United States was like a Shirley Temple dream. So Palestine it was.

The modern Zionist movement, whose goal was the creation and settlement of a Jewish homeland, had been started at about the turn of the century by Theodor Herzl, an Austrian journalist. Since the Balfour Declaration of 1917, it had focused on the British territory of Palestine. And since the rise of Hitlerism, emigration to Palestine and worldwide interest in Zionism had both increased.

The people who ran Wartheim weren't Zionists themselves, but they must have realized that when the war was over most of us would be destined for Palestine, so they were receptive to Zionist ideas and representatives. As early as 1940 I mentioned Herzl in a letter, and the next year I noted in my diary that we had had a "celebration" for him.

An organization called Youth Aliyah was devoted to attracting young people to Palestine. It was very active during the war, and organizers from the group came to Wartheim and gave us all our introduction to the cause. The first visit came in May 1942, and here is how I recorded it:

Now I have a lot to write. Yesterday a gentleman named Nathan Schwalb was here. He came representing the Youth Aliyah to Palestine. To make a long story short, I may—even more than may, it's more sure than not sure—go with them to Eretz [Hebrew for "the land of," also used to refer to the country itself] Palestine, with Rita, Klärli, Hannelore, Hannah, Appelschnut [literally "applemouth," and my nickname for Mathilde, whose last name was Apelt], Rosa, Nathan, Max. In Eretz we have to study half a year to learn about the country. The next six months we are going to study half a day and work half a day. Then comes a whole year of work, with studying in the evening. Then I hope I can go into the children's house and become a kindergarten teacher. Now I have to study and study Hebrew. In school we now have it three times a week instead of two. Nathan Schwalb is a very nice person. Now I have to write my life story for him, and then we are going to get books in Hebrew that we have to read. I'm going to be sad when I have to leave this dear Wartheim, but I can't stay here forever. . . . Dear God, please help that I can go with them to Palestine. I'm going to pray very hard every evening. Then I would also see my uncle Lothar again.

Why did the idea of going to Palestine have such an immediate appeal? For a lot of reasons. The organizers were brilliant in instilling enthusiasm and knew exactly how to appeal to adolescents who were both idealistic and emotionally needy. They warned us that there would be a lot of hard work on the kibbutzim, but they also gave us flags and showed us pictures and told us stirring tales, like the story of Hannah Senesh, a Jew who was captured behind Nazi lines and despite being tortured, wouldn't reveal the strategic information she knew. And they taught us dances and songs. I still remember the lyrics to one of them: "Every human being in this world has his own country, and that's where he is at home. Only one people in the world has no homeland. Wherever he goes, someone kicks him out, and every single day the eternal Jewish question is posed in front of him: 'Jew, where are you going, who accepts you in the world, where do you feel protected and do not have to worry about the next day?' " The answer, obviously, was Palestine.

They were spirited people, and they told us that we had a responsibility to create something for the refugees who would come out of the war (somehow everybody assumed that the Allies would win) homeless and broken and with nobody to take care of them. (It never occurred to us that that was precisely the condition we would be in.) Equally important, after we'd been kicked out of Germany and given a grudging reception by Switzerland, here suddenly was a country that not only appreciated me and all of my friends, but enthusiastically wanted us to come live there! And so my sentimental outpourings were now directed toward a new object—Palestine, and working the land, and the Jewish people. I copied songs and poems into my diary—one about life in the camps where people prepared for life in Palestine, and one about the mother lighting the candles on Friday night, and one about the Jews and their hurt. I can't sing, but I still remember all those melodies in my head.

It didn't hurt, of course, that most of the organizers were good-looking young men. There was one in particular, by the name of Itzhak Schwerzeng, whom I had a crush on. I confided in my diary, "Now I want to be very honest. Is it only his personality or the entire philosophy of the organization that was attractive to me, or is it because I'm attracted to anything new?"

I never got anywhere with Itzhak, but I did enter into a romance of sorts with someone named Werner, a leader of a Zionist youth group. For some reason he had started corresponding with Klaus, Marga's boyfriend, and I joined in the correspondence. Our letters became more and more intimate, and one day I received one from him that contained, as I exclaimed in my diary, "My very first offer for marriage!" We still hadn't met each other, but this kind of thing wasn't unheard of—getting engaged would save one entry visa into Palestine after the war. Fortunately, I was smart enough to tell him that I was too young. This decision proved to be doubly fortunate later, when it turned out that not only was Werner not really a Jew, but that he had been in a Nazi youth organization before the war.

One thing I remember being concerned about was the zealousness of some of the Zionists. After all, I had wonderful non-Jewish friends, like Helli; these people sometimes seemed to condemn everyone who wasn't Jewish. I wrote: "I want to understand and be loyal to all people, not, like the fanatic Zionists, condemn everybody who is different! . . . After the war Eretz Israel will need human beings, not fanatics; people who are willing to build and help each other." When we went to Palestine, we would live on collective farms called kibbutzim, and I presciently had doubts about that, too: "I'm ready to be part of a collective life, but I'm afraid that the individual will get lost in the group."

Eventually, though, my doubts were resolved. And as usual I was not shy about recording my feelings in my diary:

> What does it mean to be a Jew? I realize it more and more: we must have our own country. Even if not all Jews can live there, they will have a nationality, a state that will protect them, they will no longer be so helpless.

We need strong new generations. We demand Jewish honor.

I have promised to remain faithful to my people, my language, and my culture, that means the Jewish culture, and I will keep this promise, come what may.

∞∞∞∞∞∞

The war is over, that means it is peace. But the war will not be over for a long time! I don't know what to think. Of course I am glad that the bombing and killing have stopped, but I cannot be really, truly happy. Now that the cannons are silent, our hearts are beginning to speak again.

> —*diary of Karola Siegel*
> *May 7, 1945*

This time the war really was over. But our reality was far different from the gleeful celebration I had envisioned in my essay three years before. Instead of rejoicing and reunion, there was more waiting. I should have expected it—this was Wartheim after all. The main thing we were waiting for was news of our relatives and loved ones. And this the people from the home handled stupidly. Every week the Red Cross published lists of people who had survived the concentration camps. And instead of first reading the list themselves and then privately calling in any child with a relative on it, they made us all gather together and they read us the entire list. This may have been in case a relative or friend was on the list whose name they didn't recognize, but they needn't have bothered. No parent's or relative's name was ever read. I wrote in my diary, "It is a terrible feeling to read these lists, looking for two or three names, holding your breath—and then, finished—nothing. Cold and empty!"

Again, I should not have been surprised at how insensitively this was handled. A couple of years earlier, when Putz was sent a card saying that his mother had been shipped east, Frau Berendt read it aloud in front of a whole group of children. Putz started laughing hysterically, until she slapped him.

With the war over, there were important decisions to be made. Having gotten my household degree, I wanted to continue my education, and just before the fighting ended I had been accepted by a kindergarten-teacher academy called Sonnegg in the town of Ebnat-Kappel in the eastern part of the country. I was to start in October, and I was very much looking forward to going. For one thing, in addition to paying the tuition of 150 francs a month, the Swiss organization that helped Jewish refugee children was going to give me ten francs of pocket money every month. This wasn't enough to buy much of anything, but you have to remember that this would be the first time in my life that I would have had any money in my hands at all, even to buy a candy bar. So it was an exciting prospect.

But even though we would be going to Palestine with nothing, just a knapsack and our old clothes, the pull of Zionism was too strong. What's more, I knew that even if I stayed in Switzerland, I would have to leave after I got my degree. It had been made very clear to us that we were not to stay in the country forever. So I wrote to Sonnegg, thanking them for accepting me but saying that, regrettably, I would not be able to attend.

And it wasn't just that I decided to go to Palestine. I was so enthusiastic that I influenced a number of other children, some of whom were younger and looked up to me, to go as well. Later, some of them told me that they resented me for this. And in fact if I had known at the time how much bloodshed and hardship lay ahead, I might not have been so insistent that they go. But I've never regretted my own decision.

Each of us was given what was called a Nansen passport. I had no passport, you see; in fact, I had no nationality. So an international group issued these documents to people who were stateless. But it still was not a sure thing that we would be allowed into Palestine. The British, then trying to appease both the Arabs and Jews who lived in their mandate, had established strict immigration quotas, and many settlers had to go there illegally via places like Cyprus.

There was one more decision to be made. We were told

that, once we got to Palestine, we could join one of two
groups—the Youth Aliyah, whose members studied half a
day and worked half a day, or the Chalutzim, where you
worked the whole day. Putz—with whom I was still
friendly—chose Youth Aliyah. You would have thought that
I would have, too, considering my burning desire for education. But no, my Zionist zeal took precedence. I decided
that the Jews needed workers, not intellectuals. And I went
with the group that worked a full day.

Most of the fifty or so children at Wartheim decided to
go to Palestine. My friend Ilse, another girl named Ruth
Kapp, who later became a good friend, and a few others had
relatives in Switzerland and stayed there. Mathilde went to
England, where her parents were. One girl, Klärchen Rothschild, the daughter of an Orthodox rabbi in Frankfurt, actually went back to Germany to rebuild. She later became a
communist and opened a bookstore in Frankfurt. The rest of
us left Wartheim on July 7, 1945.

We took a train to the town of Bex, where we were to
spend about two months preparing for the journey to Palestine. I had bought a new diary, bound in leather and more
adult, rather than the composition books I had used in Wartheim. I suppose it's not surprising that my entries in it, at
this point in my life when I was about to totally uproot myself
once more, reflected more uncertainty and more of an "inferiority complex" than ever. Adding to the travail was my
longing for a male "friend." One of the leaders in Bex, Franz,
was interested in me, but *I* had a crush on his handsome
colleague, Michael, who didn't even notice me.

July 12, 1945. Bex. With my new life I'm starting a
new diary. Despite all my doubts I'm going to Palestine. I have no idea how everything's going to turn
out. I have to be more quiet and even-tempered, to
define problems more in their depth, and to control
myself. Above all, I am trying to find a friend.

July 13. Am I satisfied? Am I already used to being
here? I don't know. I live with 150 people and I'm
alone. In which youth organization, with which per-

son do I find what I'm looking for? When will this looking stop? Everything here is so foreign, so hard to understand. Am I a Zionist? Do I really want to give up my personal life to live in a collective? I feel so strange and alone.

July 15. Today Charles and Marga came. I was happy to see Marga again, and still—am I jealous that Charles is Marga's boyfriend? Am I so small and narrow-minded that I begrudge someone else a friend? It hurts me. I also would like to have a friend. . . . I know that others also have difficult problems, but a little bit of sunshine is part of it. Is it my fault? Partly, I'm sure, but I don't have any solution other than not to think so egotistically and to concentrate on communal living. I do want to accomplish *something.* "Our way is not soft grass, it's a mountain path with lots of rocks. But it goes upwards, forward, toward the sun."

July 16. Why don't I find the way to God? Everything would be so much easier.

July 22. All my thinking and my aim is directed to one point—to find a friend. Now I know. I am superficial. I am sorry to admit it, but I, who thought I was deep, with deep inner feelings, am empty. I fall in love with somebody only because he looks good, without looking at his inner qualities.

July 31. Why am I so short and ugly? If I would be of normal height, everything would be easier. . . . Am I not going to grow any more?

August 2. I had to go to Zurich. I had to be among a lot of people, to disappear in the crowd. I must forget Michael.

August 4. Tomorrow morning I am going back to Bex with Franz. What is his significance for me? I don't know yet. In any case, he is sympathetic, and he understands me quite well. This was the last time in a bourgeois milieu for a long time. The evening was fantastic. The clear lake. The starry sky. One could dream so well. It was beautiful to be in a boat, being rowed on the lake. The many lights around the lake, the colorful neon lights. Everything impossible to describe, like in a fairy tale.

August 6. Am I going to get used to this place? I think that I'm much too joyous and happy (despite the fact that I know this is to a great degree artificial, in order to hide my anxiety and cowardice!). Or am I really like this, do I really not take life seriously?

August 8. I have a feeling that I do not fit into this collective. I don't have an answer and I'm so alone and I'm sick and tired of thinking about it. It's not going to help anyhow. I'm with 120 like-minded people, and nobody likes me.

I do want to perform. I want to replace for refugees and orphans that which I missed the most—the love and understanding of parents. But what are the Jewish people, language, culture, to me? My whole development—body and mind—stopped. Everybody knows more than me. (Inferiority complex.) It looks to me that I'm thinking like an eleven-year-old and not like a seventeen-year-old. Previously, I always saw a clear way, a clear goal, but now neither the way nor the goal is understandable to me. Did I end on a one-way street? Where is the clear truth? I know so little about Zionist history and I became a Zionist. Wasn't that a little fast? Before, I always criticized people who did things without thinking about them.

On August 29, the day before we left Bex, we took a train to Geneva, where we were given a farewell party. I was asked to make a speech. I don't remember exactly what I said, but I do remember the theme. I addressed the people of Switzerland, and I said that we were all very, very grateful.

I was grateful, but then again I wasn't. Yes, we were saved from the certain death we would have suffered had we remained in Germany. We were fed and clothed and sheltered. But my gratitude is tempered not only by my resentment at the insensitive and sometimes cruel way in which we were treated by the Swiss Jews, but also by the knowledge that many of the Swiss were anti-Semitic, were sympathetic to Hitler, and that they refused to let other people in. When Switzerland sent them back over the border, they were sent to their certain death.

Maybe because they have been surrounded for hundreds of years by larger, unfriendly neighbors—but whatever the reason—the Swiss have never been overly concerned about the welfare of outsiders. Some other Swiss quirks are less hostile, but nonetheless idiosyncratic.

The Swiss are a strange people. Here they have this magnificent country, with those amazing mountains, and the best pastry in the world, and so many are not happy. You walk on the Bahnhofstrasse in Zurich, a magnificent, beautiful street, and you see many sad faces. Some can sit in front of a wonderful cake at the Sprüngli pastry shop, and all they care about is whether the table is set properly. Of course when I go back now, I'm received with open arms by everybody, Jews and non-Jews alike. But that's because of who I am. When I go back, I go to Sprüngli twice a day. And I go into shops all up and down the Bahnhofstrasse and buy some beautiful clothes. I think about how when I was in Switzerland as a girl, I had no money. And I giggle.

But, as I said, Switzerland gave me and many others life, and for that I really am grateful. We had a hard life at Heiden, but as I discovered when I did the research for my master's thesis, not so hard that we didn't make something of ourselves. Of the hundred children who came to Switzerland in the Frankfurt transport, including the group who went with me to Heiden and the group of older children who went to Basel, almost half ended up in the United States, almost the same in Israel, and the rest scattered around the world. As far as I can tell, all of them went on to live normal, well-adjusted lives. Few of them remained in the occupations they had been trained for in Switzerland, and quite a few of

them became successes. There is a social worker, several
businessmen and farmers, a shopkeeper, a psychotherapist,
several nurses, some teachers, a professor of zoology, a hotel
manager, a baker, several housewives, a man (my friend Fred
Rosenberg) who started as a watch repairman and now owns
many of the duty-free shops at Kennedy Airport, and at least
one sex therapist and television personality.

Obviously, Wartheim did not warp us entirely. In a group
letter he wrote to us in the 1970s, our old teacher Ignatz
Mandel paid tribute to how we had overcome the trials of
our adolescence:

> What marvelous people you all grew up to be! You
> are the proof that not everything could have been
> done wrong. Despite everything, life at Wartheim was
> rich and full. You yourselves provided that fullness,
> through your friendships (and sometimes the oppo-
> site), in fulfilling your duties, in play, excursions,
> skiing, sledding, scouting, and whatever. Once, in
> my first year at Wartheim, when I was very close to
> despair, I wrote a verse in my diary, as encourage-
> ment for myself:
>
> > If you sow flowers, you can soon pick a nosegay.
> > If you plant a tree—it will be a long time before
> >   you can reap the fruit.
>
> Today this seems to me like a promise fulfilled.
> You all grew up to be strong, straight, tall trees; you
> have your families, your work, a place in society. Yes,
> now, thirty years later, the trees are yielding fruit.

Yet in the same letter, Ignatz acknowledged the depri-
vations we had experienced and that we would always suffer
their effects:

> [I] realize how weak the pedagogic cooperation at
> Wartheim was. We adults (and I do not exclude my-
> self, by any means) cooperated very little with each
> other. There were no discussion groups, no meetings

in which we discussed any of the problems that arose. The result was—it had to be—that for some of the adults the work was purely routine. Each one tried to restrict his own duties to as small an area as possible, to do as little as possible, and let the others do it. In other words: to pass the buck. As much work, as many duties as possible, were delegated to the others. That, of course, had to lead to misunderstandings, to squabbles, to intrigues. And you were the ones who suffered most under it. Each one of you, but we adults, too, we all still carry the scars—and sometimes even the wounds—that were inflicted in those days.

As for me, well, I tend not to think about the scars. But then that was probably the main effect Wartheim, and the entire experience of the war and the Holocaust itself, had on me: a dogged determination to look on the bright side of any situation. In all of the diary entries I wrote while I was there, so many of which proclaimed my displeasure with myself, never once did I venture to criticize Switzerland or the people who ran the home. The closest I came was once in 1943 when I wrote, "Now that I'm getting older, I do understand things that I would not have paid attention to before. I think they should take care of us a little more. Maybe it will happen when we are no longer children." I never took up the topic again. Even the subject of my master's thesis—how successful the Wartheim children had become—was a way of saying, Look, it wasn't so bad after all.

This shows up most clearly in the way I dealt with the issue of my parents. Even though their names were never on any of the lists, I refused to admit to myself that they were dead. When I got to Palestine, the people there told me I had to adopt a new first name—Karola sounded too German and the Zionists wanted nothing to do with anything German. I picked my middle name, Ruth, because that would make it easier for my parents to find me.

They never did, because they were exterminated at Auschwitz. I'm fairly certain that that is where they and my grandmother ended up, because I know that the Jews from the Lodz ghetto, where they were, were shipped there. My Wiesenfeld grandparents undoubtedly were killed in concentration camps. Of their children, my aunt Ida died with them; my uncle Benno managed to survive a labor camp and was able to go to England in 1938, where he died some years ago; one brother went to Shanghai and is now in San Francisco; another brother, Lothar, went to Palestine before the war (he died a couple of years ago).

Even fifteen years later, in the early sixties, when I was living in the U.S., I hadn't quite come to terms with reality. I had some short-term psychotherapy with Dr. Arnold Bernstein, and in the first interview, after I described my background, he said, "So, you're an orphan." I was shocked. Until that day I had never thought of myself in those terms. I think one of the reasons I felt this way was an irrational sense of guilt on my part: even though it had no basis in fact, for many years I felt that if only I had stayed in Germany instead of going to Switzerland, I could have saved my parents. Gradually I was able to shed that feeling and replace it with an admiration of what my parents had sacrificed to save me. I don't think I would have the courage to send my children away forever, even if I knew it was in their best interest.

Even when I came to grips with what had happened, I tried to avoid the topic. Although I carried them with me every step of my life, I never once looked at my diaries and letters from my parents until I had to in preparation for this book. I would never go to Auschwitz. I never made a concerted effort to find out precisely when and where my parents died. And I never registered their names in the Holocaust memorial in Israel, although my daughter did it for me recently. I tried not to think about the gas chambers where they probably died, although when I see a shower head or a fire sprinkler, I can't help thinking: This is how it happened.

I now know that, even though I am not a concentration camp survivor, I was exhibiting the psychology they often display. Some survivors talk incessantly and obsessively about their experiences, to the point of burdening their friends and family; others, such as myself, tend to keep it all to themselves. I never talked to my children, Joel and Miriam, about what had happened. I was aware of the other extreme, of the parents who unwittingly put the whole burden of guilt on their children, who accusingly say, "I never had what you have." I wanted to avoid that, and maybe I went too far in the other direction. When Joel, at a very young age, asked me, "What was it like for you to live without a mommy?" I quickly changed the subject. And I know that both my children have told me that they don't think I talked about it enough.

It's ironic. One result of my experiences is that I look on the bright side of any situation. But another is that, deep down, I sometimes expect the worst. Thirty years ago, when I first came to this country, I met a woman named Hannah, a German Jew who would become one of my dearest friends. I liked her very much when I first met her, but I said to her, "I do not want to like you." Because whenever I liked somebody they disappeared.

And now I have to look on the bright side. Hannah did become my friend, and she didn't disappear, and I have a wonderful family, and I did become Dr. Ruth. So that now, forty years after my ordeal, I have begun to learn an important lesson: Good things can happen, too.

chapter

4

In the late summer of 1945 we took a train from Bex to Marseilles, from where we were to sail for Israel. It was a long train ride, and it couldn't help but bring to mind the last such trip I had taken. Once again I was leaving the familiar for something completely new. But at least this time the destination was of my own choosing.

Michael, the leader of our group, was really only about twenty, but I thought of him as incredibly mature. He was also very good-looking. Michael (pronounced MIK-eye-el) was a Polish Jew whose family had managed to escape to Belgium only to find that country occupied by the Nazis. At that point he and his sister had set out for Switzerland, over the Alps, by foot. They had Belgian papers, and Michael dyed his hair blond so that no one would think he was a Jew. They made it, and Michael was taken in by a Swiss non-Jewish family. Later he worked as a waiter and became a Zionist organizer.

As I said, I definitely had a crush on him. But most of all, I was ecstatic that people such as him, Franz (one of the older German Jewish children who had spent the war years in Basel), and a third guy, named Abraham, who was a hunchback and was very, very smart, were actually paying attention to me. Abraham was so smart that I remembered feeling extremely honored that he would even talk to me. After six years in Heiden, I was suddenly in the company of people fascinated with ideas, and I loved it.

Franz and Michael were only two or three years older than I was, but they acted almost like our parents. We had left Heiden with nothing; a big point was made that we wouldn't *need* anything, not even a coat hanger, that everything would be provided once we got to Palestine. (I later found out that this was something of an overstatement.) But while we were in Bex, we girls decided that we were going to need brassieres. I was the unofficial leader, so it was I who went to Michael and asked him to buy them for us. And he did, as if he were our father.

Michael knew how devoted we were to him, and he was good at manipulating us. We boarded the train in Basel, each of us carrying maybe one knapsack and one suitcase with all our earthly possessions, and before we did he asked me to look for something in his rucksack. I was delighted to be asked, so I scurried away to do it. Inside I found a gun in a holster. I took it to him and said, "Michael, what are you doing with this?" He said that the gun had been used by his father, who was a partisan in France, and that he wanted to take it to Palestine as a souvenir. He told me that the Swiss and the British (who would be supervising our ship to Palestine) were very gentlemanly and wouldn't be likely to search a young girl. Would I carry the gun? Of course I said I would. I wore the holster under my arm, and nobody searched me. Later, when we had gotten to Palestine, Michael told me that it was all a lie. The gun hadn't been his father's; he had brought it for the Haganah, the Jewish underground army, which needed every weapon it could get. What he didn't say was that he had endangered all of us: if the gun had been found, we all might have been thrown off the train. Young people—especially young people devoted to a cause—do crazy things.

I don't remember much about that train ride. I remember that I organized songs, just as I had done six years before.

And I remember looking out the window at the bombed-out stations and burned-out villages of France, which had only just rid itself of the occupying Germans. At one station we had a long wait. It turned out it was to let another train pass, a freight train. When it went by, I saw that it was filled with German prisoners of war. We were close enough to see their faces. They looked tired, pale, unshaven. Our parents might have been transported east in just such a train. And the men we were looking at—they might have run the concentration camps in which our parents were killed. What I don't understand is why nobody went out and started shouting or did anything. We just stared at them in silence. I suppose part of it was our own German restraint. But I do remember looking at the men and thinking, I wonder where you were?

I was sad, but I also remember a sense of adventure. Here I was on a train with my comrades, going to a country I knew nothing about except a romanticized idea of sand and beautiful Mediterranean Sea. And before that we would be in Marseilles. As the train chugged through the French countryside, I didn't sleep the whole night, waiting to see the sea for the first time.

When we got to Marseilles, tents had been set up for us on the beach. We spent two nights there. I remember the stars were bright, and I remember that we all huddled together for warmth and comfort, and I remember that I spent the night in the arms of Franz. I loved it.

We took a train to Toulon, where we were to board the ship for Palestine. And there Michael pulled another maneuver. He was in charge of getting six hundred young people on the ship—which was a British naval ship called *Mataruah*—but at the last minute he was told that he would have to get on another group of about six hundred more. He noticed that the English soldier who checked papers wasn't doing a very efficient job. So after Michael got us on, he collected all our papers and left the boat, telling the guard he had forgotten something. Then he gave our papers to the next group, and they got on, too.

As a result, the boat was very crowded. There was only enough food for half the people on board, so rations were slim. Marga and I gave our cabin to a mother and two children who had gotten on illegally. We slept on the deck, under stars brighter than I had ever seen before. Once again I slept in Franz's arms. It was a festive ride, full of songs and dancing and anticipation. But there was a sadness, too, because now that I was going to Palestine, I would never—or so I thought—see Europe again.

Here is how I described it in my diary:

September 4, on the boat. The whole thing still feels like a dream. What is going to be when I wake up from it? Happy and finally satisfied, or again disappointed? . . . We are sailing toward our destination. (Is it also mine?) . . . Everything that happened before should stay in the diaspora and on the bottom of the ocean. Is it possible? This water, this white, endless surface, sparkling, full of waves and then very quiet, is just beautiful. It is so beautiful that I can't describe it— one has to experience it with all of the force and feelings that a human being has. One wave falls into the next and a new one is created.

After six days at sea, at three o'clock in the afternoon, we arrived in Haifa. And I was in for a shock. Instead of immediately going to a kibbutz to help build the land, we were taken to a camp called Atlit. Here we waited while the British sorted out who was to go where, who had papers and who didn't. Luckily, no one was sent back, not even the people Michael had illicitly snuck on board. I was upset by that camp. By this time I had seen pictures of concentration camps, and being in this camp with a barbwire fence all around it and with Jews inside, I couldn't get them out of my head. And so, when my uncle Lothar came to see me, the same brother of my mother who had brought me chocolates in Germany and had gone to Palestine before war broke out, I couldn't even embrace him or kiss him through the fence. He had brought me chocolates again, exactly as he used to when I was a child, and fortunately these could be passed over the fence.

We could talk, too, and Lothar said he wanted me to go with him to his kibbutz, an old, prestigious, wealthy one called Ashdot Yaakov. It was a tempting offer. I would be associated with someone already established and not be a complete newcomer; maybe I would even have the chance to go to school. But I knew that I had promised Marga and Michael that I would go with them and a group of about thirty-five new immigrants, so I thanked Lothar and said no.

After a few days in the camp we set out in a convoy of covered trucks for the kibbutz. I had already been struck by how hot and dry Palestine is—especially after six years in the Swiss highlands. Now, traveling through the country-side, I saw how stark the landscape was. There was not a cloud in the sky and very little green on the land.

The kibbutz movement was vitally important in the history of Zionism. It had existed since 1901, when the Jewish National Fund was instituted for the purpose of buying land in Palestine for Jews to cultivate. The Fund had accumulated a great deal of land over the years, which it leased to kibbutzim, of which there were probably about two hundred, scattered throughout the country. Kibbutzim were (and are) collective farms in which members receive no salaries but all the necessities of life—housing, food, clothing, medical care, recreation, and vacations—in return for their labor. Kibbutzim were an efficient way to build a country, but they were just as important philosophically: the whole idea of collective, communal living became an integral part of the Zionist ethic.

Our kibbutz was called Ayanot. It was near the town of Nahalal, which is not far from Haifa and is the birthplace of Moshe Dayan. Ayanot, which had been around since the 1920s, was, like most kibbutzim, primarily agricultural—it produced olives, oranges, apples, grapes, grapefruit, and tomatoes, and there were cows there, too. About three hundred people lived there, of all ages.

It was really quite lovely. Outside the kibbutz the ground was barren, rocky, and dry, but inside there were well-tended lawns and many trees. The farmland and cows were nice for me, too, because they reminded me of my grandparents' place in Wiesenfeld. There were a few dozen one-story stucco residential buildings, each with four one-room dwellings. The nicer ones had their own bathrooms, but some were more like shacks, with tin roofs. There were also a few tents—my eventual housing. The communal areas, like the dining hall, were much nicer, and the children's buildings were beautiful, with their own little toilets and showers. This was because, in a country in its infancy, children were considered national treasures. At Ayanot they even had their own little zoo.

For the adults life was hard. There was enough to eat, but many things were in short supply—milk, for example, which we only had once a week. Even the oranges, for which the country was famous, weren't very good; the best ones had to be exported. There were no personal possessions, and no one got any money except at the end of the year, when you were given a small amount to go on vacation. We were all given just two outfits—a white shirt and a pair of pants for Saturdays, and a shirt and a pair of shorts, almost like bloomers, to wear while working during the week. We worked a full day and slept on mattresses filled with straw, four to a tent. This may sound romantic, but it wasn't, especially in the rain. There were no sidewalks in the kibbutz, so they put asphalt squares here and there, and to avoid the mud you had to leap from one to the other. The worst was when Shaul, one of my tentmates (all of them were male, by the way), got malaria. I walked around with a chamber pot and really took good care of him.

Of course I didn't mind all the hardship—it was what I had expected. I even volunteered to live in the tent; some of my colleagues were in shacks. What I did mind, and resent even more when I think back on it now, was the way we were treated compared to the rest of the kibbutz. It was almost exactly the same as what had happened in Switzerland, except that there the people taking advantage of us had been Swiss Jews, while here they were Polish Jews. Part of the reason for their attitude was that these people had all left for Palestine long before the war. In us they saw not only German Jews, who had traditionally looked down on them, but people who weren't able to see the handwriting on the wall, who stayed around too long. And in a way they seemed to blame us for that. That may have explained why they were so insistent, from the moment we arrived, that we had to change our "German" names. A girl named Hannelore be-

came Aviva, which in Hebrew means spring, Marga became
Dahlia, Franz became Dror, which means freedom, and I
became Ruth. As I said, I was worried that my parents wouldn't
be able to find me, so I not only took my middle name, but
used K as my middle initial. I still use it today, and when I
decided to incorporate a couple of years ago, I called my
corporation Karola.

They assigned one member of the regular kibbutz to be
a liaison to our group, but I don't even remember her name,
which shows you how much attention she paid to us. What
resulted was that we became a kind of little kibbutz within
the big kibbutz—a little kibbutz where life was noticeably
harder. They slept in barracks; we slept in tents. And as in
Heiden, we did all the most menial tasks. Most people worked
in the fields; Franz (now Dror) became a cowhand. At first
I picked olives and tomatoes in the fields, then I switched
to housework. I worked two hours in the kitchen, two hours
cleaning toilets, two hours doing something else, until I had
completed my eight hours of work a day.

They really should not have permitted a seventeen-year-
old girl to be treated this way. I know that I had made the
choice to work all day and not to go to school, but there was
a high school at the kibbutz. They should have said, "Never
mind what you are saying about working a whole day. Since
you are the age of my child who goes to school, I want you
to be in that school and work after school." Instead they used
our ignorance, our idealism in wanting to be pioneers, and
got all their dirty work done. They didn't even teach us
Hebrew. Part of that was because they didn't really speak it
that well themselves—being Polish Jews, their language was
Yiddish, which we could understand a little bit because of
its similarity to German. But part of it was that they really
didn't take responsibility for us.

Of course I didn't complain. But I did allow myself to
be unhappy about one thing. I really wanted to work in the
kindergarten at the kibbutz—being a kindergarten teacher,
after all, was the profession I had chosen back in Switzerland.
It was an important job on the kibbutz because children are
taken care of communally, and I was very much looking
forward to it. Unfortunately, I fell victim to some intrigue.

Another girl was chosen to be the assistant to the kindergarten teacher. At the time I thought this was because the girl, who was much prettier than I thought I was, flirted with the teacher's husband, who convinced his wife to choose her. But I recently learned that it was more complicated than that. Michael was in charge of the work assignments for our group. When he was visiting me recently in New York, Michael (who married Marga a couple of years after we arrived in Israel and, after working as an electronics repairman, now teaches electronics in a trade school) told me that it was he who assigned the other girl to kindergarten teaching and me to toilet cleaning. I asked him why.

Michael said, "The answer is very simple. Say a mother has two children. One is a good boy and the other is not so good. She will always give the easiest jobs to the bad boy and the toughest ones to the good boy. She says to him, 'You are my favorite child. Please do this for me.' It was the same with you. Our relationship was good, so I could tell you, 'Look, the most important person in the kibbutz is the one who works everywhere. You're needed.' "

Michael was young and inexperienced, but he was a good psychologist. He knew that with my Zionist zeal, I really would believe that cleaning out garbage cans was helping to build the Jewish homeland.

This was 1945 and 1946. I had already lived in three countries and experienced more tragedy and drama than most people do in a lifetime, but I was still only seventeen years old. A teenager. I had brought my faithful diary with me across the ocean, and the entries for the first year in Palestine show that I was still suffering from a teenager's longings, self-doubts, and soul-searching:

September 18, 1945. I *must* try to forget Michael. I have to control myself, and he can't know. I have to get over it, whatever the cost. I hope it works out with Dror, that he can think more clearly. Why did all this have to happen with Michael? I would be much happier and freer without these feelings.

September 24. I'm asking myself why and about what do you keep your diaries. Do you want to write that the whole problem of uncle and parents are so great and that you are suffering so deeply in your soul? Do you want to write that you are so lonely for Michael even though you know very well that he likes Henni and not you? Life, I now think, is like a chicken ladder—there is so much dirt that you can't advance. Michael, why all this? "Life is a struggle! Conquer!"— Goethe. When I go back to Ayanot I'm going to be strong, I'm not going to let Michael know anything, even if I die of it. It has to be all right, I have to fight. But . . .

October 20. I don't know. Everything is dead, gray and empty. I don't live; I only vegetate. Eating, sleeping, working, eating, sleeping, and it all starts again. I don't have enough energy, not even to study Hebrew, even though I know I must learn it in order to get to my goal. Shaul says that this is the first time that I'm out in life, and I, who always thought that I had a certain *Weltanschauung*, am capitulating with the first difficulties. What's going to happen? Not even in my free time do I do anything. . . . The group here doesn't give me anything. Do I give the group anything? No, because everyone is more educated than me. This is not an empty inferiority complex—I really feel that way, that I'm coming from a lower milieu, and I don't dare to start anything. In Heiden I had to take the initiative because nobody else was there and nothing would have been accomplished, but here I'm like a sheep that runs with the herd. Exactly what I did not want to do, and I don't have the inner power to change it.

November 25. I had decided to stop writing in my diary in order to end this period of being a silly teenager. I want to stop with this stupid talk of boys, and I'm going to devote myself to other problems of daily

living to stop this superficiality. If I find a deeper way
or a person that I'm looking for, okay. If not, I will
try to achieve a balance with friendly relationships,
because they are even more worthwhile! (This way of
looking at things is all from the conversation I had
with Michael this evening.)

November 27. My God. What is this death? I can't get
rid of the picture in front of my eyes. Dark, stars,
wind, lanterns, people, corpses put into their graves
and done with. Is this life? What higher power makes
those decisions? Why? And who is it? Give me an answer. How did my parents die? Where do they *lie*?
Did they die all alone, without people, without *love*?
Were they gassed? They did not deserve that, no
more than all the other thousands did. Mommy, why
are you not here anymore? I would work for you, I
would work very hard. But there's nothing, not even
a stone to show that there's a grave.

December 31. I would like to describe the beauty and
truth of life here in the land of Israel. But why I'm
not happy—in addition to the work problems—I
don't know. Is it still the inferiority complex? I don't
understand anything of music. I can't sing. How can I
be a kindergarten teacher? I know nothing about art
or literature. How can I give a man something, how
can I build a life (except in sexual ways, and that's
not enough), because I'm going to bore him to death.

January 16, 1946. Everything is difficult. I have to fight
for everything all alone and it hurts. Is life never
going to be different, only full of sorrow and sleepless
nights? I want to be young and happy like the others.
Is it only because I'm small and ugly?

Beginning of April. With my life, nothing worthwhile is
going to happen. Why not end it? I'm nervous, I'm
moody. I only live for my inferiority complex. It's aw-

ful. All of them know and are more than me because they went to school.

I know that this may be hard to believe after reading the foregoing, but my whole life was not drudgery and despair. For one thing, my uncle Lothar was supportive of me—and you can imagine how good it felt once more to have a family member close by. His kibbutz was near Lake Kinneret, about two hours away. The first time I went to visit him was just two weeks after I had arrived in Palestine. I wrote in my diary: "I get along with Jehudah [the Hebrew name he had adopted] very well. An intimate relationship we do not have, but we first have to get used to each other."

Lothar did some nice things. Once a year at his kibbutz, the rules against personal possessions were relaxed: all members were allowed to choose one book to have for their own, and it would be given to them. Since Lothar knew I was interested in studying and learning, he always gave his entire book allotment over to me. I remember especially that he gave me two volumes of Bialik, a famous Hebrew writer.

I also did something nice for him. He met a woman at a kibbutz, divorced with two children. He was a lifelong bachelor, and he couldn't decide whether to marry her or not. I said, "Marry her," and he did. They had a child together and a happy marriage until he passed away about three years ago.

During the War of Liberation in 1948, Lothar still hadn't married, so he was chosen to be a truck driver—a dangerous job because Jerusalem was under siege. He would drive on what was called the Burma Road, a route built to circumvent the main road to the city, which was under heavy fire. His was among the last convoys to get into Jerusalem before the city was completely cut off. On that trip, a bullet was shot into the cabin of his truck. It whizzed right over his head and went out again. Lothar was saved because he was short! Since that day I haven't been so resentful of our family trait.

I also don't want to give the impression that we didn't have fun on Ayanot. A kibbutz nearby had a swimming hole, and we would go there often. There were movies every once in a while. But what I really loved at Ayanot was folk dancing, which was always a big part of life in Palestine. This was because dancing together connotes enthusiasm and collectivism—the feeling of group festivity, in which you don't have to be an expert and everybody participates, doing the same steps. We would never dance a waltz or anything two by two—it would be too bourgeois. Also, folk dancing was a cheap form of entertainment. All you needed was a room and one person with an accordion—sometimes just a harmonica. We had a dance every Friday night, and I loved it, even though sometimes people didn't like to dance with me because I was so short, and the old-timers wouldn't dance at all with us newcomers. (Except for Michael—he was probably accepted because he was so good-looking.) So we had to dance among ourselves, but we danced all night.

Incidentally, as you can probably gather from the fact that our dances were on Friday night, our kibbutz wasn't Orthodox—the first time in my life I had been in such a situation. People traveled on Saturday and worked—after dancing I got a couple of hours of sleep, then started cleaning toilets. This wasn't just the case in our kibbutz, but all over Palestine. Religion was not emphasized. You observed the holidays, but the holidays were more secular than religious—Passover, for example, was related to the earth and the harvest more than to the biblical story of Moses. I was already aware of this new way of looking at religion just ten days after I arrived in the country, when I wrote in my diary, "Today was Yom Kippur. I fasted, not out of conviction but for the sake of my parents, because I know they would be unhappy if I would deny so radically everything that has to do with religion." I still considered myself a believing Jew, but my life in Israel did not revolve around religion. I didn't even go to synagogue. I think that the synagogue, and religious life generally, is a much more important symbol of Jewish identity in the diaspora than it is in Israel, where Judaism permeates every aspect of life.

The thing that was most important of all for my morale, despite my self-doubts, was that I had boyfriends. One of them was Dror (Franz), the boy in whose arms I had slept on the beach in Marseilles. He always cared more for me

than I did for him. One evening I was in the room that he
and Michael shared, talking about some problem or other;
like most other teenagers, I really enjoyed blowing up any
little thing into a major production. Dror walked in. Michael
was lying on his cot, and I was sitting next to him, my hand
on his knee. We may have been kissing a little bit. When
Dror saw us, he immediately picked up his knapsack and
stormed out of the tent—and the kibbutz!—in a jealous rage.
This was dangerous—there were Arabs all over. Michael ran
out and caught up with him and slapped him because he
was in a state of shock. He said, "Where are you going in
the middle of the night? Wait till tomorrow, tomorrow morning you can leave, but tonight you have to stay." Dror came
to his senses and returned.

I have to admit that I liked all that attention being paid
to me. And Dror soon realized that there wasn't anything
romantic between the two of us. He eventually became a
social worker, coming to Canada to get his degree and then
returning to Israel, and we're still good friends.

There was someone else who had a crush on me—Shaul,
my tentmate. He also had come from Switzerland, I'm not
sure exactly where. Like Dror, he was an older man, and
also like Dror, his feelings for me were stronger than mine
for him. Things were never really serious between Shaul and
me, but we had fun together. When we ate meals at the
kibbutz, you couldn't choose where you sat—you had to fill
up each table, one after the other. But I wouldn't let that get
in the way of my sitting next to Shaul. I used to figure out
when he would come in off the fields for lunch and time it
so that I would wash my hands and enter the dining room
at exactly that time.

I know exactly when things between Shaul and me really
ended—the day his younger brother, Kalman, appeared on
the scene. Kalman had been in Palestine for a longer time
than his brother—three or four years—and during the war
had fought in the British army against the Nazis on the
Egyptian front. When I first saw him he was still in the army,
and he looked like a movie star in his uniform. I've already
said how I felt about soldiers—that they were angels descended from heaven—and Kalman looked particularly an-

gelic. He was slim with brown hair and gorgeous brown eyes and I said to myself, "That's it." We quickly fell in love. I told Shaul what had happened, and he took it well. I remember perfectly the conversation that he had with Kalman. He said, "Take good care of her," and then walked off. Kalman used to come visit me every Friday night, and he gave me a gold bracelet with the name Ruth on it. I still have it today.

It was also on the kibbutz that I first had intercourse. I won't say whom it was with, because I am still good friends with him *and* his wife. But I can say that it was a beautiful, romantic experience. It was something that I knew would have to happen, and one night, when we both were ready, we walked hand in hand under the starry sky to a barn on the kibbutz where hay was stored and climbed up a ladder to the second story. (We probably chose that as our location not only for privacy, but because we knew it would be softer than our hard beds.) We spent many nights in that barn, sleeping there till morning, but I remember that first time most vividly of all, because it shows that when two people are in love, the first experience can be very enjoyable. One thing I'm not happy about is the way we dealt with the issue of contraception. I know much, much better now, but in those days I thought that hoping was enough.

The attitude toward sex on the kibbutz was interesting. Americans see movies like *Exodus*, and they get an image of free love, of people hopping into bed together left and right, but that wasn't really the way it was. Certainly some of the left wing tried it, but they found that it didn't work because of jealousy and possessiveness. At one point, they tried to have boys and girls shower together until the age of eighteen. They wanted to instill equality, the idea that there is nothing wrong with your body. It didn't work. As soon as the girls started to develop pubic hair, breasts, the secondary sex characteristics, it changed. Six girls would go into the shower and leave the seventh at the door to watch, so no boys would come in. And boys felt the same about *their* shower. Maybe in Western culture there's an inherent modesty. In Hebrew, it's called *tzniut*.

But ideas about sex were definitely far more liberal than what I had been used to. From the beginning I saw that they didn't separate men from women in sleeping quarters. And marriage wasn't necessarily a prerequisite to sex. Being monogamous was. There was a tremendous pressure to couple up, both internally, because there was little else to provide emotional satisfaction, and externally, because the members of the kibbutz were naturally interested in producing families and therefore more members. If a guy was seen two weeks in a row with a girl, people would start saying, "Do you two want a room?" Of course they did, and the fact that couples got their own room was probably the best way of encouraging pairing: the alternative was sleeping in tents or barracks. Then if they were thinking of having children, the pressure would be to get married.

But I wasn't ready to get married. And I was beginning to realize there were some other things I wasn't ready for either. I had come to Palestine with a burning idealism, but I was starting to lose some of it. Originally, I loved the idea that it was socialistic, from everybody according to their ability, to everybody according to their needs, with everybody contributing. I thought that was a great way to build a country. It doesn't exactly work that way. There were people, like us, who pulled their weight, and people who didn't.

I also had a problem with the way women and families were treated. Once a child was born, it stayed with its mother only one month. After that it went straight to the children's house, where it was brought up by nurses and teachers. For the rest of its childhood, it spent virtually all its time in the group; the parents visited two hours a day, from five to seven in the afternoon, and that was it. Raising children collectively like this saved money, but it was also done for philosophical reasons. On the kibbutz everything was collective—you had no possessions, not even a coffeepot or a radio in your room, just one set of clothes for weekdays and one set for weekends. The same way of thinking extended to children. Also, women were supposedly free and equal, and now they would be spared the drudgery of the kitchen and laundry and so forth. Again, it didn't work out that way. As soon as the child was born, the woman went right back to the kitchen.

But I had just spent six years in a collective environment, so a family, with stress on individual life, was exactly what I was hungering for. And the whole attitude of the kibbutz —and Zionism in general—that the important thing was not what was happening right now, but the building for the next generation, posed similar problems. If we were already so concerned with the next generation, where did that leave me? I was still only eighteen. Would there ever be a time for *me* to develop?

Our group's plan, as I said, was to stay at Ayanot for a while and then leave to start our own kibbutz—either in the Negev to the south or in Galilee to the north. But as time went on it became obvious that this plan was not going to work. At one point Michael went to see the people in Tel Aviv who managed all the kibbutzim in the country. They weren't encouraging. When I spoke with him last year, Michael said, "They told me, 'That's all well and good, but first we have to help the kibbutzim that already exist. You can't go out every day and build a new kibbutz.' " There was also a reluctance on the part of the people at Ayanot to let us leave: it so happened that the old-timers there had few children our age, and they needed us to do all the heavy chores.

After you had been on the kibbutz for a year, you were entitled to a two-week vacation. I took mine visiting my uncle. When I returned to Ayanot, I had a big shock. In the two weeks I had been gone, most of my group had left the kibbutz to take jobs and join other kibbutzim around the country. I felt abandoned. But after letting the news sink in, I realized that I couldn't really blame my friends—things had obviously happened suddenly and since there were no telephones in those days, they would have had no way of getting in touch with me. The important thing was that I had a big decision to make. I could stay at Ayanot. That would have been the safe option. Marga and I were the two youngest members of our group, and at eighteen we couldn't really have been expected to strike out on our own, especially since we had no money, no family, no language. Or I could leave.

I left. Despite the difficulties I knew I would face, I saw that now, finally, there was a chance for me to pay some attention to myself. Looking back on my decision, it seems like a courageous one—going into the world by myself after spending seven years in the security of group environments. But at the time I didn't see it that way. It was just something I had to do.

I had heard that another kibbutz, closer to Haifa, had its own kindergarten-teacher seminary, and I decided to go study there. Unfortunately, in order to attend you either had to be sent by a kibbutz or pay tuition. I wasn't being sent by a kibbutz, and I had no money. But I worked out an arrangement whereby I would work in the kibbutz's kitchen for a year in exchange for being allowed to study for a year, and so on, until I had completed the three-year course. And so in the fall of 1946 I left Ayanot, taking with me one suitcase that contained my going-away presents—a sleeping sack filled with corn leaves and the one pair of pants and one shirt people were given after each year's work on the kibbutz. Also inside were my diaries, all my letters from my parents, and the one washcloth that I still had from Frankfurt.

I was excited about starting this new chapter in my life, but there was one disappointment. When I left Ayanot, my boyfriend, Kalman, suddenly became worried. He thought that since I was now leaving the security of the kibbutz, I would become dependent on him. I remember he said to me, "I can't have a stone around my neck," and he broke up the relationship. I was sad. He disappointed me terribly because he said good-bye at the time when I needed him the most.

Yagur, the new kibbutz, was very different from Ayanot for me, because I was no longer a member of the kibbutz— just an employee. I lived and ate my meals there, but I wasn't really part of the collective life, which suited me fine. Not that my life was easy there. I found myself working in the kitchen under the supervision of one of the horrible women I seemed to attract like flies to honey, and she made my life miserable. Every day she said to me, "Ruth, if you drop those dishes, you're out." And of course I dropped the dishes.

On my own, life was more adventurous. At one point Marga came to Haifa to try to find a job as a children's nurse. She had no money and no place to stay, so I hid her under my bed and stole food from the kitchen to bring upstairs to her. In addition to my tuition for the following year and room and board, I was paid a small salary. This was the first time in my life I had ever had any pocket money, and I loved it. I remember exactly where I used to buy chocolate bars. Of course I didn't have so much money that I could afford to buy a car, or even take a bus when I traveled, so I hitchhiked. Once, when one of the girls from the kibbutz and I were hitchhiking, we were picked up by two Arabs and ended up spending the night on a rooftop in Nazareth. Accepting a ride from them was really stupid—they could have killed us. But there we were on the rooftop, and they started fooling around—nothing serious, just fondling. I started talking to them really fast, saying things like, "This is *not* why we left Europe, to be taken advantage of." I talked so much that they left us alone. Once again my gift for gab had come in handy.

I had to wait a year to enter the kindergarten-teacher seminary, but I wasn't going to wait that long to continue my studies—I dove into them on my own. Thinking back, I marvel that I should still have had such a zeal to learn; my only explanation is that it must have come from my father. At Yagur I started to learn Hebrew, a language that anyone who's studied it can tell you is one of the most difficult in the world. I still have the notebooks that I filled up, page after page, with Hebrew grammar and vocabulary. I also used to go once a week to a nearby village called Kiryath Motzkin, where friends from Ayanot had settled. Many people from our group used to go to these people's house and socialize on the weekends. I used to bring them meat, and in return they tutored me in mathematics and French—two subjects that I felt woefully unprepared in. I was worried about how I would do in my seminary studies, since the other students, unlike me, would have high school diplomas.

After a year at Yagur, I realized that this arrangement wasn't going to work either. I hadn't even started my real studies yet, and it would take me a total of six years to complete them—three for the course, three for the work I'd have to do in between. Once again I found an alternative. Through a distant relative of my mother's in Jerusalem, a woman named Liesel, I had met and become friendly with some friends of hers, a couple called the Goldbergs. The husband had been a lawyer in Germany, but wasn't certified in Palestine, and so had been trained and worked as a cabinetmaker. They were wonderful people, and through Mrs. Goldberg's influence I got accepted at a kindergarten seminary in Jerusalem.

I wrote with glee in my diary on February 1, 1947 (and now I was writing in Hebrew): "I am so happy. They accepted me into the kindergarten seminary, and now I have the chance to prove myself. God help me succeed."

I left Yagur, but there were still three months before the course was to begin, so in the interim I took a job as a babysitter and maid. You know how bad some of my previous jobs were—and there were more bad ones to come—but this was probably the worst of all time. I cleaned the house, took care of the children, did the laundry and cleaning—all of which would not have been so bad, except that the people I worked for didn't feed me enough! I was always hungry. It got so bad that once, when I was all alone in the house boiling meat for dinner, I stole some meat from the pot. And I was horrified. The place where I had broken off the piece of meat was bright red, much different in color from the rest. I was sure I would be found out and punished. Luckily, after a few minutes it changed to the same color as the rest of the meat, and my crime was never discovered. I repeated it a few more times before those three months were over.

Later I got a job as a waitress, which I liked much better. The only problem was that there was a coffee shortage in Palestine at the time, and I was instructed not to fill the customers' cups up all the way, but only three quarters. I just could not get my hand to stop, and I filled them up. After being reprimanded a few times, I was fired after just three weeks on the job.

I loved being in Jerusalem. It was unique among the cities of Palestine for being of mixed population: there were Jews, Arabs, and Christians, for all of whom the city was a holy and sacred place. The city is on a hill, and driving up to it, seeing the beautiful golden sunset on the "Jerusalem stone" of the buildings, I felt a deep sense of history and continuity. Even in Frankfurt every Passover we would say,

"Next year in Jerusalem," and now here I was. There were many Orthodox Jews there; ever since the turn of the century they had come from Europe to live in the sacred city. When I arrived, the Old City (later the Arab sector) was open to everybody. I went to the Wailing Wall, the only remnant of the Temple of Solomon. I saw that greenery was peeking out between the cracks of the ancient stones, and I thought to myself, "That's a little like our surviving."

It was wonderful, too, to be on my own in a big city—don't forget, I had grown up in Frankfurt but had just spent six years in a Swiss village and two on a kibbutz. The noise of the city, the buses and the bustle, was like a tonic for me. I couldn't afford to buy anything in the shops, but I loved to go window-shopping.

Most important of all, I was finally a student. I wrote in my diary at the end of April 1947: "Now I've already been studying one whole week, and as of today I have stopped working. What I was wishing for for three whole years, now I have. . . . It is very, very difficult, *again everybody* knows more than me. But I will study and I will learn." I couldn't resist adding, "About myself I don't want to write anything. On the outside I'm happy and joyful. The inside is nobody's business."

In my classes we studied the work of educators like Montessori, Froebel, and Pestalozzi, as well as practical things, like how to sing with children and how to teach them arts and crafts. I learned how to play a recorder—and I still love to play it with my daughter, Miriam. But the curriculum didn't just relate to kindergarten teaching. The school was postsecondary, almost like a normal college, and there were also academic subjects: Hebrew grammar, Bible, philosophy, literature, history, and English. As I expected, I had a hard time, especially with grammar. In fact, I never managed to lick that one: the certificate I got at graduation says, "She has passed every course except grammar."

Part of the problem was that I had virtually no time to study. My scholarship didn't cover all my expenses, so every afternoon I went to work as a baby-sitter in a household where the wife was a pianist and the husband a potassium engineer at the Dead Sea. They were nice people, but again, they didn't feed me enough, and I was still too much the good German Jewish girl to tell them I was hungry. I used to feed their kids soft-boiled eggs, and when they didn't finish what was in front of them, I did. While I was eating it I remembered that my father used to feed me strips of bread soaked in soft-boiled eggs when I was a little girl. Ever since, that dish has always found a soft spot in my heart.

But I still needed more money, so at night I would baby-sit for other families. Now, baby-sitting in Israel at that time wasn't like baby-sitting in America today, where when the kids go to bed you can do your homework or watch TV. No, while they were sleeping I had to iron or sew. Luckily, I had had good training in Switzerland so I could iron fast and maybe get in an hour of studying before I went home. Then, lying in bed, I'd study till I couldn't stay awake anymore.

I lived in a residence for young women, like a Y or youth hostel, and I had my own room for the first time in my life. From the first I was popular, and I loved it. Later I moved into a room in the second story of the house of the widow of a famous Israeli. I got it for almost no rent in return for doing errands and watching over her. One night a fellow visited me, and when it came time for him to leave, I couldn't get the door open. It was unthinkable that he should stay there overnight—this was not the kibbutz, after all—so I tied two sheets together and he climbed out the window.

I made a good friend in the kindergarten course, a girl named Judith, who was a Yemenite. At that time there was a big influx of Yemenite Jews into Palestine, because they were being persecuted in Yemen; they were flown in on what was called the magic carpet. Her father was a Torah scribe: he would sit all day, his legs folded underneath him, copying down every word of the Torah. I loved going over to visit her family because it was like taking a peek into a different century.

In Jerusalem I had my eyes opened to a lot of things. Liesel, whose husband, a physician, had passed away, was good to me, although sometimes she made things difficult. To her, my mother was a kind of poor relation, and she was clearly worried that if I came to Jerusalem, I would be a burden. I remember her saying, "It's not such a good idea."

But once I got there she redeemed herself. She was a cultured lady, and it was in her apartment that I got my first taste of things like classical music. They had books and played records and had intelligent conversations, and I thought, "My gosh, if only I could have a household like that!" Mrs. Goldberg was good to me, too. For one thing, even though I was working, I still didn't make much money, and she gave me all the old clothing of her children—I was so short that it fit me. I used to eat dinner at her house, and the thing that really impressed me was that they had dessert after every meal. I said to myself, "Look how bourgeois people live!"

A couple of years before, of course, I wouldn't have anything to do with anything that was bourgeois—I wouldn't even do a waltz! Now I hungered for it. I knew I'd never go back to a kibbutz; I think I had been permanently spoiled for collective living. Many years later in this country, after I had married Fred Westheimer, a friend of ours named Howard Epstein suggested that a few couples get together and buy some brownstones on the West Side of Manhattan, make a joint courtyard, and have a sort of commune. I said, "I don't think so, no more communes."

In truth, it wasn't the dessert that impressed me so much, it was the family life. That was what I wanted. I used to walk the streets of the city on Friday nights and look into all the windows of all the houses lit with candles and feel so strongly: They all have families. They all have somebody to be with. Why can't I?

There was still some time before I was to have a family of my own, but there was some immediate good news. One day a woman showed up at the residence to visit me. Her name was Dr. Nettie Sutro, and she was the head of the Swiss agency that had arranged for all of us to be housed at Heiden. There was apparently some money left over from the agency's operating fund, and now Dr. Sutro was finding all the children who had been under its charge and dispersing the money. We each got two thousand Swiss francs—about five hundred dollars. The grant meant that things were much easier for me, and it also meant that I could go out and buy, for the first time in my life, some dresses and shoes.

It was during this time that I wrote my last entry in my

wonderful friend, the diary. It is dated June 4, 1947, and says:

> Nineteen years. Nobody congratulates me, nobody knows that I have a birthday. All of the congratulations I'm giving myself. It's very sad, but one gets used to everything. One day everything is going to change. I know that I need *so much love*!!! But I will achieve my goal!

ᴏᴏᴏᴏᴏᴏᴏᴏᴏ

During all this time the political situation in Palestine was getting more and more tense. Jews and Arabs, each given their own territories, were finding it impossible to co-exist. Finally, on November 29, 1947, the United Nations adopted a plan whereby the British would leave Palestine and the country would be divided into a Jewish state, an Arab state, and a small internationally administered zone surrounding Jerusalem. This was good news, but its announcement brought on a kind of guerrilla war between the Jews and the Arabs. There were bombings and shootings all the time.

And not only soldiers were involved. Civilians were encouraged to join the Haganah, which was the Jewish underground army. I decided to join, while still continuing my kindergarten studies, even though my friends tried to dissuade me. But I hadn't lost all of my idealism, and I was convinced that every citizen should do his or her part to defend the Jewish people. As part of my basic training, I learned how to take machine guns apart and put them together again with my eyes closed (I can still do it!), how to use a hand grenade, how to shoot. For some reason I was an excellent marksman—I could always put holes right in the middle of the target.

After I finished with training, I would be asked to do different assignments. Because I was so short, I was often used as a messenger. For many nights I stood on a rooftop, dressed in my khaki shirt and trousers and armed with a machine gun and hand grenades, watching over a barricade where the Israeli soldiers stopped each car to check it at the entrance to the city. My job was to be on the phone if anything happened down there, and to shoot if necessary. Thank God I never had to fire. I remember thinking that if I ever did have to shoot anyone, I would tell him to stand with his back to me, so I could shoot him in the legs and he would fall over, but I wouldn't have to kill him. The closest I came to having to put this plan into effect was one night when we were walking in the outskirts of Jerusalem, and someone came to us and didn't know the password. In situations such as that you really were supposed to shoot. Mickey Marcus, the American who was an Israeli war hero, and about whom the book *Cast a Giant Shadow* was written, didn't know the password one night because he did not remember the Hebrew term, and was killed. But in this case the person came to his senses and remembered it before we had to do anything.

It was a dangerous and difficult time. Kibbutzim were isolated, and supplies could only be brought in under great danger. There were great shortages. In Jerusalem we were given a ration of one egg a week per person. A friend of mine was pregnant, and every week I went for Friday dinner at her house and brought her my egg. Because she was Swiss, she had Nescafé, and in return I got a cup of that coffee.

But the problem was more than just food shortages. In a period of just five months, about 1,200 Jews were killed, more than half of them civilians. Once a convoy of forty doctors and nurses bound for the Hadassah hospital was ambushed; the Arabs killed them all. I remember that there was a park separating the old city of Jerusalem, which was the Arab city, from the new city, which was Jewish, and the Arabs used to shoot into the new city. As my luck would have it, I had to walk past that park to get to my kindergarten seminary. I walked fast. After a while a boyfriend gave me a bicycle so I could get to the seminary even faster. Finally a wall was built so we could walk past with no danger. (This was a good thing, because the boyfriend broke up with me—he was angry after I had gone out with a cousin of his—and took back the bicycle.) When I think back on that time, I can still remember the constant whistling and exploding of the bombs.

ooooooooo

On May 14, 1948, following the UN plan, the British High Commissioner for Palestine left the country. On that day David Ben-Gurion proclaimed the independence of the State of Israel before the members of the Provisional State Council in Tel Aviv. I'll never forget that day and the following night. A bunch of us piled into a truck and rode through the city. All through Jerusalem, people were dancing and singing in the streets.

But we didn't have long to celebrate! That very day, the armies of Lebanon, Syria, Jordan, Egypt, and Iraq all invaded Israel. There was fighting all over the country. June fourth was my twentieth birthday. I did my regular duty of surveillance and at about noon came home to the youth hostel where I was living. As soon as I got in, I heard the sirens scream; that meant I had to go to the shelter in the basement—a big room lined with benches and lighted by candles. On my way out the door I said to myself, "I don't want to be bored sitting in that shelter with nothing to do," so I ran upstairs to my room to get a Hebrew novel someone had given me for my birthday. If I hadn't gotten that book, I would already have been in the shelter, but as it was, I had only made my way back down to the lobby when there was a tremendous explosion. An Arab bomb had exploded right outside the building, sending shrapnel everywhere.

The shrapnel tore into the walls of the lobby and sent plaster flying. People were screaming; dust was raining down from the ceiling. A soldier and two girls were killed, one of them standing right next to me.

I don't know how I got there, but all of a sudden I was sitting against a wall. I felt a searing pain in both legs. Hannelore, a girl who had come from Heiden and also lived in the hostel, was trying to unlace my new shoes, which I had just gotten for my birthday, and I wondered why she was doing that. Then I looked down at my feet and saw that they were covered with blood. I said, "Do I have to die?"

I was taken to an ambulance, and while I was riding in it I did not allow myself to lose consciousness. I was determined that I should be taken to the Hadassah hospital, and

I carried on until I had convinced the driver to take me there. I wanted to go to that hospital because I knew one of the surgeons there, a man named Eli, who was Putz's cousin and had been on the boat with us from Marseilles. His wife, Vera, was the pregnant woman to whom I used to bring an egg. Only two months earlier I had given him a dynamo-run flashlight from Switzerland, and I knew that he had performed many operations by its light. As it happened, Eli wasn't there, but another surgeon worked on me and did a wonderful repair job. I had been struck with shrapnel all over my body, including one piece in my neck, but the worst damage was to my feet. The top of one foot was all gone, I had multiple abrasions just above both ankles, and little pieces of shrapnel were embedded all over. I was fortunate, because I could have lost both feet. As it was, there was no lasting effect. Today I ski as if I had never been injured.

I did have to undergo a lengthy convalescence, however. The hospital had formerly been a cloister, and I was led to an upstairs room. But I was very scared of being bombed again, so I asked to be taken to a sheltered area. They brought me to the basement, which was a big room that used to be a library. Now it was filled with convalescing soldiers. There were no more beds left, but I was so small that I could fit on a bookshelf, and that's where they put me.

Some of the soldiers were in bad shape. One man had lost both hands and both eyes from a hand grenade. He lay there dying. I think he asked his brother to give him something that would get it over with. But the spirit there was generally good. The people weren't sick, just wounded, and psychologically there is a great difference. They all tried to help each other, and morale was high. I used to play chess with another man, who had been blinded. I had a lot of visitors, including my relative Liesel, who came every day even during the worst of the siege, when it was dangerous even to cross the street. She really redeemed herself by doing that. I also got a visit from the director of my youth hostel. She had a sheepish look on her face, because all buildings in Jerusalem with doorways facing the Arab sector had been supposed to build concrete walls in front of the door, so that bombs couldn't get in. If our building had had one, I wouldn't be in the hospital. The director assured me that a wall was being built right away. I didn't know English idioms at this point, so I didn't tell her that she was closing the barn door after the cows had escaped.

Another thing that no doubt helped my morale was the fact that I was the only woman among all the men. I particularly remember a male nurse whom I was infatuated with, a handsome, strong blond who had studied medicine in Romania but hadn't been able to finish school before coming to Palestine as a refugee. I pretended that I couldn't eat by myself so that he would feed me. Also, in order to change the bandages on my feet, he had to take me in his arms off the shelf, and I loved that.

On June 11, a week after I was injured, a truce was declared, which was to last four weeks. The nurse would come to pick me up, take me in his arms, and carry me outside, where he'd lay me down under a tree in the sunshine. I loved that. I must have been very good at flirting with him, because after I was released from the hospital, he got in touch with me, and we had a short, happy love affair.

My idyllic convalescence was spoiled one day when a supervisor of the hospital, a woman, saw me in the library and decided that a woman shouldn't be in a room with all those soldiers. This was really stupid—what could we have done? But no matter how much I argued, her decision stood, and I was brought upstairs to a room full of sick women who were complaining and moaning all the time. I got very sad. Finally, when I couldn't take it anymore, I got hold of Eli the surgeon, and I said, "Eli, I have to get up, and if you don't help me, I'll do it myself. I'm going home, and if you don't come there and change my bandages, I'm going to do *that* myself, too." He agreed. I walked out of the hospital on two crutches, and Eli would come to the hostel to change my bandages until I was better again.

On July 18 a final cease-fire was imposed by order of the UN Security Council, and in late January 1949 final armistice agreements were reached. Israel had not only won the war, but had increased its territory by about one half. But this time there was no dancing in the streets. Too many people had died; virtually every family had lost somebody. I know

I did. Along with thirty-five other members of the Palmach, the elite youth organization of the Haganah, Liesel's son had been ambushed and savagely killed while carrying out a mission. Even though he was the apple of her eye, I never saw her cry about his death. I guess that's the way we German Jews are. We do our crying in private.

My mother, Irma.

My paternal grandmother,
Selma Siegel.

My father, Julius.

My maternal grandparents, Pauline and Moses Hanauer.

The maternal grandparents' Wiesenfeld farmhouse, surrounded by geese.

My aunt Ida and my maternal grandmother, Pauline, in front of the same farmhouse.

My maternal grandmother, and my mother, holding me.

My parents with me in Wiesenfeld.

My first day of school. I am 5 3/4 years old.

Me at a summer camp in Bad Nauheim, 1937 or 1938.

Me at the age of 10, just before leaving Germany for Switzerland.

My uncle Lothar, later called
Jehudah Naor.

My uncle Max.

My aunt Erna.

Group picture in Heiden, 1939 or 1940. I'm standing on the ladder trying to appear taller.

Saturday afternoon at Heiden — all reading. Inge and Ruth Kapp — the twins; Elsa Katz, Marga Schwartz, Rosi Mayer, and myself. Inset: Mathilde Apelt.

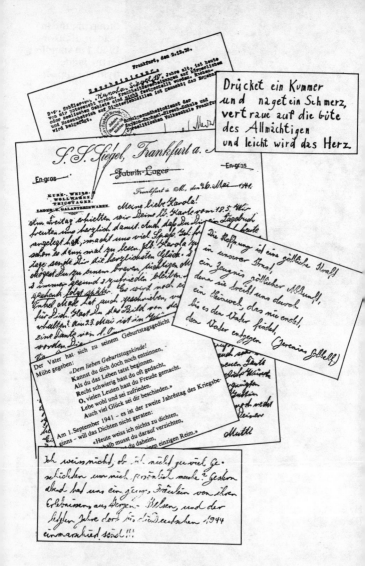

Excerpts from my diaries and a letter from my mother.

My early boyfriend Walter (Putz), now Ezra Nothman.

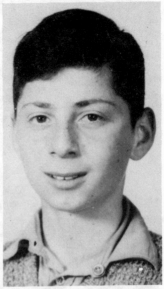

Max Laub (now Mordechai Lavi) at the age of about 12.

My girlfriend Ilse Wyler-Weil.

Ignatz Mandel —
the devoted teacher.

Here I am in Heiden —
"the youngest and
shortest kindergarten
teacher in the world."

With a group of girl scouts at the children's home, Wartheim, in Heiden. I'm at the far left.

Me taking care of the young children. Here the boys get their weekly scrubbing at the children's home in Heiden, Switzerland, about 1943 or 1944.

In Jerusalem, 1947 — pensive — what will the future bring?

The identity card issued by the British Mandate officials. Note my occupation is listed as farmer.

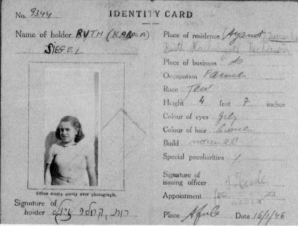

In Israel, at an exhibit of arms used during the War of Independence, 1948, the Sten sub-machine gun among them.

Shaul and me on the kibbutz, 1945 or 1946 — look at that smile.

Good friends then and still today — Marga and me in Israel in 1946.

My first position as a kindergarten teacher with Yemenite children in Eshtaol, near Jerusalem.

**Wedding portrait —
December 10, 1961.**

**Look at that happiness — my
firstborn, Miriam.**

Fred and me preparing for a
costume party.

Here is Miriam in the Israeli army — her idealism and Zionism shining through her smile.

Unbelievable! We have a gorgeous son!

What a fabulous occasion — Joel's Bar Mitzvah! Fred, me, Joel, Miriam, and Fred's parents — Else and Artur.

Another milestone — right after the award of my doctorate from Columbia University Teachers College, 1970.

Joel — Princeton graduate, 1986.

What a day! Miriam's wedding to Joel Einleger, June 22, 1986. To the right of the groom, Fred and our son, Joel. Look at all those happy faces!

chapter

5

I finished my studies in the spring of 1949. Despite the deficiency noted in my Hebrew grammar, the Ministry of Education assigned me to a job—my very first!—teaching kindergarten to Yemenite children. The school was in a hill town called Eshtaol, which was between Jerusalem and Tel Aviv; I had to get up at 6:00 A.M., take an hour bus ride, and then climb up the hill to the village. I had some familiarity with the culture through my friend Judith's family, and it was exciting for me to work with people who were from such a different world, so exotic that they seemed out of stories. The Yemenite men had two wives, one younger and one older; they would get an apartment with one room and a terrace, so that one wife was always out on the terrace and one was inside. After a while, they switched. At the kindergarten it was almost as if I single-handedly had to bring an ancient people into the modern world. The mothers as well as the children came to school, and I taught the women many things, including how to give a shower to their kids. These women weren't used to abstract instruction, so I didn't take just one child to make an example. I washed each child so each mother would know how to do it.

It was at this time that David came into my life. I met him through Eli the surgeon. Eli's sister, Miriam, had a boy-friend named Nachum, and David (pronounced Dah-VEED) was his best friend. He was from Tel Aviv, which was and is Israel's biggest city, but at the time he was a soldier in the Israeli army, stationed near Jerusalem. On weekend leaves he would see his friends. The first time I met him, the four of us went to a movie and then danced at a coffeehouse. I thought, "Oh, boy, what a great life. These people must be very wealthy." I liked David immediately. He was handsome and intelligent, wore glasses, and he was a good dancer. He also had four qualities that were sure to be attractive to me: he was a soldier, he was well educated, he wanted to be a doctor, and he was short. He liked me, too, and we immediately started going steady. A few times he sneaked out of his camp to see me, climbing over a high gate. David, Nach-um, Miriam, and I had a lot of fun together, going to the movies every Friday night, and going dancing a lot. The thing that sticks most vividly in my mind about those evenings is the huge Jerusalem moon.

David, who was three years older than I, had moved with his family from Romania to Palestine when he was three. They had never lived on a kibbutz; the father had gone into business in Tel Aviv and done well. At the time, he had his own fence-making factory. Even more impressive, he had a car, which in Israel at that time was something only mil-lionaires could afford. They weren't quite rich enough for David to have a car for himself, but he did have a motor scooter and a bicycle. He gave me a bike, replacing the one my Indian-giving former boyfriend had snatched back, and we would go for excursions outside the city, packing a picnic and having a wonderful time. I remember the first time I went with David to meet his parents, at a restaurant in the Hotel Sharon, one of the fanciest hotels in Tel Aviv. The lobby was so luxurious that I stood there open-mouthed—it was like nothing that I was used to. I also liked the fact that the hotel was right on the Mediterranean Sea. I had passed through Tel Aviv before without spending much time there, and I found that I loved the city. Ever since the first time I had seen the ocean, at Marseilles, I had had a special feeling about it, and I thought how wonderful it was that in Israel there should be a city right on the sea.

Here I was meeting David's parents—you can probably tell that things were getting serious. After we knew each other only a few months, he proposed. David apparently loved me, which came as a pleasant surprise to me—I still thought of myself as unattractive and short. But he saw something special in me, a fact I am certain of because I still have the mushy love letters he wrote me! The immediacy with which I said yes to his proposal had something to do with this low self-image; I remember thinking to myself, "How lucky I am that someone is willing to marry me." But there was more to it than that. I wanted so much to have a family, and not only could I now have children, but I immediately could adopt a whole set of ready-made relatives. David had aunts and uncles and a younger brother I liked very much; once I married him, they would be part of my family, too. I liked both his parents, but his father wasn't wild about the idea of his marrying me. He thought David was too young, but also that he should marry someone from a good family, not a refugee orphan such as me. We later became good friends, but his mother, who had had a stroke and was hard of hearing, liked me from the start. She had never understood Hebrew, but she knew French, and I had learned enough to have conversations. That was enough to endear me to her.

We got married in November on the terrace of my relative Liesel's apartment in Jerusalem, overlooking a yard with beautiful old trees. It was a lovely wedding with about fifty guests. I wore a short off-white dress. Many of David's relatives were there, but only Liesel and Lothar came from my side. When the prayer over the wedding was said, I remember thinking, How sad that my parents and grandparents can't see this. In the same way, all of my occasions of joy since then have been tempered by sadness.

But it was a happy occasion. Especially when Hannelore, my friend from Heiden, came over to me and said, "My gosh, you're marrying into a rich family." She had never been particularly nice to me—she was the one who had won the kindergarten job I had wanted at Ayanot—and I remember a distinct feeling of pleasure at her comment.

By this time David had been discharged from the army and was ready to pursue his medical studies. In those years, there was no medical school in Israel; people who wanted to become doctors had to go abroad. We had decided that we would go to Paris; he would study and I would find a job. His parents agreed to pay his tuition. For a few weeks we rented rooms in a lovely apartment in Tel Aviv not far from the ocean, and in December of 1950 David left for Paris. A month later I followed.

Germany, Switzerland, Israel, France—I had now lived in four countries in my twenty-two years. I guess one of the things I had learned was how to adapt, because the adjustment to life in this new country was surprisingly easy. By the time I arrived, David had already found an apartment— a cold-water flat in the twentieth arrondissement, a lower-working-class neighborhood. I was excited because it was the first apartment I had ever had in my life. We weren't there long, because it turned out to be too far for David to commute to his studies in the Latin Quarter. So we found another place, right around the corner from the Sorbonne. This was a prime neighborhood, so our money didn't go as far. The new apartment was an unheated furnished room on the third floor of a walk-up with cold water and no bathroom. The bathroom was two floors down, a stand-up French toilet. If you had to go in the middle of a cold night, it was *very* cold.

We didn't live in such a primitive way out of choice, but necessity—his parents paid his tuition, but not much beyond that. Obviously, I had to earn some money. Through some friends, I found out about and got a job as director of a kindergarten for Jewish children run by an international Jewish organization called Les Femmes Pionnieres (The Pioneering Women). The job was a little bit under the table, because as a resident alien I was not really permitted to work full-time in France. But people looked the other way. There was another problem—language. First of all, many of the children in the kindergarten had come from other countries—China,

Morocco, Yemen—and were on their way to Israel. They didn't understand the only languages I knew—German and Hebrew. German was a particular problem: many of the kids' parents had come from concentration camps, and they certainly didn't want to hear that language. So I set about dramatically improving my Yiddish and French, both of which I spoke a little bit. Luckily, I seem to have a facility with languages. I learned them both quickly. On the whole the women who ran the kindergarten were satisfied with my performance, but they did criticize me for one thing—my voice. I have never been able to carry a tune, and singing is an important skill for a kindergarten teacher. The ladies made me take singing lessons with an old gentleman, but nothing helped. I finally solved the problem by singing softly and letting the kids lead the way.

After a while our financial circumstances became even worse, because a law was passed in Israel setting strict limits on the amount of currency that could be sent outside the country. David's parents managed to send us a little bit on the black market, but I still had to take another job. I found one teaching Hebrew to French Jewish children. This was the first time I had worked with older children, and I discovered that I liked it. I would take about seventy of them on excursions to the theater or museums. It was quite a sight—little me crossing the street with an army of kids.

One interesting thing about the job was that, early on, I noticed that next to the school was an artist's studio, or atelier. I made friends with the artist who lived there, an Israeli who made odd little mobiles, and quickly realized that he was even poorer than we were. So every Sunday from then on I brought him breakfast. Many years later, when I was living in New York City, reading about a renowned Israeli-French sculptor named Yaacov Agam, I realized that it was one and the same artist. From then on I followed his career and one day read that he was coming to New York for a reception. I arranged to go and told him who I was. He didn't remember.

I also had to work when school was not in session, and the first two summers I took a job at a camp on the French coast. The next year a thought occurred to me: there was a summer camp that I knew like the back of my hand. Wouldn't it be interesting to go back there as an educated professional and see how it compared with my memories? I made some inquiries and easily got a job as a director of the summer camp at Heiden. The place was exactly as I remembered it. Oddly enough, it wasn't emotional for me to be there. It was only a little bit sad when I remembered some of the bad times.

I was to be very glad that I had taken the trouble to learn French, because the French people are proud of their language. They're sometimes called haughty and arrogant, but they usually only act that way to visitors who don't make an effort to speak French. David spoke well, too, and we both found the people quite pleasant. We made a lot of French friends, while most of the rest of our circle, who were Israeli students like us, kept pretty much to themselves.

It also helped that a cousin of David's lived just outside Paris. This was a doctor named Ernst David, a general practitioner who had emigrated from Romania before the war. We used to spend our Sundays there, with the doctor and his friends, who were all French. Dr. David and his wife were good to us. They had an adopted daughter, Irene, and I think they thought of David and me as their children as well. He would always fondly shake his head and make comments about "you young people. . . ." For my part, I loved having a family. Once I was sick and Dr. David made a house call and walked up all three flights to our apartment. They would take us on excursions to restaurants—they taught us how to drink wine—and like David's parents, they actually had a *car*. Once, Mrs. David took me to her dressmaker, and I got my very first couturier dress. I don't have it anymore, but I remember it as if it were sitting in front of me— a skirt and a top in a black-and-white check. A couple of years ago, when I was in France making the movie *One Woman or Two*, I called up Dr. David. I wanted him to see what had happened to me, all the different things I was doing! I was told he had died just two days before.

Except for Sundays, we lived Spartanly. We were part of a group of about twenty Israeli students in Paris, and despite having no money, we had a wonderful time. We'd eat in student cafeterias, and sometimes we'd illicitly share the ticket that entitled you to a meal. I had a good friend, Bracha, who is now a psychiatrist in Israel, and whenever I see her, we laugh about our crimes against the state. Our favorite haunt was a coffeehouse in the Latin Quarter right next to the Luxembourg Gardens, called Le Petit Suisse. Two of us would go there and order one cup of coffee. One would stay there with the coffee, the other would go across the street to eat lunch and come back to the same coffee. How the place made a living, I don't know.

I loved the culture of Paris. We used to go to the Comédie Française and sit in the cheapest seats, which were in the very last row of the theater. It was called the *poulailler*, which means "chicken roost." I remember the first time we went to the theater. When I saw how much material—yards and yards and yards of it—had been lavished on curtains and costumes, I actually got upset. I had been used to wearing the same clothes for years, and I literally couldn't comprehend such extravagance. (I got a similar reaction the first few times I passed by butcher shops and saw rows and rows of steaks and roasts. Such abundance after the scarcity I had been used to made me physically sick.) After I got over that reaction, I became a real theater fan. I would wait outside the stage door to get the stars' autographs. An assistant would collect everybody's autograph books, bring them in to the star to sign, and return with the autographs. Once, I waited two hours to get someone's signature—a famous French actress. When the books were brought back, somebody tall behind me reached over my head and took mine. That experience cured me forever of autograph hunting.

I also loved going to museums and movies. In order to get student tickets to the movies, which was all we could afford, you had to stand in line a long time, but that was no problem. The conversation was so good that the line became almost like a party. The other bit of French culture I really took to was music. I liked Edith Piaf, "the Sparrow," but I loved Mouloudji. His songs were romantic love songs, often sad, but with a hopeful message. There was one song that always got to me. It's about a woman lying in a field, her breasts exposed, waiting for her lover. It always reminds me of the song in the Hebrew literature where there is such a reference.

After a while, David and I got a Lambretta motor scooter, which increased our transportation options. Unfortunately, I couldn't drive it by myself. I knew how, but my foot couldn't reach the gas pedal—if I got down that far, the scooter would tilt. So somebody had to be sitting behind me. Once, we took the scooter on a camping trip all along the Côte d'Azur. We didn't eat much, because we had to feed the scooter gasoline, but we had a wonderful time. When we got to Monaco, we decided that we wanted to visit the casino. This cost money, so that night we didn't eat dinner—we just bought a *baguette* and some chocolate. We used our money for the admission fee and spent the evening watching the gamblers.

I enjoyed my kindergarten-teaching job very much, but after a couple of years it began to wear on me. I realized that I was starting to talk to my friends as if *they* were kindergarten children—I'd say things like, "*Let's* go, one, two, three." Also, among our group of Israeli friends, I was unique in two things. I was the only one who had no parents, and I was the only one who wasn't a student. The first I couldn't do anything about; and for a long time I didn't think I could do anything about the second, either. I used to walk through the Sorbonne, touch the old cobblestones, watch the students walking to their classes, and say to myself, "If only I could be one of them!" In terms of knowledge, I had a tremendous inferiority complex. I had no high school diploma, had never had a course in physics, chemistry, mathematics. The idea of continuing my education seemed outside the realm of possibility.

Then I heard about a special program at the Sorbonne called the *année préparatoire*. Because of the disruptions caused by the war, many people had had their educations interrupted; the French government decided that people without high school diplomas could take a one-year course, and if they passed an exam at the end of the year, they could then enter the Sorbonne. I decided to enroll. All you had to do to get in was complete some forms, but I remember how hard my heart was beating while I was filling them out.

I took the one-year course, while continuing with my kindergarten job. I studied French, history, psychology, and other subjects. It was hard, especially since everything was in French. I read Sartre and de Beauvoir. I didn't understand what they wrote, but that was all right: I loved the fact that I was reading these great philosophers *and* living in the same city with them. The subject I liked the best was psychology. I liked it so much that I decided I was going to be a clinical psychologist. It seemed a natural choice, with my penchant for introspection and my lifelong interest in other people's problems. And it would be almost like being a doctor.

I passed the exams at the end of the year and entered the Institute of Psychology at the Sorbonne, working toward a *license*, which was somewhere between a bachelor's and a master's degree. I felt as though I had died and gone to heaven. It wasn't so much any particular thing I was learning as just being there, walking down the hallways, attending classes in auditoriums named after Richelieu, Michelet, and Descartes. I felt like shouting to everyone, "Look at me!" In that period there was a real sense of excitement at the Sorbonne. The lectures were held in amphitheaters, and even though they were large, you had to get there at least an hour early in order to get a seat. With all the things I was doing, I rarely had that much time at my disposal, but I quickly discovered a solution. I got someone tall to lift me up and place me on a window ledge. It was the best seat in the house.

My courses were difficult. I had no problem with some, such as administering the Rorschach test and psychopathology. But when a mathematical or scientific background was required, as it was in things like physiology, I had a rough time. Usually, I was able to pass the course by learning the necessary information by heart, without really understanding it, and figuring out some other things I could use. But I did flunk a few exams, one of them in the same classroom where we filmed a scene for *One Woman or Two*! After a test they would post in the halls of Sorbonne the names of the people who passed. When I'd go there and read name after name and my name wasn't there, I felt a little as I did back in Switzerland, when they would read out the names of the people who had survived the concentration camps.

In one physiology exam I did a very stupid thing. Even though I really knew the material, I had no confidence in myself, so I cheated by hiding some notes in the seam of my dress. Naturally, I was caught. The professor was incensed. He said, "Never, never did anyone in my classes cheat!" I tried to explain, but he refused to listen to me. He told me that I'd have to take the exam again, but I was too ashamed to do so. As a result, to this day I do not have credit for a physiology course.

Most of the professors were helpful. I always wrote on my exams that French was not my first language or even my second, and they usually gave me the benefit of the doubt. One of my professors was the famous psychiatrist Lagache. I'll always remember something he once said, walking to and fro in front of the classroom, his thumbs stuck in his little vest: "Famous people go to the bathroom just like everybody else." I understood what he meant, but I was always amazed when people such as him or the psychologist Piaget, who was another of my teachers, would not only talk to me, but were actually nice to me! Piaget's course was hard, and the only reason I was able to pass it was that one of his students took full notes of his lectures and published them in a weekly publication called the *Bulletin de Psychologie*, which I studied intently. In 1957, a year after I had come to this country, a woman called me, saying she had studied psychology at the Sorbonne and wanted to know how to get her credits transferred to this country. It turned out that she was Francine Ruskin, the woman who had taken the notes of Piaget's lectures. We have been good friends ever since. As a matter of fact, as I write this, I'm conducting a rehabilitation seminar with her husband, Asa.

While my educational life was thrilling, my personal life was not going so well. David and I had grown apart over the years; I think we had both come to realize that we had married too young. He also had decided that he didn't want to be a doctor and arranged to go back to Israel to get a master's in Middle Eastern studies. In the summer of 1954, we went back to Israel together; at the end of the summer I would go back to Paris to finish my studies and he would stay. During the next year I became even more convinced that the marriage was over, and I asked him for a divorce. He reluctantly agreed, and it was all arranged by a group of rabbis in Paris and carried out by mail.

After getting his degree, David went to work for the Israeli government; today, he's a spokesperson in the finance department. We're still on good terms. It's interesting that he and my husband Fred always get along well whenever they meet. Fred says to David, "Why didn't you keep her?" and David says, "I'm glad you have her!"

After I was separated from David, I fell in love with a man named Dan. I met him in a coffeehouse through some Israelis—he was a French Jew, but he had lived in a kibbutz for a few years before returning to Paris. He had very little family, and he wasn't doing much of anything in Paris; in the parlance of a later day, he was still trying to "find himself." He was good-looking, kind, sweet, and we started a wonderful love affair.

Soon afterward, completely unexpectedly, I received a check for 5,000 marks—about $1,500. It was sent by the West German government, which had decided to make restitution to people who had suffered from Nazi war crimes and had not yet finished their education. I had made a point of never seeking out any restitution from the Germans—I still haven't. But I was not about to refuse money that was right in front of me.

At this point I still had a full year before I would finish my course of study at the Sorbonne. I decided not to finish it—I would be going back to Israel anyway, working as a kindergarten teacher and continuing my studies, so a Sorbonne degree really wouldn't do me any good. I said to Dan, "Come with me to the United States."

The United States had always meant something special to me, ever since those glimpses of American soldiers during the war and those Shirley Temple movies. I thought of America as a kind of paradise, where everything was available. In fact, all during my years in Paris, I kept with me in my wallet a ten-dollar bill. I don't remember how I got it, but I do remember thinking that nothing bad could happen to me—I had ten dollars! The plan was that we would spend a few months in the States, where I would visit some friends from Heiden and my uncle Max, who worked as a baker in San Francisco and whom I hadn't seen since I was three. Then we would go back to Israel.

We bought a fourth-class ticket—the lowest class available—aboard the *Liberté,* and with the rest of the money I bought a suit for Dan, who didn't have one, and a shirt and shoes. I think there was enough money left over to buy me a dress. I was so excited on that trip, even though we were in the bowels of the ship. The last night I didn't sleep a wink, staying up to see the Statue of Liberty.

We were met by some friends in New York, went out for a night on the town, and stayed in a hotel on Lexington Avenue. Our room cost seven dollars a night, and after the first night we realized we couldn't afford it. I knew that there was an important German Jewish newspaper in New York, called the *Aufbau.* It served as the center of a kind of network of German Jews all over the world—giving information about people's relatives in foreign countries, support groups, and many other things. I picked up a copy, hoping to find a room with a family where Dan and I could live cheaply while we stayed in New York.

Flipping through the pages, a big advertisement caught my eye. It was placed by the Graduate Faculty of Political and Social Science of the New School for Social Research, a university in New York, and it announced that a scholarship was available for a master's degree in sociology for a Nazi victim. The second I saw that ad, I said, "Hold it. I'm going to go down there. If I'm already in the U.S., while I'm here, I'm going to pick up a master's."

That very day I went to the school, which was a kind of university in exile created mainly by scholars who had come to the U.S. from Europe—in particular Germany—to escape the Nazis. There were people such as Hannah Arendt, Hans Jonas, Robert Heilbroner, Kurt Lewin, and Max Wertheimer. Luckily for me, everybody there spoke either German or French, so I had no language barrier. Within twenty-four hours I got that scholarship.

chapter

6

_____

Besides the ad for the New School scholarship in the *Aufbau*, there was also an ad for a room. Dan and I took it our second day in this country. It was an apartment on Cabrini Boulevard in a hilly northern part of Manhattan called Washington Heights, near the George Washington Bridge. Today, I live four blocks away. It isn't surprising that I should have ended up in that neighborhood, because it had been the main haven for German Jewish refugees since the 1930s. Anyway, for seven dollars a week we got a room with kitchen privileges with a German Jewish family. It was wonderful for me that they spoke German and knew what it was like to be in a strange country.

The same day we moved, I announced that I wanted to go to Times Square, which I had heard about all my life. Someone said, "Where's your car?—it's about seven miles away." I laughed and said, "I don't have a car. I want to walk." And so I walked all the way down Broadway to Forty-second Street. The main thing I was struck by won't be surprising—the tall buildings. I felt even shorter than usual, because everything was so big that I constantly had to be looking up.

Even though I had my scholarship, we needed money to live on. Our landlady on Cabrini Boulevard told me she had a friend who needed a housemaid. I realized that I didn't have much chance of using my training as a kindergarten teacher, much less a psychologist. Not only did I not speak English, but as a foreigner, I wasn't legally allowed to have a full-time job. So I said to myself I would swallow my pride and use the training I had gotten in Switzerland to be a housemaid. The woman I worked for was named Eva Stroh, and she paid me seventy-five cents an hour. When we started talking, it turned out that she was also from Frankfurt—though from a much wealthier background—and had also gone to the Samson Raphael Hirsch School, several years before me. Her husband, Oscar, had studied law in Vienna and worked here in a shipping company. She later became a good friend of mine, and she now loves to remind me of something I said during that first conversation: "I don't know how to do mirrors or windows."

Shortly afterward, Dan, who knew people in the French community in New York, found us jobs at the cultural division of the French embassy. We were both hired at the grand wage of one dollar an hour to do things such as prepare exhibits for schools, hang pictures, and sweep the floors. I remember being so grateful that Eva Stroh didn't give me a hard time when I told her I had found something better.

The New School was geared for working people, with classes held in the late afternoon or early evening, so that I could go to work, then go to classes, and then go home. I loved studying there, and it was the perfect place for me. Most of the professors had European backgrounds, so they understood me and I understood them much better than if I had been at a place like Ohio State. This may sound funny, but one of the problems was that I was just learning English and they had such strong accents—I almost expected French or German to come out of their mouths.

After taking and passing some summer courses to get the equivalent of a B.A., I began studying in the fall for a

master's degree in psychology. A lot of the courses I took
were things I was familiar with, like the Rorschach test, but
they were still difficult for me because of the language problem. Then I solved that problem. One day, sitting in the
classroom of Prof. Florence Miale, I heard some people behind me speaking German. I turned around and started talking to them. It turned out that they took notes in German
of all the classes, and I arranged for them to make copies for
me to study. That's how I passed my courses.

The notetakers were Else and Bill Haudek, who became
good friends. They were both from Germany; she was studying for a degree, but he had become well established as a
lawyer here and was taking classes just for his own edifi-
cation. She was the daughter of Kurt Goldstein, a famous
psychologist who had done pioneering studies of aphasia
and was now teaching—where else?—at the New School.
After class they would take me home, and on the way we'd
stop at a Schrafft's restaurant on lower Fifth Avenue near
the New School, "for a cup of coffee." I was usually starving,
but knowing that Bill would pay, I was too polite—and too
stupid—to order something to eat, even though Bill wouldn't
have minded if I had had a steak. So I always ordered a milk
shake. Luckily for me, Else always ordered an English muf-
fin. I waited patiently, knowing that most of the time she
didn't finish both halves. She'd ask me if I wanted it, and I
tried to say yes very casually.

I was passing my courses, but I found to my surprise
that I didn't really like experimental psychology. I wasn't
particularly interested in rats and abstract experiments; I was
interested in people. On the other hand, I loved the academic
atmosphere of the New School; for the first time in my life
I felt that I was in a community of scholars. I switched my
area of concentration to sociology, the study of society. I had
read and enjoyed Max Weber, Durkheim, Talcott Parsons,
Robert Merton, and in the related field of anthropology, Mar-
garet Mead and Ruth Benedict. I found I was much more
interested in the broader social issues you could tackle in
sociology, especially the study of the family.

This would soon be of practical use to me, because I was
about to start a family of my own. When I found out I was

pregnant, I was surprised and overjoyed: I had always assumed I was too small to have a baby. After we got the news,
Dan and I decided to get married. I was in heaven. I threw
up every morning for three months, but with a smile on my
face.

We didn't have the money to go to a private hospital
when it was time to give birth, so I had arranged to go to
Municipal Hospital in the Bronx, where an Israeli doctor I
knew worked. Unfortunately, when I got there he was off
duty, and a nasty woman doctor was assigned to me. I could
have used some sympathy, because after seventeen hours of
waiting, labor still hadn't started, and I was told I'd have to
have a cesarean. In those days that was a big deal. I thought
it meant that I was going to die. But I got no support from
the doctor; she told me to stop carrying on. For the operation
they gave me a spinal, so I could watch. At one point I asked
if they were almost through; she told me to shut up! Another
doctor said, "You've had your fun, now you're going to pay
for it."

But it was all worth it when Miriam was born. Babies
delivered by cesarean section don't have to go through the
birth canal and so are in tip-top shape, and when I saw the
beautiful, magnificent child I had produced, I was shocked.
It was an amazing, almost transforming experience for me.
I thought it was the miracle of the century, that no other
woman had ever given birth. My entire life I had been convinced, deep down, that I was unattractive. But when I saw
Miriam, my self-image started to change. When she got a little
older, she got even better looking, with blond curls and a warm,
bubbly personality. I know it wasn't just me who thought she
was so wonderful, because when we were outside walking,
people constantly would stop and exclaim over her.

I wanted to name her after my mother, but Irma didn't
seem the best name for a little girl in 1957. So I rearranged
the letters to come up with Miriam. To give equal time to
my father—I assumed that I would never have another
child—I rearranged some of the letters of *his* name, Julius,
in Hebrew and gave her the middle name of Yael.

We, of course, didn't have much money to spend on
Miriam, but our friends helped out. Eva Stroh had a wealthy

sister who had befriended me. She told Eva to go with me to Gimbels to buy her a *layette*, the French term for the complete outfitting of a baby. We bought six undershirts, six pairs of underpants, six pajamas, and six receiving blankets (one of which I still have), for the price of fifty dollars, which seemed to me the kind of money a millionaire would spend. Somebody lent me a gorgeous French baby carriage, which was almost as tall as me. One day I took it all the way from Eighty-second Street on the East Side of Manhattan (where we were living temporarily) to the New School, a distance of four miles, so I could show Miriam off to everyone.

When Miriam was one year old, in 1958, Dan and I separated. We did it amicably. He was good and kind with Miriam, but we both had come to realize that what we had had together was a fabulous love affair and not much more, certainly not something that would last for a lifetime. We had different interests; for my part, I was a little bored. Also, I knew that he wanted to go back to Europe, whereas I was planning to return to Israel.

I knew he wouldn't help out financially, because he had no money. I didn't expect him to—that wasn't the way I looked at things. I had been on my own since the age of ten and had learned to make do with what I had. I never had the notion that somebody had to support me. On the contrary, during the years in Paris I had helped to support David and myself, and I had paid Dan's way to America. There was no question but that Miriam would stay with me, and I felt that, since that was the case, it was up to me to support her.

I had no qualms about the decision, except for one thing. I was worried that Miriam would now have no father. At the same time, deep down, I felt that one day I would remarry, and then she would have somebody.

Soon afterward, Dan and I got a divorce, arranged by my lawyer friend Bill Haudek. Miriam and I flew to San Diego, took a taxi to a courtroom in Tijuana, and got a Mexican divorce. Outside the courthouse a Mexican boy serenaded Miriam with his guitar. Then we walked back across the border and went to San Francisco to visit my uncle Max. He was the reason I had come to America, but I still hadn't seen him. He was working as a baker, and though he's now retired, he still sends me wonderful cookies.

The period of being a single mother, living with Miriam in an apartment at 80 Seaman Avenue—also in Washington Heights—working by day and going to the New School by night, was difficult but also exciting. The first thing I had to do was learn English. Most of the words in the language have their roots in either French or German, and I knew both, so that was a plus. Also, after learning Hebrew, no other language seems difficult. And necessity helps very much. If you have to walk into a supermarket and buy milk for your little daughter, you had better learn fast how to speak the language. When I was in Paris trying to learn French, I used to buy cheap romances. They were written simply, and they held my interest—I always wanted to know, Will these people get married or not? Here, I didn't have the time or money to take classes in English, and I knew I wouldn't be able to understand Dickens or Shakespeare, so I bought *True Confessions* magazine and read it cover to cover. Somebody gave me a television set and that also helped me absorb the language. It was also useful on Saturday mornings, when Miriam would watch cartoons and I would finally have some time for myself.

It didn't take long before I could understand and speak enough to get by. When I was searching for a word, I found myself going through an interesting process, which I still do today. I would first think of the word I wanted in German, then translate it into Hebrew, French, and finally come up with the English. Of course, my English still wasn't up to grappling with Shakespeare, and to this day I have some trouble with idioms. For example, once I called an office and asked for a friend of mine. The receptionist told me, "He is no longer with us." I thought he had died. It also struck me that Americans had a mania with initials—like the UN, FDR, NBC, the FBI, and so on and so on. For a foreigner, it's difficult to figure out what people are talking about. I always wondered why Americans were so obsessed with the time they would save by using initials. My attitude has never been that time is money. I could gladly sit at the kitchen table talking for hours, but in America, long, leisurely conversations seem to be frowned upon.

Later, when I became known as Dr. Ruth, I discovered another peculiarity of the American language. I would meet people and they would say, "Call me for lunch." So I would dutifully call them, and when they answered they would sound embarrassed, as if they really didn't want to hear from me. I finally realized that saying "call me" doesn't really mean "call me"; it's just a way of being polite.

Of course, I still sounded like a foreigner. People would tell me that if I wanted to stay and work in this country, I should take speech lessons to lose my accent. I said, "Okay, okay. I will." But I never had time. Thank God that I didn't.

The biggest challenge was economic. I left the French embassy and got another job doing market research, calling people up on the phone and asking their opinions about one thing or another, but I was still only making a dollar an hour. With that I had to pay our seventy-five-dollars-a-month rent, clothe us, and feed us. I'm still really not sure how I did it. We led Spartan lives. We subsisted on sandwiches and eggs, and I *never* bought new clothes, except for one outfit I bought when I was pregnant. It was a black corduroy outfit and I had three blouses—that was what I wore the entire pregnancy. I brushed it and washed it and wore it again and again until it fell apart.

I was determined that our straits wouldn't prevent me from having fun. I didn't have money for baby-sitters, so I would throw parties at our apartment. I provided the room and the potato chips, and the guests provided everything else. They were fabulous parties. I also went to parties at other people's houses. Again, I couldn't afford a baby-sitter, so I would bring Miriam with me. My friend Lou Lieberman tells me that what I did in those days was revolutionary. Instead of saying, "Shhh. There has to be quiet for the child, and she has to be in bed by six o'clock," I would put Miriam on the bed where people had piled their coats, clear a little space for her, and she would go to sleep right through the noise.

I definitely had help. At first an organization called Jewish Family Service paid for Miriam to stay with a foster family during the day while I went to work and classes. The family lived about ten blocks from our house, and I would wheel her there in the morning and pick her up at night—which was not easy in the rain and snow and ice. The family would feed her, but when I picked her up, I hadn't eaten, and I'll always remember how hungry I was. When she was three, Jewish Family Service paid for her to go to a German Jewish Orthodox nursery school, which was wonderful. The people loved her—they were like grandparents to her—and the atmosphere was exactly what I would pick to have Miriam raised in. Best of all, a car came to pick her up and take her home!

And I had a *lot* of help from my friends. From the first days I was here, I began making friends, most of whom I'm still close to today. Although none of them ever knew how little money I had, because I don't believe in complaining, they became a support system for me. I never needed to ask for money, but I knew that if I really needed help, they would be there to provide it.

My friends helped me in a lot of little ways. A woman in my building named Grace Griffenberger had two young children and was also going to school; she and I used to baby-sit for each other. I discovered that I had a distant relative in Washington Heights named Babette Adler, whom I called Tante Babette. Through her I met another distant relation, Rachel Schramm, who was married to a man named Max and lived in Teaneck, New Jersey. They had two daughters who were a little older than Miriam, and Rachel gave us their clothes when they outgrew them. Miriam wore them, and later, so did I. Shoes were still a problem, but somehow I managed. And I loved having family around.

When I think back on those years, I marvel at how many really good friends I was able to make in so short a time. At the New School, I met Debbie Offenbacher, who had also gone to my school in Frankfurt, and Ruth and Howard Bachrach, and Cynthia and Howard Epstein; all five are good friends to this day. One day I went to a party at Columbia University and then afterward to a Chinese restaurant. In our group was a guy I didn't know. I was impressed with the way he talked. He discussed skiing, which I thought only rich people did in this country; I also remember that he mentioned the sculptor Bernini and his "fine movement." I said to myself, I have to meet this guy. I did, and Dale Ordes has been my friend and skiing partner ever since.

Francine Ruskin was the woman whose notes to Piaget's class I had studied at the Sorbonne; I became friendly with her and her husband, Asa, a doctor at Montefiore Hospital in New York at that time. I had no health insurance, but I always knew that if anything bad happened, Asa would take care of it. One day Miriam hurt her forehead in kindergarten. The school called me and I got in a taxi, picked her up, and took her right to Montefiore. Not only did Asa take care of her, but he drove us home afterward.

One day I got a letter from the Immigration and Naturalization Service saying that I had to leave the United States in twenty-four hours. When I first came to this country, I had a visitor's visa; then, when I worked in the French embassy, I got a special embassy visa, and now I had a student visa. There was apparently some irregularity with it, and I panicked. I called up Bill Haudek, who had taken care of my divorce at no charge, and he said he knew an outstanding immigration lawyer. This was Martha Bernstein, who fixed the problem in no time flat. Martha and her husband, Henry, who is also a lawyer and who used to be the head of the United Jewish Appeal in New York, became great friends. I used to go see them in their apartment on Central Park West in Manhattan every other week, which was nice because it put a little elegance into my life.

My friends didn't help me out only with professional services. They all knew that I was interested in getting married again, and they periodically tried matchmaking of their own. Once, Asa and Francine decided that a handsome psychiatrist they knew would be perfect for me, so they invited both of us to a party. I had some folding chairs and he had a car, so to throw us together even more, they asked him to pick up me and the chairs. I was excited about it, and I had even bought a new dress in the children's department of Best & Co. for twenty-eight dollars, which was an enormous amount for me. The dress was lilac and white and was made of heavy wool; it went all the way up to my neck, which all my dresses did until very recently. I don't know why, but I always felt that I had to cover my chest and neck.

Anyway, the psychiatrist picked me up, and I liked him right away. He was cute, intelligent, and tall. But when we got to the party, disaster struck. One of Francine's friends had asked if she could bring a woman friend of hers along, and this woman turned out to be beautiful. Not only that, she wore an extremely low-cut dress. All evening, the psychiatrist talked only to her. I thought, never mind, he still has to take me home with the chairs. I knew I was a good talker, so I could invite him up for coffee or tea and I would have my chance. But it didn't work out that way. When he took me home, he took the woman in the low-cut dress in the car with him. She waited in the car while he brought me and the chairs up; there was no coffee and no tea. The next day, Asa and Francine felt so bad that they took Miriam and me to the zoo. Every once in a while we take out the pictures of that day and have a good laugh over it.

The best friend I made was Hannah Strauss. One summer Dan and I stayed at the apartment of one of my New School professors, Julie Mayer, at 80 Seaman Avenue in Washington Heights, and while she was gone we found an apartment for ourselves in the building. It wouldn't be ready until a few weeks after Julie came back, so she arranged for us to stay temporarily with Hannah, who was a friend of hers—also a German Jew, and also taking classes at the New School. She's the one to whom I said, "I don't want to be friends with you, because I always lose the people I'm close to." Luckily, I didn't follow through on that threat. We had an immediate bond, and I would stay up with her till all hours talking about the fate of the world, just as I had in Switzerland with Helen.

Later, after we had become friends, I learned that Hannah had some interesting first impressions of me. When she first saw me, she asked a friend, "Who is that interesting-looking woman over there?" She later told me that what had attracted her to me was that she saw some sadness in my face, even when I laughed, and that she could tell I was courageous—the German word is *tapfer*. She was also the first person ever to tell me that I was pretty!

I was thrilled that Hannah liked me so much, because she's just the kind of person I have always been impressed by to the point of intimidation—intelligent, cultured, educated. She came from a remarkable Jewish family in Germany. Her father was a famous attorney, and her mother was the first woman ever to study medicine in that country. Her mother went to Israel before the war and wrote a book about Jewish life in Germany called *We Lived in Germany*. When I found out about the book, I was *very* impressed. I said to myself, "I'm friends with someone who's written about in a book, and whose mother wrote it!"

When I met her, Hannah's husband had recently died, and we spent a lot of time together. We would go for long walks in Fort Tryon Park—she lived and lives in Washington Heights, too—or just sit around the kitchen table and talk for hours. I think one of the things that attracted me to Hannah must have been that she bears some similarity to my mother, aside from the fact that she's short. Besides her intelligence, she certainly has one rare and wonderful quality—when you are talking with her, all of her attention is completely focused on you. It's a quality I try to emulate in my therapy, both in private practice and on the air.

When I met her, Hannah had studied both Freud and Jung extensively, and she eventually became a Jungian therapist. I never had any real therapy with her, but she was always generous with her wisdom and insight. Whenever I had an interesting dream, I would tell her about it, and she would write it down in a notebook she still keeps. I know I'm not the only one intimidated by her intelligence, because in my real therapy, after I told a therapist a dream, he would sometimes ask, "What does Hannah think?" Lately, Hannah has gotten a strong dose of humility. She'll sit at the kitchen table and say, "I don't know anything anymore." Then I found the trick. You sit her down with rye bread, butter, and cheese. Once she has eaten, all of her wisdom tumbles out.

When I started the road to becoming Dr. Ruth, Hannah was skeptical. She would say that talking about sex was going to be a fad. She doesn't think so anymore. She likes to remind me that in the old days, before Dr. Ruth was even a dream, I used to say that I only wanted two things in life: a Frigidaire and a housekeeper once a week.

More friends. A handsome young man named Lou Lieberman was in a sociology class with me at the New School, and he helped me get my first A in this country. We collaborated on a project where we observed some people in a small group in terms of leadership and tried to look at what the qualities are that determine a leader, how fast they go into effect, whether there is a hierarchy of leaders, and so on. We discussed what we were going to say, and then Lou wrote the paper. He got an A, and the professor, who understood that my English was still poor, gave me an A−.

Lou is now a sociology professor at John Jay College in New York, and we still collaborate—right now we're working on a book called *Morality and Sex: The Transmission of Values* for the Academic Press of Harcourt Brace Jovanovich. Earlier this year, Lou bought a co-op apartment in my building, which made me happy for more than just personal and professional reasons. Lou is a gourmet chef, eater, and Chinese-food buyer, and with him downstairs I know that I'll never have to worry about food again.

Through Lou I met his friend Al Kaplan, who'd been with him in the merchant marine. I can thank Al for introducing me to two things: the music of Gilbert and Sullivan —I loved it when he sang "Tit Willow" from *The Mikado*— and the natural beauty of upstate New York. We used to go on great camping trips, and also went on one not-so-great trip with Cynthia and Howard Epstein in which our tent blew away in a windstorm. Al used to criticize me for being like all Europeans in this country—constantly putting down the United States. (Remember, this is when I still planned to return to Israel.) He kept trying to convince me that New York was such a wonderful place. Another song he used to sing was from the musical *The Windjammer*:

From Norway to New York,
It's lemon juice and pork.

Where the wine and songs and the girls are good,
In the village of New York.

I guess his campaign worked.

In the old days at the New School, Lou and I would go
to an Israeli coffeehouse called the Sabra, where you could
buy cheap coffee and talk for hours. A whole group of us
would meet there, and an interesting group it was. Besides
Lou and me, there was an Episcopal priest; an Egyptian Copt
named Eddie George; and an Israeli guy named Abraham.
He had been a member of the Stern gang in Israel, a group
much more militant than the Haganah, and occasionally things
between him and Eddie would get very tense. That's when
I found out that I was a born mediator. I would say "Cut"
—even though I wasn't on television yet—and get them to
stop fighting.

Eddie and I were both active in the student organization,
and we became good friends. That was a strange feeling. In
those days, much more so than today, Egyptians were the
enemy. So here I was, being friends with someone from a
country that killed a lot of Israeli soldiers. I was able to resolve
my conflicts, partly because the Copts had themselves been
persecuted by the Moslems, and partly because he was such
a nice guy. He thought I was nice, too, so much so that he
asked me to marry him. I realized that would be a mistake,
that being Jewish was too big a part of my identity to be able
to marry an Egyptian, and he understood. He quickly married someone else and today is a professor of economics at
the University of Texas.

The Episcopal priest wanted to marry me, too. He had
been a bomber pilot during the Korean War and had made
a pact with God: If he got out alive, he would become a
priest. He had a dream that we would get married, and
people would come to our house, and I would read the Scriptures in Hebrew and he would read them in English. He was
tall and handsome, but I realized that he was not the guy
for me either, and he too married someone else. I lost touch
with him, which is unusual for me; I lost so much as a child
that now I make it a point to hold on to people. If you're
reading these pages, please get in touch with me.

∞∞∞∞∞∞

I got my master's degree in sociology in 1959 with a thesis on the experience of the one hundred German Jewish children, including myself, who had spent World War II in Switzerland. The Haudeks threw a beautiful garden party for me at their country place in Harrison, New York. I was thrilled. What especially impressed me was the fact that there were waiters.

I enjoyed being affiliated with a university and a discipline and would enthusiastically go to sociological conventions at big hotels. I was always popular at these events, for a specific reason. Whenever the sociologists are conversing with each other, drink in hand and name tag on their chest, they are always looking about to see if there is anyone more important around, whom they would be better off talking to. I never had any difficulties getting a crowd around me, because they could talk to me and at the same time have an unobstructed view of everyone else in the room.

But there was trouble on the horizon at the New School. For an academic discipline like sociology, a master's is only a stepping stone on the way to a doctorate, which requires additional courses, a written exam, an oral exam, and a dissertation. I passed the necessary courses and (on my second try) the written exam, but I failed the oral exam.

Part of the problem was that in the upper realms of sociology, the emphasis is on theory, on abstract construction and models with which the sociologists weave their webs. I'm not a very good theoretician to start with; I'm very much down-to-earth and grounded in reality and practicality. So I had a hard time understanding the material. What aggravated it was the setup of my oral exam: there I was surrounded by five eminent professors, grilling me. This was an intimidating situation in itself, but making it worse was the fact that the main thing these people were trying to do was impress each other with how smart they were, not test me. So their questions were not only theoretical, but sometimes incomprehensible.

There was something else at work as well. At that time, in the late fifties and early sixties, the dominant people in the field were known as "the angry young sociologists." In a way they prefigured the New Left of the late sixties: their main agenda was a scathing critique of the oppressiveness of American society. I had a hard time with that. I knew of the discrimination in this country, and of poor people—I was one of them myself! But I couldn't understand how people could criticize this magic land, the country that had done away with Hitler and the Nazis and that had taken me in and provided me with a great education.

The upshot was that I flunked my orals twice. The second time, I felt sure that I was going to make it, so Else Katz, the woman who watched Miriam and Joel for me, had baked a cake at home to celebrate. I had to call her in tears and say, "Put that cake away. I didn't make it."

There is a doll in Germany called a *Stehaufmännchen*. It has lead in its base, and when you put it down flat, it stands right back up again.

That's me. Instead of being devastated by this failure, I went right on to the next project. And I came to realize that what had happened was really a blessing in disguise. If I had passed that exam, I would have gone on to become a boring professor of sociology somewhere.

It also helped that by this time I had someone to comfort me. One day in the winter of early 1961, I got a call from Dale Ordes saying, "Ruthie, my friend George Blau has a car. Let's go skiing for the weekend." I said certainly. I left Miriam with the Schramms in New Jersey and the four of us—Dale, George, Hans Keizer, and I—went up to Bel Air, a ski area in the Catskills. Hans was a friend I had met while I was doing market research. He was Dutch and already had his sociology degree from a university in Holland. We worked next to each other, and since I immediately took a liking to him (he was handsome), I started talking as I worked. It turned out that he didn't have the same ability I did of doing two things at once, so he finally said, "Stop talking already, I can't work."

Here I have to inject another story about Hans. One year when Miriam was very small, I felt sorry for him at Christmas because he was so far away from home. Here it was, Christmas Eve, and he had no Christmas tree. So he and I went into the streets and found a tree that hadn't been sold and had just been left there. Then we went to Woolworth's and bought a record of Christmas music for $1.29. We took it all back to my apartment, and I thought, "My God, I have a Christmas tree and Christmas music in my house—I hope lightning doesn't strike me!"

In any case, up we went to the Catskills. Dale is much too enthusiastic a skier for me. Whenever he sees snow, he disappears into the mountains, and you don't see him again until evening. Not only does he enjoy skiing, but he thinks that the more runs you take, the better a bargain your lift ticket is. He's lost a lot of girlfriends that way. Anyway, that left me with Hans, which was fine except for one problem. The ski lift was a T-bar, an arrangement in which two people sit on a bar of metal that drags them up the mountain. The problem was that Hans is over six feet tall and I am four foot seven: when the bar was under his behind it was under my neck, and when it was under my behind it was under his ankles.

At the top of the mountain, I was introduced to a guy who was the president of the ski club that George belonged to and that had arranged for our lodgings. He was short, so I said to Hans, "Listen, next time I'll ride up the mountain with that short guy, and I'll meet you here and we'll ski down together." On the way up, the guy and I started to talk. We kept it up all day, and then that night until two in the morning. I crawled back to the room I was sharing with a female member of the club, and she said to me, "He's mine. You keep your hands off." I just went to bed. The guy's name was Manfred Westheimer.

When I got home, I called my friend Debbie Offenbacher. I said to her, "I found the guy that I'm going to marry." She said, "How can you say that? You just met him." I said, "We'll just see."

I don't know why I was so sure so immediately about Fred. A lot of it had to do with the similarity of our backgrounds. He's a year older than I, and he's also Jewish, from southern Germany—a town called Karlsruhe, where his father owned a furniture store. In 1938 the family left for Portugal. But his parents worried about what would happen if Hitler got to Portugal, so in 1941, when he was fourteen, they sent him to live with an aunt in Louisville, Kentucky. He graduated from high school there, served in the U.S. Army, then studied engineering at Pratt Institute and at Brooklyn Tech. When I met him he was the chief engineer with a consulting firm and living, of course, in Washington Heights; his parents were still in Portugal.

I think I also realized that Fred and I complemented each other. I am a little impulsive; he is sensible. I like to go out; he likes to stay home. I like to spend money; he likes to save it. He is an excellent shopper; I can't be bothered with which soup is cheaper. He likes routines; I always like to do something different. He hates noise; I don't mind it. I realize that in some cases this set of differences would be grounds for divorce, but somehow I realized that in this case opposites would attract. Plus, he was handsome, intelligent, employed, short, had a car, liked children, and played Jewish folk songs on his harmonica. What could be better?

My prediction turned out to be accurate, but it took some doing. When I started going out with him, Fred was still seeing another woman, and I knew that she was my biggest competition. He had left a guitar over at her apartment, and I really didn't want him to go there to get it. So with the assistance of Dale, I went out and bought Fred a *new* guitar. It cost twenty-eight dollars—a fortune for me in those days—but it was worth it.

I also know that it would make a good impression on him if he thought I was a good cook. Unfortunately, I wasn't. I had passed the household course in Switzerland, true, and I knew how to put a little meal together from my years in France, but for more than twenty years I had subsisted for the most part on the food in various collectives and student cafeterias. So I used some feminine wiles. I invited Fred over for dinner on the Jewish holiday of Rosh Hashanah, then asked a distant relative I had discovered and become close to, Käthe Bauman, to prepare a meal, which I picked up and brought over to my apartment, presenting it as my handiwork. I had also asked all the other guests to exclaim over how good the food was. Freddie has never forgiven me for that maneuver.

He also took me to see his relatives, obviously presenting me for their approval. I usually passed the test, although his aunt Recha, whom I came to like very much, later told me that she thought to herself, "Who is this little girl he is bringing?" And another relative, who shall remain nameless, said, "You shouldn't marry her because she has a child. You don't need that." Fred reported this to me, and that is where I learned that you don't always tell the truth, the whole truth, and nothing but the truth to your spouse.

As soon as I met Fred, I heard him talk about Oscawana. This turned out to be a lake not far from New York City where he and a lot of his German Jewish cronies used to rent bungalows during the summer. It's a beautiful lake with hills all around that was particularly attractive to his friends because it's so European. They were so protective of it that they would never even say the name around outsiders.

I wanted to rent a room in the same house Fred did, but I couldn't because they didn't allow children, and I wouldn't go without Miriam. But I didn't like the idea of his being up there every weekend and my being in the city—especially since the other woman also rented a room in the house! Then someone said that the bungalow next to Fred's house was for rent, for six hundred dollars. I, of course, didn't have six hundred dollars, but my mind quickly went to work. The place only had three bedrooms, but with the living room and the porch, I figured we could get six shares out of it. I said to myself, Okay, I can afford one hundred dollars, and Fred is going to spend another one hundred dollars, because he can only go to the other house every other week and this way he can come up every weekend. So I already had two hundred dollars. Then I went to Howard and Cynthia Epstein. Cynthia was a sociology student I had met at the New School. Howard was a journalist (he's now president of the publishing company Facts on File) who had done well. They had a two-seater MG that I used to call an asocial car because there was no room for Miriam and me. Anyway, I called Howard and told him that he should trust me, that the place was beautiful and he should take two shares sight unseen: four hundred dollars. Dale and his girlfriend agreed to join the group, and so did my friend Debbie after I told her that it was so quiet up there that she'd make great progress on her doctoral dissertation. So in just one night, I had the bungalow.

We had a great summer there, because we had a perfect division of labor. Cynthia knew how to cook; I knew how to talk and did so enthusiastically while washing the dishes; Dale and Fred knew how to fix things around the house. Even so, it took me a while to win Freddie. You see, he still had that half-share in the other house, and the woman there gave great back rubs and made great herring salad. Fred slept in our bungalow, but went to the house every other weekend to eat—he figured he had paid and he should get his money's worth.

By the end of the summer I had a feeling that when it came to our getting married it was now or never. Freddie was thirty-four, an only child, and seemed to be on the edge of being a lifelong bachelor. After living for years in furnished rooms, he had just moved into an apartment where his only rug was *The New York Times*, and he decided that he should buy a real rug. So one day he took me and Edith Oppenheim, the wife of one of his oldest friends, Walter Oppenheim, to go shopping for rugs. I knew that if he bought one he would never get married. Edith must have been thinking the same thing, because after he had agonized over his decision for an hour, she said to him, "Why don't you wait awhile?" and he agreed. I breathed a sigh of relief.

I think the moment Fred realized the inevitable was one day when he, Miriam, and I were out driving in his Renault. Miriam said, "If you two get married, is this going to be our car?" Fred almost drove into a ditch. He popped the question not long afterward, while we were hiking on Balsam Mountain in the Catskills. He gave me two conditions: first, we had to get married before the end of the year, for tax reasons, and second, I couldn't tell anyone the news until he talked to his parents in two days. Anyone who's read this far will know which one was harder for me.

I didn't meet Fred's parents until the day before the wedding, when they flew into New York from Portugal. I got along well with his father, who had gone to Portugal with no money and had built a big office-supplies importing business with fifty employees. I had some trepidations about his mother, because Fred had told me that she was superneat. My apartment was even messier than usual at the time with the added burden of getting married along with my studies, work, and daughter, and I gathered up all the papers that were lying around the apartment, stuffed them into a rolltop desk, and closed the top. The Westheimers came over for dinner, and at one point, forgetting what I had done, I opened the desk and everything came pouring out. I have to give my mother-in-law credit. She took this calmly. Not only that, but despite her neatness and my sloppiness, she has never opened up a drawer of mine (probably because she knows what she would find there).

On December 10, 1961, we had a lovely wedding at the Windermere Hotel on the Upper West Side of New York. All my New York friends were there and so was Mathilde, my childhood friend from Germany, which meant a great deal to me. We spent our wedding night at a hotel in the Poconos, and the next day Fred had to fly to Kansas City on business. If he ever starts complaining about all the traveling I do now (he hasn't yet), I will remind him of that, and of the many business trips he had to take in the early years of our marriage.

After we were married, I had to face a sobering realization: I would probably never go back to Israel. All during my time in Paris and New York, I had thought of myself as an Israeli student, completing her education before going back to Israel for the rest of her life. I even spoke Hebrew with Miriam before English, and her first words were in Hebrew. But Fred was not that much of a Zionist. He likes the cold weather and the change of seasons, and he was very much an American. I suppose I had become one, too. I felt a little guilty about this, especially since my life, even with all its hardships, was much easier than the life I had lived in Israel. I knew that in Israeli terminology, someone coming to the country is called an *olah*, meaning one who goes up, while someone who has left it is a *yored*, or one who has gone down. Even though I was to return to Israel often—I taught there for nine years in a row—and sent both my children to Zionist summer camps, I had to face the fact that

I was now a *yored*. I made the process official by becoming an American citizen in 1965. I was so scared when I took the exam that I brought Martha Bernstein with me for support. But I remembered how many were in the House of Representatives and on the Supreme Court, and I passed. It was a moving moment for me, because I had come to think that the United States was the greatest country in the world. I certainly don't agree with everything its government does, but no other country has been so generous to refugees such as me.

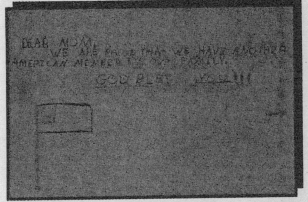

Miriam and Joel's note on my becoming an American citizen.

The other adjustments to being married again were not so difficult. We easily found an apartment in, naturally, Washington Heights. And Fred and Miriam's relationship was good from the beginning. When we got married, I told her, "You can call him Daddy or Freddie, it's up to you." She called him Daddy from that day on. When Joel was born and he would cry or something, Fred used to say to Miriam, "You used to do that too when you were small." And Miriam would answer, "How do you know? You were not around!"

We both wanted to have a child, and about six months

after the wedding I got pregnant. Just as with Miriam, as soon as I could feel movement, I walked around all the time with both hands on my belly and a big grin on my face—I loved that feeling of a baby inside. I said to myself, "My gosh, look what I can do, I can have babies." Cynthia Epstein and I were pregnant at the same time, and about six weeks before Joel was born, Howard called me from the hospital to say they had had a boy, Sasha Alexander. This upset me because I superstitiously thought that there were only a certain number of children of each sex to go around, and since I already had a girl, I really wanted a boy. I thought that for Cynthia it wouldn't make any difference; why couldn't I have the boy? I resigned myself to another girl, but, lo and behold, there was at least one more boy left.

The experience of giving birth this time was different, to say the least. I now had insurance, and so the hospital I went to was Columbia Presbyterian, very elegant and right in my neighborhood. The birth was by cesarean section again, but there were no complications, and my doctor, Emmanuel Friedman, was excellent. He lived in Tenafly, New Jersey, and I live a few blocks from the hospital, but when I called him to say I was going in, he got there before I did. I still don't know how he did that. I even had my own private room. To give you an idea of how much I enjoyed myself there, let me tell you that when I left, my phone bill was higher than my medication bill.

Miriam, who was six when Joel was born, loved having a little brother. And I, having studied child psychology, very intelligently cut off any sibling rivalry at the pass. When I came home from the hospital, I brought her a magnificent leather briefcase to take to school, because she was such a big girl. And I accumulated a surprise bag with little gifts for her. When people came with gifts for the baby, I always slipped them something from the bag to give to Miriam, so she wouldn't feel left out.

Right before I met Fred, I had a dream that I was buying some rugs. Hannah said that maybe this meant I was about to put down some roots, that my life was about to become less gypsylike. As usual, she was right.

ooooooooo

I knew I didn't want to become a housewife, but with two little children at home I also knew I couldn't work full-time, so I was fortunate to find a series of part-time jobs as a researcher with several projects having to do with patient care in the School of Public Health and Administrative Medicine at Columbia University. The leader of the projects was a woman named Charlotte Muller, an economist who taught me a great deal about research methodology. It worked out well: she worked twenty hours a week and I worked twenty hours a week. I was paid five thousand dollars, which wasn't bad for a half-time job in the early sixties. The best thing about it was that I got coauthor credit—my first!—on several articles that we published in scholarly journals. The titles will give you an idea of the subject matter: "Formularies and Drug Standards in Metropolitan Hospitals," "Drug Utilization and Costs for Patients with Acute Myocardial Infarction," and "Use and Cost of Drugs for Inpatients at Four New York City Hospitals." Not exactly *Firm Thighs in Forty Days*. I liked it, though, so much so that my plan was to go on and get my Ph.D. in public health.

Through one of the projects, I met a psychotherapist named Arnold Bernstein, who had written a book called *Anatomy of Psychotherapy*. Someone told me I should go see him as a client. Just like any other German Jew, I thought doing something like that would be a sign of weakness. Making such a to-do over yourself was nonsense, I thought, with so many problems in the world. The way I allowed myself to go was to tell myself that it was what the psychoanalysts (which he was not) call a lehr analysis, a therapy one undergoes in order to learn how to do therapy. I'm glad I went, although I held back somewhat: I didn't discuss my past in detail because it would have been too painful. He worked at a clinic, and I paid him three dollars for half an hour. Then he went into private practice, where he was only going to take patients for fifty-minute sessions. I couldn't afford his rates, but he said, "Okay, I'll take you for half-price. You talk so fast that half an hour is enough."

In 1967 the money ran out for the public health project and I was out of a job. Someone told me that Planned Parenthood was looking for a research associate. I went for an interview with Stuart Cattell, the director of research. Not only did I get the job immediately, but a week later, when the woman who was running the project quit, I got *her* job.

The project consisted of taking the contraception and abortion histories of about two thousand women in Harlem. My specific job was training and supervising about two dozen women, none of whom had ever worked in the family-planning field before, to be paraprofessionals and collect these histories. My first day of work I came home and said to Fred, "These people are crazy! They talk about sex all day long! How come they don't talk about literature, about philosophy, about politics?" But I got used to it fast. Within a week, in fact, I decided that this was a professional endeavor I wanted to get into. I didn't know that I would become a sex therapist, but I thought that teaching people how to teach sex education and family planning would not only suit my skills and experience, but would provide a wonderful service. Another benefit of the job was getting to know Stuart Cattell, who turned out to live close to Oscawana. We became good friends and did a lot of spirited hiking, talking, sailing, and eating together.

The women I trained at Planned Parenthood were all black or Puerto Rican, and most of them had never even had a job before, much less done anything like this. I'm proud of the work I did in training and supervising them. One young woman who worked for us didn't have a high school diploma. We made it possible for her to use part of her work load as school credit, and she got the diploma while the project was going on. When the project was over, I was able to find every single one of those women a better position, some for the City Health Department, some in hospitals.

After a few weeks of training on how to interview a subject, how to fill out a questionnaire, and so on, it was time for them to go out and collect data. At that point I asked the women if I could go with them as they conducted the interviews—not as their supervisor, but simply to sit there quietly and listen. Over the years I had developed a strong interest in the nature of family life and child-rearing in different cultures, and I thought this would be a wonderful opportunity for observation and learning. It was.

But there were a few hairy moments along the way. This was at the height of the unrest in Harlem, and here I was, a four-foot-seven white woman merrily going on her way and asking people about birth control! It seemed that every single time I went alone to an apartment, I could be assured that there would be wind and snow and rain, that I would have to walk up four flights in a scary building, and that nobody would be home. Also a big barking dog in the hallways.

But there were never any serious problems. I made sure never to come across as a Lady Bountiful, a middle-class white savior coming up to Harlem to dispense goodness and wisdom. We had some volunteer women from the Upper East Side, and I stressed that they too shouldn't take the attitude that they were doing a favor for the poor, but rather that all of us were working together. That helped. It was also important to me that we didn't just take information from people, but tried to assist them if we could. If we found a child not going to school, for example, we knew the name of the social service agency to call to do something about that. Sometimes the children were kept home because they had no winter clothes or shoes, and help could be gotten. Not only did this alleviate some suffering, but it helped the morale of the staff: they knew that they were effecting some change, maybe small, but change nonetheless.

Something that helped me in those years was my background: I didn't have the guilt over slavery and generations of oppression that many Americans have, and that can prove to be heavy baggage indeed. For some of my colleagues, these feelings sometimes made them incapable of performing the task at hand, because they were so afraid of doing something wrong. My life had also taught me that I always wanted to stand up and be counted, and I think that attitude came across to people in Harlem. Once I was with the director of a day-care center, who had had a falling out with the man who unofficially ruled East Harlem. Anyone who disagreed with him was simply removed. I was there on a Friday afternoon, and two big armed men came in and told the director to get out right away and leave the office as it was. But I was not about to let her be brutalized like that, so I stood up, with all my four feet seven inches, and said, "It's all right, we are going to leave. But you wait outside until she finishes gathering up her personal belongings from her desk." They were so startled that somebody such as me should speak to them with such authority that they walked out, stayed outside the door, and waited patiently for an hour while the two of us packed up her things and left.

One effect the years with Planned Parenthood had on me was to convince me of the importance of contraception and of legalized abortion. Abortion was then against the law, and I already knew how wrong this was. In Paris, because one couldn't get a legal abortion, a friend of mine had had an induced abortion by a physician. She was sent home, and her boyfriend and I stayed the night with her. I shudder when I think about that, because he and I didn't know anything. She could have bled to death. As for contraception, I had always practiced it myself—I only had two children, after all—but working with the people from Planned Parenthood and seeing the poverty in Harlem, where people couldn't afford to clothe and feed their children, made me realize for the first time how vitally important it is.

While I was working for Planned Parenthood, Joel began school. I thought that this was the time to go back to school myself for my doctorate. I started out slowly, taking one course at Columbia's Teachers College. I got an A and then went full speed ahead. I took as many courses as I could each semester, as well as during the summer, and by 1970 had my doctorate. This wasn't easy. I still had a family to care for and a half-time job. Most of the courses at Teachers College are at night, because so many of the students have jobs, and I remember many cold, miserable, rainy, snowy, *hailing* nights, standing at 11:00 P.M. on the corner of 120th Street and Riverside Drive, the windiest corner in the world, waiting for the bus to take me home.

One thing that helped me was that there were great people at Columbia, especially Hope Leichter, the chairman of the department of community and family relations, and

David Goslin, my adviser. David, who is now in charge of social sciences at the National Academy of Sciences in Washington, D.C., was particularly helpful. I was planning to make my dissertation a continuation of my master's thesis at the New School. This was a study of the orphans of the Holocaust: the people, such as me, who had lost their parents during the war. I would study the children from the home in Heiden and see how their childhood experiences had affected their lives. This subject was and is, of course, very close to my heart and would have been a major, major project. Then one day there was a meeting where all doctoral candidates had to present their dissertation topics. The person next to me announced what he wanted to write about, and David said that people shouldn't do a dissertation that would take years out of their life, that would become the be-all and end-all of their existence. He said there were thousands of ABDs out there, people who had finished All But the Dissertation and might never make it at all.

This immediately set off a lightbulb in my brain. I decided I would study the orphans of the Holocaust another time; for my dissertation, I would write about a much more manageable topic, the Planned Parenthood project in Harlem I was in the process of completing. He approved the topic and was very helpful when I was writing the dissertation. Whenever I gave him a chapter, he would return it the very next week with his comments. And when I got lax in my production, he would see me in the hallway and say, "If you don't give me the next chapter soon, I'm going to drop you." I went right home and got to work on the next chapter. Of course, it didn't hurt that he was handsome and had a Yale Ph.D.

I was awarded my degree, a Doctor of Education, in June of 1970. My grades were so good that not only did I qualify for the Kappa Delta Pi honor society and the dean's list, but I marched at the very front of the procession in my cap and gown. I have to say that it was the closest thing to heaven I ever experienced; I didn't ever want to take that gown off. Fred and Joel and Miriam were all there and so were a lot of my friends. Even though it's usually the person graduating who gets the presents, I bought Joel and Miriam each a wristwatch for being so helpful and supportive. Here I was, a person who once wasn't even allowed to go to high school, marching at the great Columbia University.

I had more on my mind that day than just my degree. Freddie and I had wanted another child for some time, but I also wanted that doctorate. So we made the agreement that I have a baby after I got the degree. And as I was marching in the procession, I was already pregnant.

But my joy was tempered because I knew the child wasn't developing properly. My doctor had told me he heard a heartbeat, that everything was all right, but I knew deep down that something was terribly wrong. My fears were confirmed one day in early July when I found that I was bleeding. I knew this was not a viable pregnancy and I would have to go to the hospital and have the fetus removed. And I wanted to do it right away. But there was a problem. On July 1 abortion had become legal in New York State, and as a result the hospitals were jam-packed. I knew that in order to get a bed I would have to use some strategy. So I waited until Fred had left for work and Joel had left for day camp (Miriam was away at sleepaway camp), and I called the hospital and pretended that I was hysterical. I started to cry and said I had to come in right away. It worked.

But there was a catastrophe waiting. My doctor performed a procedure called a D&C, for dilatation and curettage, and when he tried it, I went into shock. If I had not been in a hospital with all the support staff, I would not be here today. I had to have a partial hysterectomy, in which they removed my uterus but left the cervix and the ovaries, and stay in the hospital for ten days.

Every once in a while, I'll think about that baby. As I write this, he or she would be seventeen years old.

chapter

7

In the summer of 1970 I got my first teaching job. There was an opening in the Secondary and Continuing Education Department at Lehman College in the Bronx, which is part of the City University of New York, for someone to teach a course in the Psychological Foundation of Education. I got the job because I was flexible. At first they didn't know if there would be enough students registered to take the course, so I said to the chairman of the department, "I would love to teach here, but I don't have to know your decision now. If you don't have a spot for me, that's all right too." I got that job, and I loved it. I said, "If you have a place for me, I would love to stay here."

So from being a guest lecturer for the summer, I became an instructor, then an assistant professor, and after just a year and a half, an associate professor, which was an advance of unprecedented rapidity. I progressed so quickly partly because I knew how the game was played; I was no twenty-five-year-old straight out of graduate school. I published in scientific journals, I participated in all the departmental meetings, I served on all the committees they wanted me to serve on. And I loved being there. I walked around that campus as if I owned it.

The only problem was getting there. We only had one car, Freddie's Volvo, and I journeyed to Lehman on the bus. Classes were again in the evening, and I had to go around to my colleagues every night at 10:00 P.M., with all my books and bags, to see who could drop me off on their way home. It wasn't that I didn't know how to drive: Eddie George, my Egyptian friend, had taught me back in the New School days. Actually, I didn't really learn very well, and the only reason I got a license was that I engaged the guy who gave me a driving test in such an interesting conversation that he didn't notice my mistakes. Shades of the burned carrots in my cooking test in Switzerland.

The reason wasn't that we couldn't afford a second car, either. But Freddie and I both had a European prejudice against being extravagant. It was the same way with the telephone. I didn't have one in Israel or Paris, and when I got a phone in this country in my apartment at 80 Seaman Avenue, I thought it was the height of luxury. But when Miriam became a teenager and wanted to talk on the phone with her friends, and I wanted to talk to my friends, it created quite some tensions in our apartment. But both Freddie and I thought that you don't get a child her own telephone. Finally, against Fred's wishes, I gave Miriam her own line for her sixteenth birthday. It was actually an even better gift for myself, and it was one of the best decisions I ever made.

One day Elaine, a beautiful blond woman who was the dean's secretary at Lehman, walked in and said, "Look at the sexy car I bought myself." So we went to the parking lot and there she had the most gorgeous little sports car. That day I said to myself, "Hold it, I have a doctorate now, I'm teaching, I will get myself a car." I borrowed some money, and I took Al Kaplan, who knows a lot about cars, with me to a showroom on Fordham Road, and I bought a beautiful little Toyota Carina for $4,700. I loved that car. I had always thought that I wouldn't be able to drive because my feet wouldn't reach the pedals; the Toyota's seat could be pushed all the way forward, and I could reach everything. (Thank God the Japanese are short.) Al improved my driving technique by imparting to me what he called the zen of driving, including the notion of how not to think about driving while you're driving. It sounds strange, but it works.

At Lehman, I developed a specialty—teaching teachers and prospective teachers how to teach sex education. When I first came to the school, the chairman of the department asked me what courses I could teach and this came to mind as a good fit, considering my training and background. Over the next few years the demand at Lehman for this kind of course increased, because people knew that sex education would have to be better addressed in the schools. Within a few years courses relating to family life and sexuality made up my whole teaching load. I liked the topic and knew I was providing my students with something useful, but I soon realized that while I knew enough about education, I did not really know enough about sex. Students would ask me questions whose answers I did not know, and then in the hallways of Lehman College, my six-foot-tall colleagues would lean down to me and whisper questions about sex that I couldn't answer.

So I decided that I had to get some more training. In 1974 I took a week of seminars at Long Island Jewish Hospital, which was helpful, but really too far away to continue with. Then one day I saw that Dr. Helen Singer Kaplan was going to give a lecture at the Ford Foundation. Of course I knew who she was. She had both an M.D. and a Ph.D. in psychology, had worked with Masters and Johnson, had written *The New Sex Therapy*, which was the Bible of sex therapy, ran an advanced training program for sex therapists at Cornell Medical School in New York, and was probably the most renowned sex therapist in the country.

I immediately decided to go. And when I went there, after Dr. Kaplan gave a talk and some educational films were shown, there was a question-and-answer session. I worked hard to come up with one good question. I raised my hand, asked it, and sure enough, it started a good discussion. Immediately afterward I went up to her and, my heart racing to my throat, explained who I was, said I had admired her for many years, that I knew about her training program, and asked if I could possibly come visit it. She said yes. One of my characteristics is that I don't wait. The talk was on a Thursday, and the next Tuesday I was at that class.

I went every week for three months. I only opened my mouth when I was sure I had something intelligent to say, because first, I was only a visitor, and second, I was the only one there who didn't have a clinical background—either an M.D., a Master of Social Work, or a master's or Ph.D. in clinical psychology. But I was happy just to listen. The material was fascinating, and I loved the way Dr. Kaplan conducted the class. She would say, "Learn from me, but then you have to have your own way of doing sex therapy. It can't be a cookbook."

During those three months I realized that I wasn't there only to help my teaching at Lehman; I really wanted to be a sex therapist. The kind of psychosexual therapy I was learning about, which was devised by Masters and Johnson and was being refined by people like Kaplan, was not only exciting, but seemed well suited to me. Unlike traditional psychoanalysis, for which I would never have the patience, it is short-term and oriented toward results; in that way, it is more like behavior therapy. The basic idea is that certain sexual dysfunctions—such as premature ejaculation, problems with desire or reaching orgasm—can be treated with specific techniques, often done as "homework" by the individual or couple being treated. And the test of time had shown it actually worked. It seemed like something I could do and would enjoy. Now, finally, there was a way I could come close to my lifelong dream of being a doctor.

Toward the end of the semester, before the summer break, I asked if I could officially be accepted into the program. And Dr. Kaplan said yes again. In the program, once a week there was the seminar that I had audited, and once a week we observed Helen Singer Kaplan actually performing sex therapy. We were on one side of a one-way mirror, and on the other were she and a patient (who knew he was being observed and got the therapy for free). In the beginning I was embarrassed about that. Here were these people talking about the most intimate details of their sex lives, and here we were taking notes and being glued to that window. But

I soon got used to it. And I was very taken with the company I was keeping. Most of the people in the seminar were doctors, and you know how I feel about doctors.

After a few months I was assigned to a small treatment group. We took turns taking the sexual status examination of incoming clients—essentially, finding out what their problems were. In the beginning that too was not easy for me. I wasn't used to talking about sex, and when I heard some of the people discuss their problems, I couldn't help blushing. One of the trainers who helped me overcome my embarrassment was Mildred Hope Witkin, whose comfortable attitude about sexuality I tried to emulate.

Another person who helped me a lot was Charles Silverstein, a clinical psychologist who was the head of the Institute for Human Identity, a counseling center frequented mainly by gays and bisexuals. He was in the same small group with me. He realized that I needed clinical experience and said, "Look, if you want to get some experience at being a therapist, give us three hours a week, and I'll give you supervision." I said fine. He told me that he thought I should have a lesbian supervisor, so I would learn something of that way of life. At the time I didn't know any lesbians, so I was a little bit scared. But he found for me a wonderful woman named Kay, who gave me fabulous supervision. It was a great experience both ways: they got my time for free, and I got supervision for free. (Kay did make one blunder with me, though. She noticed that I was so active and talkative, and so she suggested that I try some meditation. I tried it for about two seconds and realized it was not for me. What does work in calming me down, I have found, is going to synagogue on Friday night. I sit very quietly and I hear the same melodies I heard as a girl in Frankfurt. It's soothing, and at the same time Rabbi Lehman's sermons, book reviews, and comments on current events are intellectually stimulating.)

When I was at Teachers College, I had made friends with a Catholic priest named Father Finbarr Corr, and through him I got some more practical experience under my belt. By this time he was the head of the counseling service for the Catholic Church in New Jersey, and every Saturday, through ice, rain, and snow, I drove out to New Jersey and counseled couples and individuals who had gone to him for help. (Just a few months ago, Finbarr published a book called *From the Wedding to the Marriage*, a guidebook for priests involved in premarital counseling.)

After two years of training I got a certificate as a psychosexual therapist from Cornell. More important, Barbara Hogan, who was the supervisor of my small group, told me I was ready to do therapy with my own clients; she said I could use her office to see people. My very first client, a patient of my friend Asa Ruskin, was paralyzed from the waist down after being in a car accident. He was engaged at the time of the accident, and he was having understandable trouble in dealing with the issues of sexuality. I saw him in his hotel room—it would have been hard for him to come to Barbara's office. I showed him a movie that demonstrated techniques he could use to satisfy a partner. He wanted to see it twice, and then he wanted to know if the man in the movie was really disabled or was an actor. (He was really disabled.)

Gradually I got more clients, mostly by referral, and after two or three months I took my own office on East Seventy-third Street in New York. But I didn't want to be a full-time therapist: I would never be able to sit from 9:00 A.M. to 9:00 P.M. listening to people's problems. I needed the stimulation of teaching. So I definitely didn't want to forsake the academic world.

I got involved in another interesting project during those years. Ever since I had dropped it as a dissertation topic, I had meant to pick up again my study of the children who were with me at Heiden. Once I was settled at Lehman I saw my chance. For my New School dissertation, I had sent out a questionnaire to as many of the children as I could locate, and when we had a reunion in Israel, I had interviewed as many as I could, as well as quite a few of their children. Now, because thirty years had passed since the end of the war, some important files had opened up in the Swiss National Archives in Bern. The biggest thing for me were the questionnaires—with information about background, family, where they wished to emigrate, what future occupation they wished for their children—that the parents of us one hundred children had filled out before we had gone on the transport to Switzerland. I went to Bern in the summer of 1974 and made photostats of all of them. When I read the one my family had filled out, I found out for the first time that they had applied for a visa to the United States.

That fall I was talking on the phone with Käthe Biske-Johannas, a Swiss woman whom I had met through my Israeli friend Dror, and who had become a good friend of mine. She was the head statistician of the city of Zurich. She asked me if I would be willing to give that data and a copy of my master's thesis to someone by the name of Alfred Häsler. He was a famous Swiss journalist and the editor of a prominent newspaper (now defunct) called *Détente*. He had also written, among other books, *The Boat Is Full*, later made into a movie of the same name. It was an indictment against the Swiss policy toward Jews in World War II: how it sent Jews to the border, wouldn't let them in, and so forth. I got in touch with Häsler, and he said yes, he was interested in seeing me for a three-hour interview. He thought it would make an interesting front-page story in his newspaper. I told him that I could come to Switzerland in a few weeks, when I had my Christmas vacation from school.

When I told Freddie what had happened, he said I was crazy. We would be going to Switzerland in the summer anyway to visit with his parents, as we did every year. Why spend the money for an extra trip? But I was adamant. I said, "If this famous journalist is willing to interview me, even for three hours, I am going right now. Who knows what he's going to be doing in August?" I borrowed the money from Hannah and Martha, and I flew to Switzerland for a three-hour interview.

The three-hour interview turned into ten days of interviews. I was always available for Häsler. If he wanted to talk to me in the middle of the night, I could do it; first thing in the morning, same thing. Käthe's husband, Arthur, is a retired high-school teacher, and he let us meet in his study of their apartment, which was in the middle of Zurich and very convenient. Kate made us coffee and stollen, a kind of Christmas cake with dried fruit inside that Häsler adored. Once we went for a weekend at Käthe and Arthur's country place. We talked about my experiences, about the historical background, about what I had found out about the effect of this episode on the children who had gone through it. He is an interesting man—not Jewish, by the way. He has no formal university training, started out as a printer, but by this time had written twenty books. He is also a controversial figure in Switzerland. Some people, especially younger people, say they're tired of his finger-pointing, of his holier-than-thou attitude.

Out of these interviews Häsler wrote a fourteen-week series for his newspaper. Each installment appeared in the Friday literary supplement of that paper. Running across the top of the page was a chronology showing what was going on in the wider world when we were experiencing the various events of our lives. It was an effective technique: it put our story in the context of history.

I was thrilled when the articles started to appear, especially since they were still coming out when I arrived in Switzerland that summer to visit my in-laws. On Fridays, everywhere I looked people were buying that paper and reading my story. The first thing I did was to go to a newspaper kiosk and ask the woman there for ten copies of the paper. She must have thought I was crazy, because she said, very politely, "Excuse me, but are you aware that all ten copies are exactly the same?" I got very upset when I saw the newspaper in trash cans—I was almost tempted to pick out each single paper after people threw them in. One day I was riding on a train on my way to visiting my friend Ilse, and the man next to me started to read my story. I sat up and made so much noise that he must have thought I was crazy. I finally told him it was me.

In the middle of my excitement I realized, Hold it. These are newspapers that get yellow in a month. Who's even going to read them tomorrow? I decided that the articles had to be put into book form, and I set about finding a publisher. Through two Swiss friends, Alfred Moser and Toullio Georgi, I found a firm that was willing to publish the book . . . for the price of $2,700. That didn't stop me. I put in $900 of my own money, which I couldn't afford, and persuaded two wealthy Swiss people interested in Jewish causes to put in $900 each. I certainly felt that my share was well spent when the book was published, and for seven whole days it was in the window of the best bookstore on the Bahnhofstrasse, prominently featured as the book of the week: *Die Geschichte der Karola Siegel* ("The Story of Karola Siegel").

But the book was not a best-seller. I never got any money from it, and in fact I'm my publisher's best customer. Every time I go to Switzerland I buy a hundred copies or so. I'm always worried that they'll throw out the plates, so I want to make sure I have plenty of copies of that book.

When the book came out in 1976, I was still doing well at Lehman. I was teaching, supervising student teachers, active in various programs, friendly with many people. In one more year I would be eligible for tenure, which meant I would have a job for life, and I felt confident I would get it. Then disaster struck.

As I said, for years I went back to Israel every summer to teach. I was in Jerusalem in the summer of 1976, and I got a telegram saying that my employment was terminated. At that time the City of New York was in an extreme financial crisis—it nearly went bankrupt—and the City University was told that everyone without tenure had to be let go. That meant me. I called the chairman of the department long-distance to see if there was any way out, anything I could do, and he said, absolutely nothing.

I was in a state of shock. I remember going to a little park in Jerusalem where there was a little stone wall, and I just leaned against it and cried. It was my own personal Wailing Wall. My friend Marga, from Switzerland and Haifa, was with me, and I remember that she was upset because she had never seen me cry before.

By this point I was deep into my training as a sex therapist, but I never considered dropping my academic career and becoming a full-time therapist. As I said, I needed the stimulation of teaching. For one year after I was laid off from Lehman, I taught at the school as an adjunct, which meant that I wasn't on the staff, wasn't paid much, got no benefits, and had no job security. Clearly, it wasn't an ideal job. Dur-

ing that year I got another position as an associate professor,
this one with Empire State College, a kind of college without
walls within the State University of New York. It was a nice
idea, but it didn't really work for me: I was advising people
on their independent study projects, and I had to get into
my Carina and drive all over the New York area to see them.
So I only stayed there one year.

Then I saw in the Week in Review section of the Sunday
New York Times, where academic jobs are advertised, that a
position was available at Brooklyn College in the department
of health sciences, teaching human sexuality. I said to myself,
This is for me. I went for the interview and got the job. There
was only one catch. I had reached the rank of associate professor at Lehman, and at Brooklyn they only had funding
for an assistant professor. But I badly wanted to continue in
the academic world, so I agreed.

I had to make another sacrifice, too. They asked me,
"Can you teach at eight in the morning?" I did not tell them
that I am not a morning person, that I usually do not even
like to hear the sound of human *speech* until 10:00 A.M. I said,
"Of course." So there I was, on the West Side Highway by
seven, driving to Brooklyn in my Toyota. (I had a second
one by now, a Corolla, which my son Joel still drives. I loved
the name, because it sounded so much like my given name,
Karola.) After one semester I went to the chairman and said,
"If you happen to have a class later in the day . . ." He did
and I felt much better.

I loved it at Brooklyn College. Like Lehman, it was a
division of the City University of New York, which charges
low tuition, and I had in my classroom blacks and Puerto
Ricans and Orthodox Jews and Greeks—the whole spectrum
of life in New York, talking about sex. I thought it was terrific.
My students here were not teachers but people who were
planning to go on to medical or nursing school, or training
to be counselors in hospitals or hold other positions in the
health field. That was a relief to me, because at this point
there were few jobs for teachers, and I didn't like teaching
people to do nonexistent jobs. I also taught a general course
in human sexuality, which was open to all students.

I became a popular teacher: all the places for students

in my courses were filled before the semester started, which was rare. I think that one of the main reasons for this was a characteristic of mine that I later brought to my television show: I didn't ask personal questions. At the time there was a fashionable way of teaching human sexuality to doctors and other professionals, called Sexual Assessment Restructuring, or SAR. Growing out of sensitivity training, it was based on the idea that if you want to talk about and teach human sexuality, first you have to "share" your feelings and your own attitudes and practices.

I never bought that. I always felt that a student's sexual preferences or history was none of my or any of the other students' business. I made it clear that if people were not comfortable talking about themselves, they could always refer to "a friend." (Contrary to what many people think, it is the same on my television show. I *never* ask a guest about his or her sexual practices unless he or she has brought it up first.)

The reason I don't accept this practice is that people don't forget. I always like to tell the story of a physician in his late forties who was involved in one of these sessions at his hospital. The instructor said, "Okay, let's talk about what arouses you." When it came to this doctor's turn, he said, "I'm going to reveal something I've never told anybody else, not even my wife. I get very aroused, with a strong erection, whenever I see a cow." Nobody laughed, nobody said anything, because people are polite. But no one can tell me that his assistant didn't walk into his office the next day, to get his assignments for the week, thinking just one thing: "Moo."

It wasn't just that the students liked me. Research carries more weight in academia than popularity does, and I published three academic papers that year and got a research grant. Every teacher has to be evaluated by faculty members sitting in on the class, and I received fabulous evaluations. So when I went to the school at the end of the year and asked to be promoted back to associate professor, they agreed.

At the end of the next year, just when I thought I was flying, the chairwoman of the department called me in to her office and told me I wouldn't be reappointed the next year. That meant I was fired.

I couldn't believe my ears. Here I was so popular, and

with a growing list of publications, and this woman was letting me go? I knew I couldn't sit back and accept this, that I had to stand up and be counted. I went to the president of the college and told him I had never been fired in my life. He said, "There's nothing I can do." I was in a union and I decided to use my right to appeal to an arbitrator—an independent judge who would decide if the chairwoman had a right to let me go. Normally, arbitration appeals are handled through the union, but this situation was complicated: this woman was not only chairwoman of the department, but was also head of my chapter of the union. If you think about it, this is a contradiction in terms: it means she was both a boss and a representative of the workers. My sense that I shouldn't go through the union was confirmed when I went to union headquarters on Forty-third Street in Manhattan. Everyone there was sympathetic—they kept saying, "This is *so* unfortunate"—but I quickly realized that they would not help me at all. So I hired my own lawyer and went to arbitration myself.

My case created quite a commotion on the Brooklyn College campus. There were lots of articles in the school newspaper, and a petition protesting my firing was signed by more than three thousand students. Among the faculty, with few exceptions, it was a different story. Suddenly, it was as if I had leprosy or was invisible; people completely ignored me as I walked down the halls. One person who had been a good friend refused to return my phone calls. The only possible explanation was that these people knew who had the power over their own jobs and didn't want to offend her.

The arbitration dragged on; my phone was tied up every night as I consulted with my friends on every detail of the situation. Eventually, I spent five thousand dollars of my own money on legal fees. But I didn't mind, because I was sure I was going to win. Against all my lawyer's arguments about what a good job I had done, the other side only had two tangible issues: an incredibly vague complaint that my exams weren't well prepared and a patently untrue statement that I wasn't needed. (If that was the case, then why were my classes so popular, and why were others hired to teach the same courses?) I walked out of the final hearing with no doubt in my mind that I was going to win. I lost. According to the arbitrator, the chairwoman of the department didn't *have* to give her reasons for not reappointing me; such decisions were within her power.

I could have appealed the decision, but I had spent enough money, cried enough tears, lost enough sleep. I know when it's important to stand up and be counted, but I also know when it's important to cut your losses. The one thing I regretted was that the year before I had gone to a party at the woman's house and had given her a beautiful green embroidered tablecloth imported from Portugal. I sorely wanted to call her and demand that tablecloth back. But all my friends told me that would be bad form, so I restrained myself.

Remember I said that I'm like the German doll that bounces back up when you knock it down? After finishing my training with Helen Singer Kaplan at Cornell Medical School, I had stayed on with the title of adjunct associate professor, helping with the training. Periodically, requests would come in asking for someone from the Human Sexuality program to lecture to some group or another. When I was asked if I wanted to give a talk, I always said yes, even on a Saturday night in New Jersey, and even though usually there was no fee and never was it more than twenty-five dollars. I had a strong feeling that if people were willing to listen to me, then it behooved me to go and talk to them. In the beginning I was nervous—about the subject matter, about my English, about my ability to hold their attention. But gradually I got better and more relaxed.

One day a letter came in from a local broadcasters' organization asking if one of us would be willing to address the community-affairs managers of all the radio stations in the New York–New Jersey–Connecticut area on the need for sex education. In those days the FCC had a rule that every radio station had to have a community-affairs manager, and every month they had to hear from different people about community concerns. There was no fee, but as usual I volunteered.

I called Liz Brody, the woman who had signed the letter,

and found out there had been some mistake. She said, "Oh, someone from your group already came and spoke to us a couple of months ago." I asked who it was, she told me, and we started to have a conversation. In the middle of it she changed her mind and finally said, "Why don't you come in anyhow?"

The meeting was at the St. Moritz Hotel in New York. I said to myself, "Aha. I'm going to have all these important people at my disposal for fifteen minutes. They have to be quiet while I can talk. I'm going to float a trial balloon." I talked about the need for sex education, I talked about unwanted pregnancies and all the other problems. Then I said, "You broadcasters are significant others"—the sociological term for someone who can effect change in another person's life. I told them they ought to have a program on the air that talks about these issues. I said not everybody had the luxury of sitting in my class at Brooklyn College. I got a good response, with a lot of interesting questions, but I could not have foreseen what was going to happen next.

A woman named Betty Elam was the community-affairs director at WYNY, an FM station in New York that's owned by NBC. She went back to her office and talked to Mitch Lebe, the director of news for the station and the host of a Sunday morning talk show called *Getting to Know*. She said to him, "There's a terrific sex educator and therapist that I want you to interview on *Getting to Know*." Mitch, who is a nice gentleman and who had just gotten married, said, "No, I don't want to talk about sex." She said, "I'm the boss. Call her."

The minute he started talking to me, he realized that I wasn't interested in putting anyone on the spot, that I wouldn't ask embarrassing questions, so he asked me on the show. We did it, and the same afternoon that we taped the show, Betty Elam called me.

She said, "Mitch Lebe said you can do anything you put your mind to. I have a proposal for you. We have fifteen minutes of free time on Sunday nights between midnight and twelve-fifteen. Do you want your own show?"

This was May 5, 1980.

chapter

8

Betty told me that I would have to come up with two things: a name for the show and theme music. For the music I went to Fred Herman, the cantor of my synagogue in Washington Heights and a good friend. I also happened to mention that I needed a title, and he immediately suggested *Sexually Speaking*. Within an hour he presented me with the theme I still use, a baroque dance with recorder and drum by an anonymous composer. It was perfect. (I still love it. Sometimes at the beginning of the show Susan Brown, my producer, gives me the signal to start, but I keep quiet because I want to listen some more.)

On a Tuesday afternoon I drove down to 30 Rockefeller Plaza, the headquarters of NBC, where the show would be taped to be aired the following Sunday night. On the first show I gave kind of a mini-lecture, just as if I were addressing a community group or a classroom full of students. I talked about contraception, sex therapy, about surveys and recent developments in the field, about different cases, about various sexual myths. From the beginning I was explicit, not to be titillating, but because it is my strong feeling that in talking about sexual matters you should not use euphemisms or mince words. At the end of the fifteen minutes I said, "Listen, if there's anything you people want me to talk about relating to these issues, send me a letter." At the end of the show the station's program director, Maurice Tunick, came up to me and said, "You are going to be the talk of the town." I didn't know about that, but by the third week I had a whole stack of letters, and from then on I devoted the entire show to answering them.

Someone very helpful to me at the beginning of the show was the engineer, Alex Cimaglia. He always listened intently to what I was saying, and his laughter and encouragement told me that something good was happening here. It was especially heartening when he told me that as I was taping the show, everybody at NBC was listening in on closed-circuit radio. It was also good that Alex was a married man, not some young hipster, and his reaction to my subject matter was instructive. Judging by his response, people were ready.

I was paid twenty-five dollars per show. This was actually a money-losing proposition for me, because after I had driven to Manhattan, put my car in a garage, and eaten lunch, I was always out a good deal more than twenty-five dollars. Fred said to me, "You're crazy. Why don't you go down there once a month, tape four shows, and then be able to make a little bit of profit?" I said, "Fred, you stick to your engineering, let me do my business." I knew what I was doing. If someone wrote a letter, they wanted the answer on the air the next Sunday, not a whole month later. I was willing to subsidize my radio career a little bit.

In the beginning, the program did not show up in the ratings, so I had to rely on different ways to see if anyone was listening. One was the volume of letters, which steadily increased from week to week. Another was informal sampling. More and more people I met said they listened to the show. And I knew something was happening when I was in a taxi with a friend one day, and the driver turned around and said, "Dr. Westheimer?" From that moment on, I knew I would never take voice lessons to get rid of my accent. It was my most distinctive feature.

After a year had passed, I said to Betty Elam that I would like to try to answer telephone calls on a live show. I don't know exactly how I got the idea, except maybe from my lifelong addiction to talking on the phone. Despite my affection for that means of communication, I was apprehensive, because I didn't know what kind of people would call in, and I didn't know if I would be able to give answers fast enough, and I would have to push buttons and operate machinery—not my strong suit. But I knew this was the logical next step. Betty agreed and arranged for the program to be expanded to an hour and moved to 10:00 P.M. on Sunday.

It went well from the start. The lights on the switchboard all lit up, and Susan Brown, the producer, started jumping up and down with excitement. I pressed the button like a pro and said "You are on the air," not because I knew it would become my trademark, but because it seemed the natural thing to say. The first caller was a woman who was unable to reach orgasm. I started to talk to her as if she were sitting right next to me, and within five minutes all my apprehensiveness was gone.

I got some help with the technical aspects from Alex the engineer and from Roberta Altman and Steve O'Brien, the newscaster and disk jockey who were on the air before me. (For most of the week WYNY was and is a music station.) They would always stay with me until all the right buttons were pushed and everything was set up correctly. I found I was able to get an immediate grasp of what people were talking about, both on the surface and beneath it, which was heartening but not too surprising considering my experience as a therapist. I found that I was able to use humor, just as I had done in my teaching. Even the words I used a lot in my day-to-day life, such as "terrific," seemed to adapt themselves perfectly to radio. (And when I realized that this word was becoming a trademark, too, I started to rrrreally rrrroll those *rrrr*'s.) I also found that I had an intuitive sense of how to conduct the show, of when a call was running too long or when one was interesting and I should keep the caller on the air. I never let anyone tell me how many minutes each call should last; one station manager did tell me I should speed things up, but I just laughed.

One thing that helped was that I emphasized from the start that I was not a medical doctor, and that I wouldn't do therapy on the air. What I would do was educate and give general advice, the kind that would be given by an aunt—an aunt who's trusted, well educated, well prepared, and willing to speak explicitly. I did not ask questions—or rather I did ask questions, but only ones designed to get information, to get to the real gist of the problem. I did not ask the questions a therapist would ask—"How do you feel about that?" and so forth. Anytime someone called with a serious problem, such as depression or suicidal feelings, I quickly said that they must seek professional help. That message must have gotten through, because from the start few truly desperate people called in. Susan Brown, who's still with both my television and radio shows, screened the calls, and she tells me that there were hardly any crank calls, either. So even though I had a "dump button," for a long time I never had to use it. For the most part, I found that people who called pretty much knew what I was going to say, because it usually was common sense. They called because they wanted reaffirmation: for someone to say, yes, when you are feeling that you should drop this guy, it's correct. The most popular issues that people wanted to talk about were not surprising: premature ejaculation and problems with reaching orgasm.

As of the second or third show, I had a new nickname —Dr. Ruth. This happened completely spontaneously, not through any plotting on my part. A young caller started it because she had a hard time saying "Westheimer," and it immediately caught on. I didn't mind it—and still don't—but I never refer to myself as Dr. Ruth. And I only recently started signing autographs that way, and only if there's a big crowd, with no time to sign my whole name.

In the beginning we still weren't showing up in the ratings, but I got a sense of how well I was doing when WYNY printed up a set of T-shirts that said, "Sex on Sunday? You Bet. Only on WYNY, 'Sexually Speaking,' with Dr. Ruth Westheimer." We told people to write in if they wanted one, and in no time at all we had more than three thousand requests. Many people told me they had "discovered" my show on their way back to New York City after weekends in the country. Idly flipping the car radio dial, they'd stumbled on and were transfixed by this woman with a German accent talking about sex, and from then on they listened to me every Sunday night. I loved the idea of the Long Island Expressway packed with cars returning from the Hamptons—a perfect image of a captive audience—and every one of their radios tuned to me! The knowledge that I had so many ears at my disposal would have been enough for me, but WYNY was nice enough to give me a raise to one hundred dollars a show. I thought this was a fortune.

At about that time, WYNY engaged a public relations firm called Myrna Post Associates to try to get some publicity for the station. One of its employees, a young man named Pierre Lehu, was assigned to me. The minute I met him I liked him. He was warm and sincere, not a typical public relations type, and he was educated: he had an M.B.A. from New York University. Even though Pierre was there to find out how best to publicize me, I, as usual, got him to do most of the talking, and I found out that he was French Catholic, married to a law student, with one child. Not only did I like Pierre, but I knew that, like Alex, he would be a good "normal" person on whom to try out what I was doing. Ever since, Pierre has been my trusted friend and adviser in all of my endeavors.

During that first meeting, Pierre, trying to find a peg on which to hook a publicity campaign, said something to me that stopped me cold: "There are hundreds of sex educators and therapists out there. Tell me, what is there about you that makes you different." For a minute I was stumped. Then I told him that the course I had taught at Brooklyn College on the sexuality of the disabled was the first course in the country of its kind. I was particularly proud of the fact that there were equal numbers of disabled and able-bodied students in the class; they were able to learn from each other.

Pierre thought that was a good enough angle. He put together a packet containing the T-shirt, a cassette tape of some of my shows, and a press release about my class for the disabled and sent it out to the newspapers. Pretty soon it brought results. A reporter from the New York *Daily News* came to see me (he had a degree from Harvard, which naturally impressed me), and he wrote a nice story about my class and my shows.

The *Daily News* has one of the largest circulations of any newspaper in the country, but that was nothing compared to the next article about me. It was in *The New York Times*, which was my Bible: reading it while drinking my coffee was and still is the first thing I do every morning. They sent a very nice reporter named Georgia Dullea to interview me, and on Friday, December 4, 1981, there appeared an article entitled: "A Voice of 'Sexual Literacy.' " You'll excuse me if I quote liberally from it:

> A tiny, middle-aged woman hailed a cab in the East Seventies and, in a heavy German accent, asked to be taken to 30 Rockefeller Plaza. Hearing her voice, the cabby brightened. "Dr. Ruth?"
>
> Yes, it was Dr. Ruth Westheimer, host of the Sunday night radio call-in show, *Sexually Speaking*. They talked about human sexuality, the sex therapist and the cabdriver, and before long the driver allowed as how he had "this friend who has this problem with his wife."
>
> "I see," the sex therapist said, leaning forward in her seat. "Tell me about your 'friend' and his problem."
>
> By the time they reached Rockefeller Plaza, the cabby was smiling, and the switchboard at WYNY-FM was blinking with calls from people with more problems for Dr. Ruth, as everyone calls her. . . .
>
> Dr. Westheimer differs from other so-called psych jockeys in that she specializes in sexual questions. Her warm, frank, and often funny answers are delivered in an idiosyncratic accent that invites but defies mimicry. "It's Grandma Freud," a listener remarked. . . .
>
> During the next hour, the sex therapist talked on the air with more than a dozen male and female callers, ranging in age from twelve and one half to forty-eight years. She dealt with a variety of common con-

cerns, such as those of nonorgasmic women and men with premature ejaculations. She also dealt with some questions that are not so common, stressing, as she always does, that "anything two consenting adults do in the privacy of their own bedroom is all right with me."

What is not all right with her is any sexual activity engaged in under pressure from partners or peers. For example, to an eighteen-year-old virgin whose boyfriend of one month was proposing intercourse, Dr. Ruth gave this advice:

"Don't do it. You know why I'm saying that. Because one month is a very short time. Also, because I hear in your question that he is putting pressure on you. Listen to that inner voice that says you would like to wait. Tell him that Dr. Westheimer told you that you can hug and kiss and neck and pet, but that you are just not ready."

"Wait until I'm ready," the caller echoed.

"Absolutely," Dr. Westheimer declared, "and then only with a good contraceptive."

The wife of an engineer and the mother of two, Dr. Westheimer admits to being a fanatic about contraception. Her attitude was strengthened, she says, by years of working with pregnant teenagers at Planned Parenthood. As a result, almost everyone who calls *Sexually Speaking*—regardless of age, sex, or type of problem—is asked, "Do you have good contraception?" If the answer is no, Dr. Westheimer proceeds to tell the caller where to go for help, adding, "Call me back and let me know how you are doing."

Dr. Westheimer says most of her mail comes from middle-aged people who may be reluctant to discuss their sexual problems on the air. Many calls originate from college campuses, where she is a frequent guest lecturer and something of a cult figure.

At Fordham University recently, the sex therapist, who is four feet seven inches tall, climbed atop a milk crate to tell a crowd of five hundred students amid applause: "What we need today is sexual literacy. We do not need people to go through their whole lives being sexually unhappy." At New York University, a professor of human sexuality has made listening to Dr. Westheimer's show a class assignment.

Not all the calls to *Sexually Speaking* are serious, of course. But all are treated that way. Even when Dr. Westheimer hears giggles in the background, she manages to respond to the question in a manner that is both straightforward and disarming. . . .

I loved everything in that article, except for one thing: Why did Georgia have to quote a caller who referred to me as "*Grandma* Freud"? I would have much preferred "Aunt Freud."

The article had immediate effects. Everybody that I knew called me up to say that they had seen it, and then some people whom I didn't know called. One of them was the editor in chief of New American Library, a big publishing house. She asked me if I was interested in writing a book. As it happened, I was interested in writing *two* books, one about sex, and the other the autobiography that you're reading now. I had sent proposals for both to a number of publishers, never getting even a nibble of interest. An editor from New American Library took me out to lunch, which was a completely new experience for me, and said they wanted me to write the sex guidebook. I thought that was great; I said I was definitely interested, and she said she would be in touch soon. Coming from the academic world, I felt that now the issue was settled; it didn't occur to me to talk to other publishers.

So a few days later when I got a call from Bernard Shir-Cliff, a senior editor at Warner Books, I said, "I'm terribly sorry, but I'm already talking to the people at New American Library." Bernie said, "I know, but we're very interested in you. What are you losing by just coming down and talking to us?" So I said I would.

And Bernie was smart. For that first meeting he had assembled the president of the company, Howard Kaminsky, the publicity staff, the advertising staff, and some other editors, and they were all saying that they wanted to publish my book. It worked. I signed with Warner.

Since I am not a professional writer, and since English is not my first, second, or third language, it was clear that we needed someone to help me with the literary aspects of the book. The people at Warner introduced me to a writer named Harvey Gardner, whom I liked immediately. He was well educated and warm, and he had a twinkle in his eyes. Plus, he looked a little like Alfred Häsler, the writer I had worked so well with in Switzerland. Harvey and I did work together well, and a little more than a year later *Dr. Ruth's Guide to Good Sex* came out.

The *Times* article was also followed by a media barrage. Within three months, there were major articles about me in the *International Herald Tribune*, the London *Times*, the *Soho News* (a New York weekly, now defunct), *Newsweek*, the *Philadelphia Inquirer* (this one written by Judy Bachrach, the daughter of my friends Ruth and Howard Bachrach), and the *Wall Street Journal*. I was particularly happy about the *Wall Street Journal* article because it came out on Friday, so executives would bring the paper home for the weekend and their wives would read the article. Now television jumped on the bandwagon. Again within a couple of months of the *Times* piece, I was on half a dozen local New York programs, the *CBS Evening News* with Dan Rather, *ABC News Nightline* with Ted Koppel, and at the end of February, *Late Night with David Letterman*. All of these interviews were arranged by Pierre, and by this time, he tells me, an average of seventy people a *day* were calling him up to ask about me.

In less than a year I had gone from being an obscure, unemployed college professor to a national celebrity.

What was it about me that struck such a nerve? I honestly don't know. The closest I can come to an answer is that people really had a need to talk about sex, and that suddenly here was a little, matronly woman with a German accent who did just that. I had a nonthreatening image, which helped people talk about things they otherwise wouldn't. And I think my accent helped in two specific ways. First, there was the association with the Viennese Freud, which gave me legitimacy, and second, the fact I was a foreigner let people say, "One of *us* would never talk like that," and therefore they could listen to me without feeling guilty. Plus, I am good!

Whatever the reason, I was suddenly a hot property. And that meant that the sharks started to come to my doorstep. I decided early that I didn't want an agent or a manager. I was in my fifties, not a young starlet, and I didn't want anyone to dictate my life to me. I didn't even have a literary agent to negotiate my contract with Warner, which was highly unusual. So I, with the advice of Pierre, Freddie, and my friends, weighed all the offers myself. I'm the last person in the world to call myself brilliant, but I was brilliant in two things: not permitting anybody to push me, and not being hungry. Others would have snapped up all the offers, but most of them I knew quickly were not for me. I remember one man who wanted to syndicate my radio show across the country—fifty percent for him and fifty percent for me. I didn't give him an answer right away, because I don't make decisions instantaneously, and he left a message on my answering machine that said, "Time is aflying." Right then I knew I would never do business with him, because my time was *not* aflying. I had waited this long, and I could wait a little longer.

One of the projects that came to my door led me to a man who was to become important in my life, John Silberman. I was sent a script for a movie called *Starry Night with Sprinkles*, in which I would play myself; the story was about all the people who called me on the radio over one weekend and the various ways they interconnected. I liked it, but there were some complications in the negotiations. One day I was sitting next to a big-shot producer on an airplane, the setting where I meet a lot of interesting people, and I asked him if he could recommend a good entertainment lawyer. He told me that the best in the business are at Paul, Weiss, Rifkind, Wharton and Garrison and referred me to Robert Montgomery.

I made an appointment, and when I got there Mr. Montgomery said, "Do you mind if my associate John Silberman sits in? He's a big fan of yours." It seems that John had seen my name on Mr. Montgomery's calendar and asked if he could meet me. John handled all of my work from the start, and we became good friends. I liked him not only because he is warm, extremely intelligent, a Harvard Law School graduate, and a superb negotiator, but because I could see that he was really interested in what I was doing. Now he's my main business adviser, and I sometimes take him along on trips—to China, for example, when I went there for *Lifestyles of the Rich and Famous*. John was made a partner in the Paul, Weiss firm several years ago, and at his acceptance dinner he said he's the only person who gets calls *from* Dr. Ruth *asking* for advice. (By the way, although we made a deal with MGM for the film, it was never produced.)

Most of the sharks had plans to syndicate my show, but I was reluctant to leave WYNY. First of all, they had given me my start, and I am a loyal person. I also liked having the NBC imprimatur behind me: with it I wasn't just a little woman who talks about sex, but a little woman who talks about sex on *NBC* radio.

And my loyalty proved to be useful. At one point, some nice people from a radio station in Philadelphia, Sid Mark and Lita Cohen, approached me about doing a similar program there. They proposed that I do a show early Sunday evening, and they would provide a Cadillac to get me to Philadelphia and back to New York in time for my WYNY show.

I went back to the president of NBC radio, Bob Sherman, and said I had to talk to him.

"Bob, let's discuss something. These people in Philadelphia want me to do a program there, and they are going to give me a Cadillac."

"We'll beat them. If it's a Cadillac you want, I'll get you a Cadillac."

"Do it now."

He started to pick up the phone.

"Hold it. I know a Cadillac is a big car, and I have to see if I can reach the gas pedal and the brake."

"Trust me."

I figured there was no reason to stop now. "Bob, one more thing. A car needs a garage."

He got me space in a garage, and he leased me a beautiful Cimarron, which I was able to drive perfectly. The next day I called up Sid and Lita and thanked them, but said it would be too difficult for me to do the show in Philadelphia.

Within a short time of my expanding the show to one hour, I was number one in the ratings. I knew that eventually the show would go nationwide: Larry King had proved it was possible to have a successful national talk show. But I didn't want to rush things—I was in no hurry—and it wasn't until three years had passed that I felt I was ready. I went to Bob Sherman and said, "Okay, now's the time. If you want me, let's syndicate the show. If not, I'll go somewhere else." He said he had been thinking exactly the same thing. John Silberman handled the negotiations, and he arranged it so that I, Ruth Westheimer, all four foot seven of me, am a full partner with NBC in *Sexually Speaking*. The show, which expanded to two hours, was an immediate success, being picked up quickly by more than ninety stations across the country. I loved it when I would pick up the phone and the person on the other end would say she was calling from Seattle or Buffalo. Other than their distance and their new accents (I was beginning to recognize the differences), the people were the same as the New Yorkers who had been calling me for three years—neither less nor more sophisticated, intelligent, or troubled.

This, I suppose, was the real beginning of the Dr. Ruth phenomenon. I was no longer strictly a local celebrity; now, virtually everyone in the country could listen to me on the radio.

I started to be a favorite on college campuses, where people would have "Dr. Ruth" parties, gathering in a dorm room and listening to me on the radio. I know that they laugh at what they hear, but that never bothers me: they're hearing and absorbing good information, and the laughter gives them a good pretext for listening to it. Sometimes a call gets through from one of these parties—I hear giggling in the background and I know it's a hoax. But I answer the question seriously anyway—maybe someone listening out there suffers from that very problem, and he or she deserves an answer.

Out of this popularity came an outpouring of invitations for me to lecture at colleges. (Incidentally, while I am popular with college students, young people do not make up as many of my listeners as some people think. A disproportionate number of the callers to the program are young, but that is because it takes a long time to get through and young people generally have more free time and patience than older people do. Our studies have shown that there's a wide age range to the audience.)

In the beginning I lectured wherever anyone wanted me, even if it was for no money. As I became more popular, I could be a little more selective. I now give about forty-five talks a year, most of them at colleges, with the rest divided between corporate meetings and benefits. I enjoy lecturing —it's an excellent outlet for my pedagogical yearnings—and I'm proud to say that for two years in a row I have been selected Lecturer of the Year by the College Campus Activity Board.

My newfound fame also made me a popular guest on talk shows. At first, I was concerned about going on with Johnny Carson and David Letterman. I thought, "What's a professor such as me doing on this entertainment program?" Then I thought it might be fun. And it is. I first appeared on David Letterman's show and have so far been on it about a dozen times; lately I've been more on the Johnny Carson show and on *The Late Show*. The best thing about all of them is that they've never been disrespectful and always listen carefully to what I have to say. The first time I was supposed to go on *The Late Show*, I was nervous because of Joan Rivers's reputation for being tough and couldn't sleep at all the night before. But when I got on, she listened in rapt attention every time I opened my mouth.

A lot of people ask me what David Letterman is really like, and I honestly have to say that I don't know—not least of all because when a commercial is on, Paul Shaffer's band is blaring so loudly that we cannot have a conversation. But one thing I can say is that I don't think talking about sex makes him quite as embarrassed as he pretends it does.

The one moment on David Letterman's show that every-one remembers is the onion rings story. I told David about the young man who called me up on the radio and commented that his girlfriend liked to toss onion rings on his erect penis. There was of course a big uproar, and David got up and temporarily walked off the stage. Now whenever I'm on the show, before a station break they always show a picture of a plate of onion rings. I recently went to lecture at a college and then went to dinner with some students. Before we had even ordered, the waitress put down plates of onion rings all around.

I love to tell that story, because it does something I've always felt is important. Not only does it teach a lesson—that whatever two consenting adults do in the privacy of their own home is fine—but it teaches it with humor. As the Talmud says, "A lesson taught with humor is a lesson well retained."

People always ask me if it was hard to adjust to fame. And I always say not at all. Because what had changed? Now people talked to me in the streets, which I loved, and reporters asked me questions, which I loved too, and I could always get good tables in restaurants.

The fortunate thing is that I knew enough and had lived long enough not to be overwhelmed by celebrity. I still had the same friends and family and apartment and history and values. I still saw clients in my office on the Upper East Side of Manhattan. (Often people were surprised that my office phone number was listed and that they could easily get an appointment with Dr. Ruth.) And I still taught—I obviously didn't have time for a full-time position, but I was an adjunct professor at West Point, at Adelphi, Marymount, and Mercy colleges, and starting in 1979, with Helen Singer Kaplan's program at Cornell University Medical Center. Last year I realized that I no longer had enough time to do that and stepped down. Fortunately, I got another position, which may even be better for my current purposes, as a "roving" professor in the School of Continuing Education at New York University. I have no classes of my own, but any professor can call me in to speak to his or her class at a relevant time.

And I still took courses, too. Since getting my certificate from Cornell, I have taken courses in behavior therapy at

New York Hospital, in psychoanalytic aspects of sexuality at Columbia University Medical School, and in sexuality and the Jewish tradition at two different synagogues. For my next course, I want to study art history.

My friends and family helped me keep my equanimity. Fred, as usual, took everything calmly, was supportive but certainly not pushy. Some husbands might have resented such sudden fame on the part of a wife, but only if they wanted to be in the limelight themselves—something Fred has absolutely no interest in. He gladly fended for himself when I was not around, and if I had to go away for a weekend, he was glad to go up to Oscawana (which I call his mistress, since he spends all his free time there) to putter around. In the evening, if I have to work or go out, he happily studies or watches reruns of *The Odd Couple*, his favorite television show. He also just went back to school to earn a master's in business administration, which pleased me—not only because it kept him occupied, but because I feel that the more degrees in this family the better.

Inevitably, people started to interview Fred about what it was like to be the husband of Dr. Ruth. And Freddie came up with a stock answer—"The shoemaker's children don't get any shoes." I don't permit him to come to my lectures, because I know that once the question period started he would stand up and say, "Don't listen to her. It's all talk."

One fortunate thing about Dr. Ruth is that it happened after Miriam and Joel had grown up and didn't need my time; I don't see how I could have been both Dr. Ruth and full-time mother. Miriam and Joel both support my new career, but they have their own busy lives to lead.

As it happened, both of them were away from New York when the Dr. Ruth phenomenon really started. In 1981, Joel graduated from Horace Mann, an outstanding private high school in New York. Even when we had little money, we always sent the children to good schools. I served for three years on the school's board as a parent trustee, an experience that taught me a great deal about how boards work and gave Horace Mann a verrry enthusiastic telephone fund-raiser.

Joel applied to and was accepted by Princeton. This, naturally, gave me great pleasure; I loved going down to

Princeton to visit, seeing the ivy-covered walls and standing in the lecture halls. By the spring of his freshman year, my radio show had started to catch on, and I was invited to give a lecture at the college. I told Joel that I wouldn't come if it would embarrass him, but he gave me his blessing. And as it turned out, he stood up and asked the first question: At what age should sex education start? I said, "I won't say from whom this question comes," which got a good laugh, and then gave my answer: Like it or not, sex education starts the moment a baby is born, because that is when attitudes about sexuality begin to be transmitted.

Along with a mechanical aptitude, Joel had inherited some musical genes from Fred the harmonica player, and by the time he was at Princeton he and a friend named Michael had formed a folk duo and were performing in coffeehouses. One time when I went down to see him play, they premiered a funny song called "Jewish Mother Blues," one of whose lines was, "I've got a mother who talks about certain things on the air." At Princeton graduations there is a tradition called the senior sing-in: all the seniors gather together outside and sing. At Joel's graduation, everybody recognized me and started applauding. The master of ceremonies handed me the microphone and asked for a song from me; I explained that I couldn't carry a tune and asked them to sing *me* a love song. Before they did, the students made all their parents, the fathers in three-piece suits and the mothers in prim dresses, shout in unison one word: contraception.

One of my most moving memories of Joel's years at Princeton came when he acted in a play called *The Warsaw Ghetto Uprising* by Susan Nanus, based on the memoirs of Jack Eisner. He played a boy killed by the Nazis, and he spoke to the audience as if from the afterlife. He said that he was proud to have been one of the partisans, but what made him proudest of all was the fact that he did not cry. This moved me so because the same thing had always been so important to me: never to cry.

Miriam was even farther away when my ship came in. As I said, I raised both my children with an emphasis on Zionism and idealism—I didn't want them to be a Jewish American prince and princess. They both went to Zionist summer camps that were modeled on kibbutzim—which meant a lot of work and no pay for the counselors. With Miriam, the message really came through. After she graduated from Barnard in 1978, with both a bachelor's degree and a master's in teaching English as a second language, she announced that she was going to Israel to live. I knew it was coming—I had *encouraged* it—and I knew I couldn't try to dissuade her, but still I felt lonely and a little bit abandoned. It hit me especially hard because ever since I lost my parents I have always found separations extremely difficult: whenever I'm at an airport or train station and see two people saying good-bye, even total strangers, I get choked up. So I cried a lot saying good-bye to Miriam. But I didn't try to stop her.

She stayed on a kibbutz for a while, then joined the army, which brought back memories of machine guns, sentinels, and shrapnel. I was scared for her, but proud, too. Every year she would come here or we would visit her there—one year I went to the ceremony celebrating the end of her basic training. One time when she came back, she heard people talking about "Dr. Ruth" and had no idea who that was; I quickly explained to her. The message came through clearer when I was able, with just one phone call, to get tickets to what at the time was the hottest show on Broadway, Harvey Fierstein's *Torch Song Trilogy*; afterward we went to Sardi's and had a drink with Harvey Fierstein and Estelle Getty, one of the stars. Miriam said to me, "You know, it's not bad to have a famous mother."

In the fall of 1984 I got Miriam back. That September she had visited for the High Holy Days, then gone back to Israel. A month or so later I got a call from Joel Einleger, a young man she had been seeing romantically for about a year. Miriam and I had both known him a much longer time—he had taught my son Joel Jewish history. When Miriam returned to Israel, she and Joel corresponded, talked many hours on the phone, and finally decided that Miriam would return to New York to give the relationship a real chance. Joel surprised Miriam with a visit to help pack and say good-byes. Upon his return Joel called me and said he had tickets to see Stephen Sondheim's musical *Sunday in the*

Park with George, which at that time was the hottest show in New York. I asked how he had gotten the tickets; he said a friend owed him a favor. I told him that of course Freddie and I would go, and he said we would meet beforehand at a restaurant in Greenwich Village. As we were eating, Miriam walked in and announced that she and Joel were getting engaged and were going to live in New York! Some people later told them that they shouldn't have done that, that Fred or I might have had a heart attack. But I was so happy that my daughter was back, and happy that I was going to gain such a wonderful son-in-law, that I wouldn't permit myself to have one. (Besides his other virtues, Joel is the best six-foot hugger in the city of New York.) I threw a big engagement party for them at the Washington Heights Young Men's and Young Women's Hebrew Association. I chose that setting because I wanted to show where my roots are, and that you can have an elegant party in Washington Heights. I have also been on the Board of Directors of the YM&YWHA of Washington Heights since 1970. Then, on June 22, 1986, they were married in a beautiful ceremony at the Water Club in New York. Walking down the aisle with Miriam, I was both sad and exhilarated, but afterward, while I was dancing for four hours, I was only exhilarated. As with Joel's Bar Mitzvah ten years earlier, I had only one regret—that my parents couldn't be there to share the joy.

Needless to say, not all of the attention I had started to get was favorable. I discovered to my surprise that just saying "Dr. Ruth" seemed to guarantee a giggle. Lee Iacocca, in discussing whether he would run for president, said that he would take me as a running mate: "I would tell everybody what to do and she would tell them how." Someone wrote that my "warm giggle sounds like a gerbil in heat." Somebody else put me on a list of the dullest people of the year, because I "managed to make sex sound boring." Even evangelist Robert Schuller got into the act. He said, "Not to take anything away from Dr. Ruth, but the authority on love is Jesus Christ." I certainly was not offended; he put me in good company! I suppose some kind of milestone was reached when I became the subject of a *New Yorker* cartoon. It showed a middle-aged man watching television while a woman, obviously his wife, talked on the phone: "We've tuned in to someone named Dr. Ruth, but we don't know what to make of it."

And *everybody*—including newspaper writers, some of whom called me Doktah Roos, Dogtah Roos, and Doctah Vooth—thought they could imitate the way I talk. Johnny Carson does a decent imitation, but few of the others do a good job of it. (For one thing, they all seem to think that I pronounce my *w*'s as *v*'s, which I do not.) One night a friend of mine went to a comedy club, and three out of the four comedians who performed did a Dr. Ruth imitation. I know that right now hundreds of people are mimicking me at parties all over the country. This never bothered me; I even had Mary Gross, who did an excellent imitation of me on *Saturday Night Live*, as a guest on my show. I'm a good sport about it all because I know that most of the jokes are in good taste and are good-natured, and that they carry my message—that contraception is important, that it's okay to talk about sex.

As for more serious criticism, the fact is that there was amazingly little of it from the start. I get some hate mail, but very little, and when people talk to me on the street, there are a thousand who tell me what a wonderful job I'm doing to every one who says I shouldn't talk about such things on television. (For those people I have a stock answer: "I'm an educator, not a missionary. If you don't like what you're hearing, please move your dial.") Even with all my talk about contraception, I have not had significant negative reaction from Catholics; as I've said, I've counseled premarriage seminars along with my friend Father Finbarr Corr. And in all my lectures, which have taken me to the Bible Belt, to Utah (the stronghold of Mormons), and to every other part of the country, there have been only two incidents.

Once, when I was scheduled to speak at the University of Oklahoma, I was told that a man who was running for governor but was far behind in the race had been trying to get some publicity by starting a campaign to stop my appearance. I called the vice-chancellor of the university and told him that if it would be better for him that I didn't come,

I would tear up the contract. He said no, it's a freedom-of-speech issue. So I came. Before I did, I read up on my critic, found out that he planned to attend my lecture and interrupt me and make a citizen's arrest on me for lewd and immoral behavior. I even found out where he was going to sit—in the front row, naturally.

When it came time to give the lecture, I made it so interesting that the guy actually forgot to interrupt me! During the talk, I kept looking at him out of the corner of my eye; he was sitting there with his mouth hanging open. After the lecture I called for questions and he stood up without even raising his hand and said to me, "Do you believe in Jesus Christ?" Before I could answer, a student said, "Sit down! She's Jewish," and the entire hall started to applaud. The guy was still standing, and he said, "Do you know what the Bible says about homosexuality?" I quoted the passage in Hebrew, and then he started to ask another question, but I said, "Excuse me, but other people want to ask questions." I finished the question-and-answer session and right afterward he came up on the stage and tried to make a citizen's arrest on me. The security people escorted him out before he could do it, but still it was not to my liking. It reminded me of Nazi Germany.

The other incident took place in Charlotte, North Carolina, where a fundamentalist group was planning demonstrations against me. Nothing happened—especially when it turned out that the counter demonstration in *favor* of me was much, much bigger. But I was still a little bit afraid, especially when I turned on the local news after arriving in town and saw that the Ku Klux Klan had been marching in town. It had nothing to do with me, but seeing them go around with their white hoods over their heads worried me all the same. So after I gave the lecture (without incident), when the university asked if I wanted the plainclothes policeman assigned to me to stay overnight in my duplex hotel room, I said yes. (I made sure to call his wife beforehand to make sure it was all right with her.) That night, he told me about his life and how he had gotten into police work, and I told him about my experiences in the Haganah, and it was 3:00 A.M. before we got to sleep.

It was a little more upsetting to me when my professional colleagues criticized me. Actually, while I know there must be some grumbling about me out there (much of it, I have to say, stemming from jealousy), I never experienced much of it directly. Still, what there was of it hurt; as you know, what I want most of all is to be liked, and criticism, especially when it comes from my colleagues, really stings.

The most dramatic incident occurred about three years ago, when I addressed the American Orthopsychiatric Association meeting in Boston. During the question period I got some hostile questions—from psychologists who also write columns and do radio shows, and one (I later found out) from the husband of one of them. The woman, in a shrieking voice, criticized me for doing therapy on the air. My answer was that I don't do therapy on the air—all I can do is educate. A man who I later learned was her husband stood up and said, "Six months ago you said on your radio show, 'It's wonderful to open the door to your husband naked.' How can you defend saying something like that over the air?" I said, "This does not sound like something I would have said. But if I did, I would expect my colleagues to call me the next day and say, 'Dr. Westheimer, you made a terrible mistake,' and then if it were true, I would go on the air the very next day and apologize." So he had to sit down, too.

Since then, the American Psychological Association has participated with *USA Today* in a special program whereby people could call in and receive advice over the phone. Coming from the biggest organization in my field, that truly was a vindication of what I do. I also feel good about the fact that no one, ever, has come forward and accused me of making a bad mistake over the air. Until that day comes, the saying about sticks, stones, and bone fractures will be my motto when it comes to criticism.

One day before the radio show went national, Susan Brown called me and said, "Ruth, guess who wants to have lunch with you? Fred Silverman!"

"Who?"

Susan, who has worked with me from the start of my

radio career, is always cheerful—full of energy and loyal. She quickly informed me that this was the former chairman of NBC, a very, very famous man in broadcasting, now running his own independent television production and distribution company. By this time I knew that if a big shot wants to have lunch with you, you should have lunch, so I agreed to see him. He took me to a fancy restaurant, and he explained how he was coming home from the airport on a Sunday night and stumbled on my radio show. He had never heard of me before and had been fascinated by the show. Would I be interested in doing television? I said of course I would. He said he wanted to fly me out to California so I could "look over" a producer. Now, I understood very well that what he really meant was that the producer would be looking *me* over, but I didn't say anything.

A couple of weeks later, a limousine picked me up at my apartment and drove me to the airport, where I flew first-class to Los Angeles, where a limousine picked me up and drove me to the meeting. Not bad. The producer must have liked what he saw because we quickly reached an agreement to shoot a pilot for a syndicated show. I still didn't want a manager, but during the negotiations for the pilot I realized that I needed an agent of some kind for a project such as this. Fred Silverman would tell me one thing, his business manager the opposite thing, and I was completely confused. So I went to Lee Stevens, the head of the William Morris Agency, who had been after me for some time to sign with them. I said, "Lee, you can be my agent on certain conditions. I will pay you a commission for the business you bring my way, but I do not want to be 'exclusive' with you or anybody else, and I never want you to pressure me into doing something I don't want to do." Lee agreed, and that's still our arrangement. It's worked out fine for me, and I think for them, too.

We ironed out the deal, and shortly afterward shot a pilot for a syndicated television show in the studio of Channel 5, a New York station. I was outfitted in a beautiful wardrobe designed by a famous Hollywood designer, which I was surprised to find out that I loved; I had always proudly described myself as the worst-dressed professor in New York. There was also a beautiful set. Clearly, Fred Silverman was used to doing things in a first-class way. But the lavishness of the production was the main problem with the pilot. While a lot of stations, including Channel 5, liked the show, it was just too expensive an enterprise, and not enough of them committed to it to make going into production worthwhile.

The same day that Fred Silverman told me he couldn't sell the show, I went to see the general manager of Channel 5, Bob O'Connor, and said to him, "Look, you wanted to take that show but couldn't because it was too expensive. Let's do our own local show right here and do it on a shoestring." And he said okay.

So, like Mickey Rooney and Judy Garland in one of the movies I saw in Heiden, we put on a show. The format was an extension of my radio show—I took calls, but now also interviewed prominent guests and talked to people in a studio audience. We were on in the morning, and we did quite well in the ratings. Another show had to move to a different time slot because of us. At the end of our thirteen-week run, the station told me they'd be signing us up for another thirteen weeks. We had a party and I danced as never before. Two days later, John Van Soosten and Paul Noble, executives at Channel 5, called me in to talk to them. The night before I had gone to Gracie Mansion and met Mayor Koch for the first time, and I thought that's what they wanted to talk about. So I walked in excited and bubbly. The first thing they said was, "Sit down." Then I knew they didn't want to talk about my dinner with the mayor. They said that their parent company in Boston had sent word down that my show was to be taken off the air.

Remember when I said that I know when to stand up and fight and when to cut my losses? Well, this was a time for loss-cutting. I could tell that canceling the show was their final decision, and there was nothing I could do about it. What I did do was turn around and ask them a question they didn't expect: Could I buy the shows I had already done? Now, I had made a thousand dollars a week, for a total of $13,000 from doing those shows; to sell the tapes and the rights back to me, they wanted $8,000. I immediately said yes. I wanted the shows for two reasons. First, I know that television people don't keep things forever, that they would eventually erase the shows, and I wanted to be able to show them to my grandchildren. The second reason should be familiar to anyone who's read this far in this book: I save everything.

The Channel 5 show probably could not be considered a success by many measures, but the experience I got doing it came in handy a couple of years later. Late in 1984 I heard through William Morris that a woman from the Lifetime cable network named Mickey Dwyer wanted to have breakfast with me to discuss my doing a cable TV show. I am not a breakfast person: I like to sit quietly with my piece of bread, my coffee, and my *New York Times* and plan my day. I like quiet around me; I don't even like Freddie's talking. But for television I made a sacrifice and had breakfast with Mickey Dwyer.

The result was *Good Sex! with Dr. Ruth Westheimer*, which premiered in September 1984. (The original title was *Good Sex with Dr. Ruth Westheimer* but the people at *TV Guide* magazine felt that this had undesirable implications; the exclamation point was added to appease them.) It was similar to the Channel 5 show, with interviews and call-ins, but there were a couple of important differences. I wanted a cohost, a *male* cohost, so that women could listen to me and look at him. Of the dozens of tapes and résumés I saw, one caught my eye—an Italian guy from Philadelphia who had graduated from Temple University and then gone to Brandeis to study acting before becoming a host of a magazine show in Philadelphia and a talk show in Baltimore. I said to myself, "Any Catholic who goes to a Jewish university to study acting is for me." So I had lunch with Larry Angelo, and as soon as we started talking, I said, "Don't send me anybody else— he is the one for me."

My initial instincts about Larry were confirmed a couple of weeks after the show premiered, when he accompanied me to a lecture at Yale. On the way up in the limousine, we read the poems of Goethe together—Larry in English, I in German. The end of that wonderful day was when Larry and I were serenaded in Mory's by the Whiffenpoofs.

Someone at Lifetime had an interesting idea for the

show—to show on the air what goes on in a sex therapist's office. I liked the idea from the start, but with one caveat: I said that my "clients" on the show could not be real people with real problems. Because, let's say a woman came on who had been molested at age twelve by her favorite uncle. I ask her about herself, and we talk about it on television, and after seven minutes I say, "Thank you very much. I'm sure many women out there had similar experiences." And then I say good-bye. Who is going to pick up the pieces? So we agreed that I would consult with the show's writers, come up with case histories based on fact, and then present them to actors and actresses who would bring them to life.

I was a natural, if I do say so myself. I didn't have any stage fright—certainly much less than when I address a convention of doctors. From the start people told me I had an instinctive sense for where the camera was; I was so good when we had to tape promotional announcements and other prerecorded material that I got a new nickname, "One Take" Westheimer. When you think of it, what we did on that program was quite daring. "Talking heads" shows are often criticized as boring, but when I answered phone calls, the viewer often only saw my *listening* head. But no one complained. I think viewers sense how wrapped up I am in the call, and that is transmitted to them.

The show did well right from the start. I can't take complete credit for that, because in an important way we were in the right place at the right time. We went on cable television at a time when cable was the only place where we could do such explicit material, and at a time when cable was taking off. Cable helped me, but I helped cable, too: television critics have said that I was the first star to emerge from the medium. Anyway, before long we could be seen in twenty-five million homes, all across the country.

The show led to a quantum leap in visibility. I could sense it on my various travels—many more people recognized me—but I also received scientific confirmation. I never knew that such a thing existed, but a friend of mine did a "data base search" on me, a computer technique that lets you find out how often a certain name or phrase has been mentioned in various publications. He found that in his sample of three big-city newspapers, I was mentioned a total of only three times in 1984. But in 1985, after the show had gone on the air, I was mentioned forty-seven times. The figure was up to ninety-three by 1986. (The interesting thing about 1986 was the number of times I was referred to simply as "Dr. Ruth," without my last name—forty-two, as opposed to just twelve in 1985. I had clearly become a household word.)

And this new level of fame led to a multitude of new offers. First of all, I wrote two more books: *First Love* in 1985, and *Dr. Ruth's Guide for Married Lovers* in 1986.

(*First Love* is the book with the famous mistake. For those not familiar with what I'm talking about: On December 31, 1985, my publisher got a call from a librarian in Ramsey, New Jersey, who said she liked the book but couldn't put it on the shelves because there was a mistake on page 195. When my editor called me, I looked, and she was absolutely right: because of a typographical error, a passage about when it is possible to have intercourse with much less chance of pregnancy read, "The safe times are the week before and the week of ovulation." This, of course, is the *unsafe* time. We sent out a press release saying we were going to recall the book, almost like a car with faulty brakes. The original book had a white cover, and Warner issued a new, corrected one with a red cover; people could turn in their old book for a new one. Few did—I think they held on to the ones with the mistake as a collector's item. Luckily—or unluckily—for me, there was no news in the world on December 31, 1985, so it seemed that every newspaper and magazine in the country printed a story about my mistake. Naturally, headline writers had a field day. There was "Don't Follow the Doctor's Orders" and "Edition Could Cause Addition" and "Sex & the Single Typo" and "Dr. Ruth Sings the Rhythm & Blues" and "Best of Times Really the Worst of Times"—I didn't think one mistake could call forth so many puns. My favorite quip was the one in *Time* magazine, which said that the new cover was red because I was blushing. The one thing I was proud of was that from the start I didn't try to make excuses—I said that I was responsible for the mistake because my name was on the book.)

It seemed that every day there was a new offer for a new project. I put out a "Good Sex" board game and a "Terrific Sex" videocassette. On Valentine's Day of 1986 I started a syndicated advice column that now appears in newspapers all over the country. And I did commercials—for Lifestyle condoms, Smith-Corona typewriters, a department store, the Brasserie restaurant in New York, Dr Pepper soda, and chocolate mousse. I went to China with *Lifestyles of the Rich and Famous*. Maybe the strangest thing I did was appear on *Hollywood Squares*, a television show I had never even heard of until I was asked to be a "square." I appeared with Steve Allen and Mary Lou Retton and Richard Simmons and Lou Rawls. I had a fabulous time. I especially liked the fact that the contestants chose me more than any other celebrity, and that one of them won a car because he picked me.

Some people criticized me for becoming too commercial, but that struck me as absurd. All of these things are *fun*, not to mention well-paying. And maybe because all of this happened to me later in life, overexposure is not my biggest worry. I also think that the sheer number of things that I do sometimes gives the false impression that I'll do *anything*. I have said no to far more proposals than I have said yes to. If something strikes me as in poor taste, or in any way questionable, I will immediately refuse it. (I also immediately say no if anyone uses one or both of two terms—"concept" and "exclusivity.") I turned down a commercial for Cadillacs because I do not believe that everyone who listens to me can afford a Cadillac. I have said no to many Dr. Ruth dolls. I said no to the idea of Dr. Ruth Therapy Clinics all over the country. I said no to an idea for a Dr. Ruth telephone line, where people could call up and get prerecorded advice. I said no to Dr. Ruth popcorn. I said no to quite a few plays and movies. I said no to a rap song. I said no to a perfume ad. I am also careful about how the projects I do agree to are carried out. In the commercial for Smith-Corona, they originally wanted me to misspell "psychology." I said I wasn't doing that, because if I didn't know how to spell psychology I shouldn't be in the business.

∞∞∞∞∞∞

On a Friday morning two years ago I got a phone call from someone at William Morris, asking if I wanted to read a movie script by Daniel Vigne. I had loved Vigne's film *The Return of Martin Guerre*, so I said of course. They messengered it over. I had a busy weekend, so by Monday morning I still hadn't read it. Monday morning at ten the phone rang. It was Daniel Vigne saying, "Where are you?"

"What do you mean, where am I? I'm at home."

"You're supposed to be at my hotel talking to me."

I quickly opened the envelope, and sure enough the note said I was supposed to meet with him at nine-thirty on Monday. Unfortunately, I had to leave to catch a plane to give a lecture. I apologized and he agreed he could wait until Wednesday. I read the script on the plane and loved it. The part I would play was a wealthy American woman, the head of a charitable foundation, who becomes interested in the work of a French archaeologist, to be played by Gérard Depardieu, who discovers the remains of the first woman on earth. Why is she interested? Because the foundation head is short, and this evidence shows the prehistoric woman to be both short and well proportioned. (Obviously, the part was perfect for me, especially since I speak French, but I later found out that when Daniel Vigne wrote it, he didn't know that I existed.)

When I went to the hotel on Wednesday, someone on the staff said that the part had already been given to someone else. I said, "Okay, I'd like to meet Daniel Vigne anyway." So I went upstairs. When I walked into his room, he took one look at me and said excitedly, "Let's do it." I don't think he knew that in my line of work "Let's do it" has a very specific meaning; it turned out that all he wanted me to do was read a scene from the script. He liked what he heard, and right away he offered me the part. I never told Daniel Vigne what I had heard about the other woman; one of my good qualities is that I know when to keep my mouth shut. (I later found out that the part had originally been written for Linda Hunt, who for some reason couldn't do it, and when I found out that I was taking the place of an Oscar winner, I was delighted.)

The executive producer said, "We'll be filming for two months in Paris." I said, "Hold it. I can't go to Paris for two months—I have a TV show and a radio show to do and clients to see in my office. Why don't you fly me back and forth? If it's too expensive, I will pay for one or two of the flights myself." They had never heard that before and were so dumbfounded that they agreed to it. (It ended up, as I suspected it would, that I never had to pay my own way.)

I loved making the movie, although I have to admit that I had trouble with one thing—remembering my lines. I missed cue cards. But it was wonderful to have the chance to work with Daniel Vigne and with Gérard Depardieu and Michel Aumont, the stars of the film. The most exciting thing was filming one scene in a lecture hall in the Sorbonne, just down the hall from a room where I had flunked an exam thirty years before, and just a block or so away from the third-floor walk-up apartment where I had lived with no hot water and no toilet.

After the filming was over we went to celebrate at a little discotheque in the village of Peranz. There was a moving electronic sign in the disco, and it said welcome to the "Cinéaste [director] Daniel Vigne et l'actrice Ruth Westheimer." It didn't say Dr. Ruth Westheimer or Dr. Ruth, but the *actress* Ruth Westheimer. I wanted to stay there dancing the whole night. I had to get up at six the next morning, so I only stayed until four. The whole time, I was constantly peeking at the sign to see my name come around again.

The movie was not a gigantic hit, either with the critics or at the box office. But I was apparently not too bad in it, because the National Society of Theater Owners awarded me their Star of Tomorrow Award, given annually to the most promising newcomer to the screen. (A past winner was Dustin Hoffman.) And since then I have starred in an episode for Shelley Duvall's *Tall Tales* series on cable TV. Michael York played Ponce de León, and I played a strange old woman he asks for the elixir of youth. I loved it!

As I keep saying, I like to take risks. I have a little brass snail that I keep on a table on the set of my television show. It reminds me that when a snail stays inside its house, it's safe, but it doesn't move. Only by sticking its neck out does it make any progress.

I took a big risk last year when the company that syndicates my newspaper column, King Features, gave me the opportunity to try a syndicated television program on broadcast television. This meant leaving the security of cable for a market where the vast majority of proposed shows don't make it to the air, and most of those that do don't last a year. But it also offered the chance to be seen by millions more people. I took the leap, and *Ask Dr. Ruth* went on the air in January of 1987.

As I write this, we've just finished taping the last of 130 shows. In many ways the show was a success. We were picked up in most of the country—often by network affiliates. We got good ratings in New York, Los Angeles, and San Francisco, and despite the fact that we got taken off the air in Boston (apparently after some advertisers put pressure on the station that was carrying the show), in no city was there any concerted effort or campaign to get us off the air. In some cities, though, the ratings just weren't very good. I'm not sure whether this was because we were competing with reruns of the cable show, because I refused to sensationalize the subject, or because broadcast TV just wasn't ready for Dr. Ruth. In any case, last spring I decided to cut my losses on syndicated television and accept an offer from Lifetime to revive the cable show. It returned to the air in the fall of 1987.

I left broadcast TV with no regrets, but with a three-word prediction—I shall return.

chapter

9

A Week in the Life of Dr. Ruth

Monday. I like Monday mornings because I permit myself to sleep a little late. My radio show runs on Sunday from ten to midnight, and I never get home till after one, so I deserve it. This morning, when I wake up, Joel and Fred are just about to leave for work. (Joel graduated from Princeton last year and for a time lived in his old bedroom, working as a part-time consultant for a computer company and also trying to succeed as a folk musician. I think it's wonderful that he is still involved in music, although I may have different thoughts if he tries to make a career out of it. Last summer he moved into his own five-flight walk-up. Luckily it's just a few blocks away in Washington Heights, so he can still bring his laundry home.)

It's just as well that I'm alone. In the morning I like to get up slowly and mooch around. Fred likes music and the news in the morning, and I like complete silence. It takes me a while to collect myself. I like to get some orange juice, a cup of coffee, and some toast, read *The New York Times*, and look out the window at the view.

The view. Every limousine driver who takes me up to

Washington Heights—which is a half dozen miles and at least half an hour from midtown Manhattan—asks me why I don't get an apartment on Park Avenue. The view is my best answer. Out of the living room window of our tenth-floor apartment, in which we have lived for twenty-two years, we have a beautiful and unobstructed view of the George Washington Bridge, the Hudson River, and the New Jersey Palisades beyond. From Joel's bedroom, you can see the Cloisters and Fort Tryon Park, just north of us, and if you crane your neck you can see the Tappan Zee Bridge. I could stare out the window for hours, watching the sun play on the water, or following the progress of a little tugboat as it tools its way up the river.

But there are other reasons why I stay in Washington Heights. Even though the neighborhood has deteriorated somewhat in recent years, it's still the center of the German Jewish community in America, as it has been since the thirties. When I first moved here, I said, "How wonderful. Here is a place where everyone comes from the same background as I do," and I still haven't lost that feeling. I can go for a walk in Fort Tryon Park, where the wonderful Cloisters museum of medieval art is located, and hear the sound of German being spoken, and it takes me back to Frankfurt. When people talk to me in the neighborhood, as they often do, they usually say they are proud of me, which may seem surprising considering that I talk explicitly about sex and that German Jews are conservative. But it was the same way with Henry Kissinger, who also comes from this neighborhood. They may not have agreed with his views, but they were proud that someone with his background, with an *accent*, could make it to the highest echelons of influence and society.

By the way, I have a good piece of gossip for you if that's what you're interested in: Fred and I sleep in separate bedrooms. The reason is that he snores. He claims that snoring is an atavistic instinct of men, that it comes from the time when they had to protect women from wild animals. I ask him how many wild animals he's seen around the apartment lately. The only reason I bring this up is to show that a good sex life is certainly possible even if two people sleep in separate bedrooms. I don't believe in that nonsense that couples have to do everything together, and that definitely includes spending the entire night in the same bed.

This is actually kind of an early Monday morning for me. At quarter to nine I'm picked up by a limousine. The driver is Sasha, a Russian émigré who's become a good friend of mine, so good that Miriam invited him to her wedding. The other driver I've become close with is Terry, who's a minister with the Jehovah's Witnesses. He gave me all the literature they use on family life.

Sasha takes me downtown to Superdupe Studio, a production facility on Madison Avenue, where we're met by Pierre Lehu and Hank Sagman, from Grey Advertising. I'm there to do a test for a commercial spot for Stove Top Stuffing. On my way in to tape the spot, I meet the president of the studio. Joel's birthday is coming up, so I arrange for him to get some studio time at a sharply reduced rate as a present.

We do a few takes of the audio; it's a variation on the line "variety is the spice of life," which naturally takes on extra implications considering that I am the speaker. This reminds me of a Dr Pepper commercial I did, where someone called me up on the radio and I said, "Do you use . . ." Then I paused, and everyone expected me to say "contraceptives," but what I really said was "ice cubes." I liked that so much that I immediately got the copywriter a raise and a promotion.

After I made that commercial, I happened to be giving a speech in Dallas, which is where Dr Pepper's headquarters are located. I arranged to have a lunch with some bigwigs of the company because I wanted to do a content analysis, with my sociologist friend Lou Lieberman, of the letters written to me asking for advice, and we needed ten thousand dollars to fund the project. I figured that Dr Pepper would be the perfect company to provide the money. When I was picked up in a limousine by the director of public relations and another vice president, they both said that they loved the idea, but that it would be hard to get it by the comptroller of the company, a man who was very, very tight with money—it was tough even getting paper clips from him! I said let me talk to him. And when we had lunch, I gave an impassioned description of my idea, and the controller said yes. I was so happy that I made everybody at the lunch—about fifteen people—applaud him. He said they'd mail me the check, but I said I wanted to go home with it in my hands. So two hours later, he personally brought it to my hotel room.

That's the kind of thing I call a Westheimer maneuver. The concept was invented about two years ago, when one day at the studio someone said, "Mayor Koch wants to talk to you." I immediately went to the phone, and the mayor said, "Will you do me a favor? Will you participate in the Inner Circle?" This is the annual show where journalists take the mayor and other politicians to task. I said, "Of course." At the time *Little Shop of Horrors* was a big hit Off Broadway, and the idea for my skit was that the mayor would be swallowed by a giant man-eating plant like the one in that musical, and I would rescue him by performing the Heimlich maneuver on the plant. But when we started to rehearse we discovered that I couldn't get my arms all the way around the plant! Then I came up with the bright idea that instead of hugging the plant, I would caress it. It worked beautifully. The plant was played by a black man with a big booming voice who kept saying "More, more . . ." until he spit the mayor out, almost as if the plant were having an orgasm.

How I got funding for the closed-captioning of my television show is another example of the Westheimer maneuver. The idea came from my son, Joel. The sister of a Princeton friend of his is deaf, and Joel learned sign language in order to communicate with her; his junior thesis was a computer program called "How to Teach Sign Language. " I knew that hearing-impaired people have a lot of problems because of prejudice and misunderstandings resulting from their disability, so I wanted my program to be closed-captioned (a process by which viewers with a special device can see subtitles on their TV screens). However, having a show closed-captioned costs money, and the company that produced the show was not willing to put out that much. One day I was on an airplane, and the man sitting next to me was the president of a big corporation. I won't say which one because they wish to remain anonymous. I explained enthusiastically about closed-captioning, and the upshot was that the company gave me a check for a hundred thousand dollars—which, added to Joel's check for a hundred dollars, provided all we needed. You can expect some more Westheimer maneuvers in the near future.

After recording the commercial, we go down the hall to take some photographs, also as part of the Stove Top Stuffing proposal. I'm met by Bill and Marga Kunreuther, Vincent Facchino, and Nicole Harris. Along with Pierre, I suppose they constitute my—for want of a better word—entourage. Bill makes all my appointments for my private practice and takes care of my checkbook. Marga, his wife, is in charge of my wardrobe. (Marga is a distant cousin of Fred's, and Bill knew Fred, and their twenty-year marriage was initiated by me. But it took me three dinner parties before they started dating.) Vincent, who does my hair, takes such good care of me that people say I look younger every year. He introduced me to Nicole, a superb makeup artist who was once a dancer in the Folies-Bergère and who has the most magnificent legs of anyone I know.

It turns out that the photographer is an acquaintance of mine, and he's delighted to see me. He takes pictures for about an hour, and Pierre has the bright idea of using one of them on the cover of this book. Also, in a typical Westheimer maneuver, I asked Miriam's friend Elaine (who, with her husband, Richard, worked with me for several years helping to answer letters) and her brand-new baby to come during the shoot so they can have photos taken.

After the photo session we all have lunch—which includes Stove Top Stuffing. I call Hank Sagman's boss at Grey Advertising to say what a great job he's doing.

At 2:00 P.M., Sasha takes me to the King Features office, where there is a production meeting with the staff of my television show. It's important to me that the staff not see me as some big television star who only swoops in Wednesday and Thursday, when the show is taped, so I make it a point to go to the Monday meeting whenever I can. I also like to stock up on books and tapes concerning my guests for the week, so I can study them at home. If the people aren't from my field or world-famous, I usually haven't heard of them.

At five, Sasha takes me to the airport. I can't go home first because Washington Heights is too far away. I suppose that's the main drawback of living there—once I'm gone for the day, I'm gone. There's no going back home to change. That's why I'm always schlepping so many things.

I have a 6:15 flight to Miami, where I'm to give a speech the next day. I'm met at the Fontainebleau Hotel by a group of ladies from the group that invited me. I talk with them for a few minutes, then excuse myself and go to my room. I know that if I sat down with them, I would be there for two hours. When I first started traveling around the country, not only would I never do such a thing as excusing myself from a group of people and leaving, I would actively seek them out. Someone from the group I was addressing would pick me up at the airport, and I would talk all the way to the hotel. I am constitutionally unable to be quiet and close my eyes when another person is there, even though I know that the other person does not need to be entertained. Then, at the hotel, I would poke around to see what was happening. I have learned that I can't spread myself so thin. I request a taxi or limousine, and when I arrive at the hotel, I go up to my room and order room service.

That's what I do tonight. Staying in hotel rooms on the road is also the only time I get to watch television—a field I really should know something about, considering that by some strange course of events I wound up in it. But it doesn't really help—I don't seem able to retain any of it. I go to sleep to the sounds of a show whose name I have forgotten by morning.

Tuesday. I wake up at 8:00 A.M. so that I can get a massage, a procedure I have recently become addicted to. I also have my hair done and my face made up, because I know the ladies I'm about to speak to will be elegant. Sure enough, when I arrive at the hall, just outside Miami, I get some compliments on my appearance. People are usually surprised at how good I look. I don't know why; it may be because my image as "Grandma Freud" makes them think of me as old and dowdy. In any case, I consider this one of the greatest things that's happened to me in my life. A friend even told me that someone asked her if I had had a face-lift! I loved it. The other thing that (tactless) people frequently say about my appearance is that they knew I was short, but didn't realize I was *this* short. I guess that makes sense, since on television I'm usually sitting down. It doesn't bother me— if I haven't adjusted to my height by now, I never will. The only time I feel a little sad is when I walk by a mother and child, and the kid says something like, "Mommy, did you see that midget?"

After the greetings are over, I give a press conference— usually I insist that the press conference be *after* my speech, so people can hear what I have to say before asking me questions. But I'm told that people here have early deadlines, so I make an exception. A reporter asks me about my background—"Is it true that you survived a concentration camp?" I politely tell her that I do not talk about these things, that if she wants to find out about them she can read my autobiography. It is simply too painful for me to casually discuss those experiences and then go on to talk about sex. It's not only reporters. Some people think that I don't mind talking about the Holocaust at a dinner party, as just one more topic of conversation. That is not for me.

I have a similar problem once the luncheon—which is a benefit for the United Jewish Appeal—begins. The first speaker is an expert on terrorism. I find what he has to say upsetting; I don't know how I'm going to follow him by talking about sexuality and excitement and pleasure. What I do is take a deep breath, a big sip of coffee, and tell myself this is something I have to do. It usually works.

I always start my lectures in roughly the same way. After being introduced—and I insist that the person introducing me list my academic and clinical qualifications—I say something like, "I'm sure that the walls of this famous institution have never heard words like ejaculation, lubrication, penis, vagina, orgasm, masturbation." That immediately disarms the audience; if they were on edge, waiting for explicit language, they can relax. I've put forward what it is I'll talk about. Then I disarm potential critics even more by explaining my philosophy of sex: that it can't be taken in isolation, that it has to be taken in the context of love, caring, companionship, and family. All of a sudden I am no longer the wild radical preaching free love; I am saying something close to what they themselves believe. I go on to say that people come from different religions and ethnic groups and have different sets of moral beliefs and values; if they want to stick to those, no one should tell them otherwise. I certainly believe all of these things, but anyone who's read this book this far knows that I say them for another reason as well: having people like and approve of me is very, very important to me.

But the next thing I say causes some disagreement. I say it anyway, whether I'm speaking in Miami or at Boston College, with Jesuits on its board, or at the University of Utah, with a majority of Mormons. I say I'm not a theologian or a politician but an educator, and from where I stand, abortion must remain legal. I go on to dispel various myths about sex, raise such issues as contraception, homosexuality, sexually transmitted diseases, and AIDS, talk about recent research findings, and discuss interesting questions I've gotten on my radio and TV shows.

I have talked in this book about teachable moments and about the importance of humor, and nowhere do these come into play more than in my lectures. For example, when I talk about masturbation and the myth that it causes hair to grow in the palm of the hand, I usually make a joke. At Stanford, I looked around and said, "You people at Stanford seem to be a very controlled group, because at the Harvard Law School I saw plenty of lawyers looking down at their hands." That brought down the house.

I also tell a story from the radio show that David Letterman does *not* know yet. A man who was about to get married said he and his fiancée had been living together, but he wanted to do something to make the wedding night different from all other nights. What could he do? For a split second I was speechless because I had never had that question before. But I know that you cannot have dead air on the radio, so I did what any good professor does—repeated the question in different words. Finally something came to me. I said, "After the ceremony and after the party, when you are finally alone, let her go to the bathroom first and into bed. When you come out of the bathroom, do not wear pajamas, wear only a tie and a top hat." I thought that was pretty good, but he topped me by saying, "Where should I put the top hat?"

Obviously I adapt my talk according to the group I'm addressing. If it's businessmen, I talk about the issue of sex in the media and about problems they may be having with their children. If it's students, I talk about the importance of contraception. Since the Miami group is predominantly Jewish, I weave into my usual lecture some elements of a talk I give called "Sexuality and the Jewish Tradition." It's a fascinating topic, and I owe a lot of my knowledge of it to Rabbi Leonard Kravitz, who is a professor at Hebrew Union College and an authority on Maimonides and with whom I wrote a paper on the subject, and to Rabbi Selig Salkowitz. Rabbi Kravitz showed me the passage in the Midrash (the compilation of Jewish laws and learning) saying that it's the obligation of the man to provide not only food and shelter for his wife, but also sexual satisfaction. The Midrash says that if you bring your wife to satisfaction before you ejaculate, you will have a son—in those days, an outcome greatly desired. The Jewish tradition actually has quite a lot to say about sex, most of it remarkably in keeping with today's thinking. It says that a man can have sex with his wife as he pleases, even from behind. (This doesn't refer to anal intercourse, but to entering the vagina from behind.) There's even support for my stand on abortion, because the Jewish tradition says that a child is only considered a soul once he or she is born. The Talmud occasionally gets quite poetic on the subject, as when it says that sex is a foretaste of the world to come. (I also like to quote a line from the Scriptures: "If a man marries a short woman, he must bend down and talk to her.")

I usually speak for about an hour, then devote another hour to answering questions. (Because some people are understandably embarrassed about asking intimate questions in a hall filled with strangers, there's some arrangement whereby they can write the questions down and leave them in a box outside the door.) Today, as is almost always the case when the audience is mainly female, most of the questions have to do with how to make your sex life more interesting—in particular the problem of the husband who wants to go to sleep immediately after sex. I say that, like so many other things, it is a question of sexual literacy. The husbands have to be taught that for a woman the resolution period is longer; they have to be introduced to the concept of afterplay, which is really nothing more than foreplay for the *next* sexual encounter.

Apparently the women like what they hear, because over one and a half million dollars is raised for the UJA.

I take an evening flight to New York, and from the airport I go to dinner with Larry Angelo. We discuss the show, and afterward he takes me home.

Wednesday. At 9:30 A.M. Terry picks me up to take me to Bellevue Hospital, a large city hospital connected with New York University, where every other week or so I do psychosexual therapy in the department of geriatrics. About three years ago I decided I needed to know more about geriatric sexuality, not only because it's a neglected field, but because it will be an increasingly important one as America gets older. Besides, as *I* get older, the topic takes on increasing relevance for me! I find the work satisfying, and not only because I am affiliated with the department of medicine—I'm working with doctors, and knowing me you can imagine how good that makes me feel. But it's also a valuable experience because Bellevue is almost a mirror to what is happening in the city. It seems that every time I walk in there, there's a prisoner being brought in or some emergency going on. Going there, I see how important it is to keep my eyes and ears open to the society around me and not get swept up in my own little protected world.

Today I see one individual and one couple. The most important thing I've learned at Bellevue is that you *can* teach older people new tricks. My clients there, many of whom are on Medicaid and are referred to me by their doctor or social worker, range from intelligent to simple people, from the very poor to the comfortably middle class. But no matter how old they are or what their background, I've found that if a couple are in good health and have a basically good relationship, one can do psychosexual therapy.

At 12:30 P.M. Terry drives me to the studio. I have my hair and makeup done, and I have a manicure. It's all paid for by the program, which means that I myself pay half, since I am equal partners with King Features in *Ask Dr. Ruth*. It's worth it. Every other week I have a pedicure, too, and this I pay for all by myself, since you can't see my feet on TV. Even so, I won't give it up; it's one of the luxuries that I relish while they're still here. (Besides, getting pedicures has made me a better dancer, hiker, and skier.)

I used to be amused by the atmosphere at television studios. Everybody would be walking around, always holding a cup of coffee, always with their sweaters slung over their shoulders Ivy League-style (even if they didn't go to Ivy League colleges). I didn't understand how they ever got any work done! I used to make so many comments to John Lollos, my producer, about "you television people" that he started talking about "you psychology people." Now I understand that there is work and there is work; television people are "creative," and even when they're walking around and drinking coffee, they're thinking of how to improve the show.

As with Larry, as soon as I met John Lollos, I knew he was the right man for me. He was experienced in television, but I could immediately see that he also had an intellect: he had done a great deal of theatrical directing, and he is an accomplished musician. I also liked his enthusiasm about doing a show that is both entertaining and educational. And it didn't hurt that he is good-looking, with a dashing snow-white beard (that makes up for the lack of hair on the top of his head). As usual, my instincts were right: it's been and continues to be a wonderful relationship.

Our routine is to tape three shows each on Wednesday and Thursday. It makes for two long and hectic days—but it's much better now with the thirty-minute syndicated show than when we were doing the hour-long cable show, three of which we also put on in a day. For today's shows, the guests are to be a journalist who's written a book on changing sex practices in the wake of AIDS; Allan Carr, the producer of *La Cage aux Folles*; and the comedian Jackie Mason. They all go well, especially Jackie Mason. I always find him funny, maybe because he's a former rabbi, or maybe just because he's of my generation. I have a lot of young comedians on the show, and while I like them and laugh to be polite, sometimes I really don't understand what they're talking about.

I also like Allan Carr. He has been on my show before, and he arranged for me to appear at a big fund-raiser for AIDS held last year at the Metropolitan Opera. The only problem was, all the other people appearing were enter-tainers—and I had no act. Allan arranged for all of the cast members of *La Cage* to make a magnificent coat for me in the Folies Bergère style of that show; each one of them sign-ed it. At the benefit, I simply put on the coat and posed. It was a Sunday night, so I had to leave to do my radio show, but I was able to get back to the Met in time for the finale. I loved it.

In the three years or so I've done television shows, I've had an amazing variety of guests, and a list of some of them will dispel the notion some people have that I only talk about sex: Beverly Sills, Nell Carter, Cyndi Lauper, Milton Berle, George Burns, Joan Rivers, David Brenner, Mayor Koch, Ben Vereen, Willard Scott, Erica Jong, Bianca Jagger, Martin Scorcese, Jerry Lewis, Joel Grey, and a rock star named Ted Nugent.

In the beginning, interviewing made me nervous and I made some gaffes that Larry and John won't let me forget. I called Henry Mancini Henry Man*KEE*nee, and the film di-rector Louis Malle—whose name I should have been ex-pected to know how to pronounce, as rhyming with doll, given the years I spent in France—I called Louis Mall*AY*. I called Henny Youngman Hen*ry* Youngman and said that I knew his most famous joke: "Please take my wife." (After-ward the staff said that the right way to tell it was "Take my wife . . . please.") My worst gaffe came when a flamboyant impressionist named Wayland Flowers was on. I was supposed to ask his dummy, which is called Madame, if she planned to get married. But by mistake I asked Wayland Flowers. John Lollos later told me that up in the control room he said, "Is that woman *blind*?"

But I've also had some memorable interviews. Probably the most difficult was with a sex surrogate. Just having her on was stretching the limits of our show, because, for one thing, sex surrogacy was illegal at the time. (Now, with the increased threat of sexually transmitted diseases, I would never recommend that someone see a sex surrogate, and I would not have one on the show.) But, after looking at films of the work of this woman (who happened to be beautiful), we decided that it was an important subject that should be addressed and we scheduled her for a program that was to be broadcast live. When she showed up we were in for a terrible shock: she had been in a bad car accident that had horribly disfigured one side of her face. I knew I had to just ignore it, because it was irrelevant to the subject at hand, and somehow I managed to pull it off.

I think my favorite interview was the one with Burt Reynolds. It was hard to get him to come—I even sent him flowers, something I had never done before and have never done since. When he finally agreed to appear, I was so nervous that I couldn't sleep the night before the show; the next day I made such a fuss over Burt that Larry later told me he had never felt so ignored in his whole life. Despite all that, it was a great interview. True to my policy of never asking personal questions, I didn't ask Burt any, and he rewarded me by saying some very intimate things. This was not long after he had broken up with Sally Field, and he said pointedly, "If you have someone you love, don't let her slip through your fingers." He also told a story he had never told anyone before. He said once he was waiting for a plane in the Chicago airport, and he noticed that a beautiful woman was reading the same book he was. They started talking, had a drink, and ended up spending the night together. He's never heard from her since. He said he thinks about the encounter often, how wonderful it was, and he wonders about the woman. Say she's watching television with her children when a Burt Reynolds movie comes on— what does she think?

On each of the three shows being taped today there's a therapy session, and they all go fine, too. I'm impressed by the actress in one of them, about a woman who had had an abortion and later regretted it; the actress actually cried. Doing simulated therapy several days a week has made me a better actress, but it's also made me a better therapist—as has answering telephone calls on radio and television. The therapy sessions have to be completed in seven minutes, and time can't be wasted in the phone calls. This sense of urgency has carried over to my practice, making me a better history-taker, a better sexual-status examiner, and also more concise. Like all professors, I had a tendency to repeat myself in order to make a point. You simply cannot do that on television, and now I tend to do it less in the rest of my professional life. (I reserve the right to repeat myself when I want to get something through to Fred.)

After the shows are completed I tape two promotional spots. The copy for the first one reads: "Dave and Maddie, Maddie and Dave, Sam and Dave. Two and a half years of foreplay. By act of Congress . . . I don't mean act of Congress. . . . You know what I mean." *I* had no idea what I meant, either. It was a promo for an episode of the TV show *Moonlighting* in which the characters played by Cybill Shepherd and Bruce Willis would finally sleep together. I agreed to do it for union scale, not only because it sounded like fun, but because the spot was to be shown during the telecast of the Oscars, an enviable place to be seen. (Later, the producer, Glen Caron, sent me a telegram that read, "I owe you one." I'm not sure how I'll ask for the payback—maybe a dual appearance of Willis and Shepherd on my show.)

Then I do a spot, for which I will be paid nothing, that will be broadcast over the Armed Forces Network. The message is that people should use condoms. It came about because the network picked up the television show, but—owing to my feelings about both contraception and American soldiers—I would have done it even if they hadn't. I was in Washington a few months before to appear at a special meeting at the National Academy of Sciences (itself a great honor), and while I was there, I went to the Pentagon to finalize the arrangement for the spot. I was thrilled to be walking down those halls, a general on either side of me, especially because of the fact that it is thanks to the American army that I am alive. Today, before reading the announcement, I change the copy. Initially it began "I love you, Armed Forces," but that didn't sit right with me. I changed it to "I respect you."

Afterward, the whole staff has fortune cookies and champagne to celebrate the rating we got in New York for our Saturday night (or rather Sunday morning) one A.M. show—an impressive 6.9, which was more than half the rating of *Saturday Night Live*, the show that comes on before us on WNBC, the NBC affiliate in New York. Jim Percelay, the bursar with King Features, ordered fortune cookies that read, "Nielsen [instead of Confucius—get it?] say 6.9."

The champagne party tonight is not a one-time thing: I make it a point that anytime there's a milestone such as this, we celebrate it. One time I had ice cream carts full of Dove Bars sent to the studios. Even if there isn't something to celebrate, I insist that there be a transition period after the show. Because when the lights go off, it happens so suddenly—there's no dimming. I think this is something that should be taught to all aspiring actors and actresses: the difficulty is going instantaneously from a situation where the spotlight is on you and everyone is paying attention to you, to one in which it is dark and all you have to do is go home. So, to prolong the sense of importance and excitement and to promote an esprit de corps, after each taping we have wine and cheese.

After the champagne and fortune cookies, Pierre, John Lollos, Larry, and I go to a verrrry fashionable New York nightclub called Nell's, where there is a party for Catherine Deneuve, who is launching a new perfume. It's a fancy party; among the other guests are Lauren Bacall, Pat Lawford, and Tammy Grimes. I find it hard to see what's going on, so on Pierre's advice, I stand on the sofa. (*The Village Voice*, a weekly newspaper in New York, later wrote that I was "leaping" around.) I meet Catherine Deneuve, who tells me in French that she has seen my movie *twice* and admires me. I try to get her to agree to come on the show, but she seems reluctant. I have no better luck with Raquel Welch. Don't these women know that I won't ask personal questions? But something good does come out of the party: I meet the president of Avon, who promises me a lot of freebies. A freebie, as anyone who knows me knows, is a small promotional item—a hat, tote bag, umbrella, radio, bar of soap, T-shirt, bottle of perfume, or anything else on which is printed the name of a radio station, television show, company, movie, hotel, or some other enterprise, and which is given away free. I'm not sure why—as I said before, I think it may have to do with the fact that my father sold small items for a living—but I love them. I insist on getting one whenever they are being given out. After I get back to my apartment, I put my booty into a big box, from which I select appropriate freebies to give to people who come to visit me.

I also get to dance at the party, which gives me great pleasure. I had always thought I was too short to dance, but lately I've discovered that I can do it and I love it. I go to discos and have a great time—although I never bring Fred. Last year we went to a party at a disco and Fred walked around the whole time with his hands over his ears. So Larry or John Silberman comes and dances with me.

After the party we go to a restaurant called B. Smith's for dinner. I am too short for the table, so I ask for a Manhattan telephone directory to sit on. I consider it a major accomplishment to be able to make this request; I always used to be too embarrassed to do it. Now, if it's a small town, I can even ask for *three* phone books! Clearly one of the major benefits of becoming Dr. Ruth is a significant increase in my chutzpah. The meal is delicious. I have mushroom soup (this was recommended to me in the ladies' room) and fish, and I finish it all, which is unusual for me.

The tradition of going out to eat with John and Larry started while we were doing the cable show. In those days the last show was over at 11:00 P.M., and after the wine and cheese we went to the Brasserie, which besides being an excellent restaurant is open twenty-four hours a day. These dinners have become an important part of the week for me. We talk about the show and we talk about other things, and we really cemented our relationship. Tonight as usual a limousine drops John off at his fancy red sports car, in which he'll drive to New Jersey, then goes to my apartment. Larry walks me upstairs, and then the same thing happens that happened when I was a little girl in Frankfurt and couldn't say good-bye to my friend Mathilde. After he walks me to my apartment, I am so reluctant to say good-bye that I walk *him* back down to the car.

Thursday. At 10:00 A.M. Terry picks me up and takes me to the Helmsley Palace Hotel, where I have my hair and makeup done by Vincent and Nicole. Then we walk over to the Waldorf, where I speak on the issue of AIDS and the media at a luncheon meeting of the International Radio and Television Society.

I have some definite thoughts about AIDS. Most important, it's imperative that we stop wasting our time blaming one group or another and get on with the critical business of finding a cure. Until we do, however, I always emphasize that there is no such thing as "safe sex," only "saf*er* sex." I recommend the use of condoms, but I know that they aren't one hundred percent effective. And when homosexuals call me on the radio, worried that they might get AIDS, I tell them that I can't answer specific medical questions—for that they have to call an AIDS hotline—but my advice is that if they don't have a steady partner, they should confine their sexual activity to masturbation. The situation is that dangerous.

As I say, the only answer to the problem lies in finding a cure, and I have donated my time to many AIDS benefits. Last spring I participated in a European-wide conference on the disease in Luxembourg. And I am proud to say that this year I received from the Fund for Human Dignity, a gay association, an award as Educator of the Year.

Sometimes people ask me if I ever get bored with the subject of sex. It should be obvious that I'm far from obsessed with the topic; indeed, people who spend time with me are sometimes surprised to find that in my social life I rarely talk about sex—and I *never* ask people about their sex lives! In fact, I always get suspicious when I meet people who talk inordinately about sex in private conversation; just what impression are they trying so desperately hard to give? But professionally, I still find the subject fascinating. Sex is not like a diet, where the rules are hard and fast; it has all sorts of ramifications and raises questions across a wide range of topics.

Sex relates to fantasy, dreams, the unconscious, the family. It is relevant to politics, religion, psychology, medicine, literature, art, philosophy, history, anthropology, and sociology. And it is an important component in every period of a person's life—from infancy until old age. And so I always say, No, I'm not tired of sex yet and I don't expect to be.

Outside the hotel I sign some autographs. Some people talk about what a silly custom that is—having someone sign her name on a sheet of paper and then keeping it. But I know that the signature is not the real reason for the custom. It's that when I'm signing the autograph, that person has me for ten or fifteen seconds for his or her very own; that experience, that individualized attention, is what they're after. I am happy to provide it. When people ask for my autograph, it's almost as if *I'm* interviewing *them*—I ask their name, whether they're a student, and so on.

Sometimes people on the street want more from me than an autograph. They'll often walk up to me and whisper a problem in my ear and then look at me expectantly. If I can help them in a minute—as I often can—I will.

I've found that I have to do certain things to protect my soul, because if I listened to everybody all the time, I would get sad. I've discovered that people are much less likely to spill their souls to me if someone is with me. They smile, wave, say something—such as they enjoy my program—but they don't ask me questions. So now, if I'm walking somewhere, I try to arrange for a companion—Pierre, John Lollos, John Silberman, Larry, or whomever.

On my way to the car I drop some change into a blind man's cup and say, "There you go." To my amazement he replies, "Thank you, Dr. Ruth."

ooooooooo

Then it's on to the studio, where we tape three more shows. The guests include the comedian Jerry Seinfeld and Peter Ustinov. I'm pleased to see that in the studio audience are two former members of my Brooklyn College class on sex and disability; one of them is blind and the other is confined to a wheelchair.

After the interview, Ustinov—whom I'm thrilled to have on the show in the first place—tells me that he has a satellite dish at his home in Switzerland, and he loves to watch my show. He said that once he watched it with a high-ranking UN official who had come for a visit from Geneva. That impressed me most of all, because when I was a teenager and the UN was just starting, I was a *very* strong believer in it. I thought it would prevent all future wars. (That really was an idealistic time for me. Besides the UN, I was a fervent believer in Zionism, and also Esperanto, then proposed as a new, universal language.)

I always operate on the assumption that Dr. Ruth could be over at any moment—no more autographs, no more pedicures, no more Cadillac El Dorado (last year I upgraded from my Cimarron), no more parties with Catherine Deneuve, no more trips to China and Kenya with Robin Leach. I guess that's part of my refugee mentality. One result of this expectation is that I enjoy these things all the more enthusiastically; but another is that I have not become attached to them. I used to think—like many young people, I suppose— that as long as you weren't starving and there was a roof over your head, money was absolutely unimportant. My attitude has changed to the extent that I realize how nice it is to have some luxury in your life and some security. While I would never gamble with my money or play the stock market, I have made investments, and it's good to know that when my television days are over, I will never have to worry about money. And it's good to be able to give to charity and to be able to take a taxi instead of the subway. I used to agonize over taking taxis because the subway was so much cheaper. No more. But as to money's making a big change in my lifestyle—no way.

In the same way, I have certainly not gotten dependent

on the idea of being a celebrity, and I know I won't have any problem adjusting when I no longer am. What I know I *will* miss is being around the people on the show. It's not just Larry and John. It's also people like Dean Gordon, the six-foot-four floor manager, who used to be a floor manager at the Metropolitan Opera; he's intelligent and attentive, and I love his graceful hand directions, almost like a conductor's. I look at Dean's reactions the way I used to look at Alex's in the old days of the radio show, and when he likes something, I know it's all right. When something strikes him as particularly good, he'll grimace and make sounds as if he were in the throes of sexual rapture. I try hard to keep from laughing, so if you ever see me smile for no particular reason on television, it's probably because of Dean.

At six-thirty a limousine takes me to the airport, where I'm to fly to Washington to speak to the American Ortho-psychiatric Association. By now you probably have the idea that my schedule is pretty hectic. I have to admit that this is a particularly busy week, but I would say I average ten hours of work a day, seven days a week. People frequently ask me how I do it. And I don't really have a good answer for them. Part of it is probably biological—I have had a lot of energy all my life, and I've always had the ability to completely concentrate my attention on the matter at hand, blocking out everything else. But it also has to do with attitude. If there's anything I don't like, it's people who complain, who are bored, who say they are tired—I have no time for that kind of thinking. I believe that if you're healthy, you can be ed-ucated to be energetic, just as you can educate children to be considerate or to love nature. Of course, it also helps that I love what I'm doing.

It also helps that I have the ability to take quick catnaps in the middle of the day at a moment's notice. I take one on the plane to Washington. When I wake up, we're there.

I love going to Washington, and not only because I often tend to do fabulous things there—visiting the Pentagon, going out on the floor of Congress (a representative—who shall remain nameless—snuck me on after I had given a report on the need to reinstitute funds to a UN family planning program), attending dinners of the National Academy of Sciences. It also happens to be the location of my favorite hotel, the Park Hyatt. Its manager is a big fan of mine, and he puts me up in their best suite; it even has a Jacuzzi. It's so fancy that, when I'm ready to go to sleep, I can't figure out how to turn the radio off. So I just close the door of the cabinet that it's in. In the morning I open the door, and there I am on the radio singing the praises of chocolate mousse!

Friday. At the meeting I'm happy to run into Povl Toussieng, a psychiatrist friend of mine with whom I used to do a lot of workshops. I remind Povl that he gave me one of the best pieces of advice I ever got. After I got fired from Brooklyn College, I told him how unhappy I was. He told me *not* to see a psychiatrist—that doing so would dampen my natural enthusiasm. In Washington I ask him if he thinks he was right. He says yes. I think so, too.

The hotel gives me the use of a Mercedes with a Nigerian driver, and that way I am able to see a wonderful Matisse show at the National Gallery of Art before I catch my flight to Kansas City. On the plane I get to talking with my seatmate, a navy officer. It turns out that his wife works for a clothing manufacturer. We talk about the possibility of her working out a deal whereby I get free dresses to wear on my show in return for giving the company credit. I tell him that I'll throw in a free lecture to a ship with five thousand men. He tells me he'll work on it.

I love picking up people on airplanes. Once I sat next to the president of a pharmaceuticals company, and as a result I am now consultant for the company. A few months ago I picked up a woman from Beverly Hills who's a dress designer. Out of that trip I got two gorgeous outfits, one black and one velvet, and also a guest for my television show—her husband, a neurologist at the UCLA hospital, who had some interesting things to say about the importance of the neurologist in sex therapy. Another time I got a guest for the radio show. I met a group of Mormons on a plane, we started to talk, and since it was a Sunday, I invited them to visit the show that night. After talking some more, I found out that one of them was studying for a master's in social work. I asked her to appear on the show to talk about Mormon family life, and it turned out to be a wonderful interview.

One of my most prized pickups was Marvin Traub, the chairman of Bloomingdale's. He was sitting in the row behind me, talking to my seatmate, and obviously did not recognize me. Takeoff was delayed, and while we sat in the Dallas airport (for three hours, it turned out), they turned on the television in the cabin. Who should come on but me! Marvin Traub did a double take, then introduced himself. I got some great freebies out of that encounter.

That night I lecture at Northwest Missouri State University. As at most colleges, I get a great reaction when I walk out—lots of clapping and hooting and hollering. But also as usual, once I start, you can hear a pin drop. I consider this my greatest accomplishment as a lecturer—commanding such rapt attention with a subject that's conducive to giggling and nervous coughing.

I try not to schedule many lectures for Friday evenings, first, because Friday and Saturday are the two nights I try to save for Freddie and friends, and second, because I like to go to synagogue whenever I can. I go because I am still a believing Jew, but also because of the memories. I like to sit and hear the prayers and the melodies I grew up with.

I recently sponsored a lecture at my synagogue in remembrance of November 9, the Kristallnacht. I couldn't attend because I was out of the country, but I was told that the place was as full as it is on Kol Nidre, the night before Yom Kippur. What pleased me especially was hearing that my son Joel went up and lit a candle, in honor of the six million Jews who died at the hands of Hitler, and in special memory of my own family. Then he read a quotation from Heine: "When people begin to burn books, the next thing they'll burn is people." It pleases me no end that, even though I didn't raise Joel and Miriam Orthodox, they still feel such a strong connection to the religion and the people. When my friend Ilse was visiting from Switzerland, she said that Joel told her that once a month he and Miriam have decided to celebrate the Sabbath together—that on Friday night they make a meal and light the candles and say the Sabbath blessings. It's wonderful to know—both for myself and for the sake of my parents—that without my having insisted on it, there is in them something of the Jewish heritage and soul that I have transmitted.

Saturday. On the flight back from Kansas City I work on my column. The procedure is that my collaborator, Harvey Gardner, screens the 250 or so letters we get a week and picks out some to be answered. I dictate the answers, and then he writes them up and sends them back to me for my approval. I mentioned that I persuaded Dr Pepper to fund a study Lou Lieberman wanted to do about the letters. Well, he's finished it, and the results are fascinating. Lou analyzed a sample of about six hundred letters. Here are some of his findings: People wanting help with sexual problems not surprisingly made up the highest proportion of the letters, forty-one percent. Thirteen percent of the letters had to do with self-image and various physical (but not sexual) problems, three percent were from people who had doubts about their own gender identity, and ten percent didn't fit into any of these categories. Two thirds of the letters were from women (but unlike the men's letters, which tended to be about the men themselves, the letters from women tended to be *about* men). Eighty percent of the people wanted advice; only ten percent wanted information. This suggested to Lou and to me that media personalities such as myself have started to fill a role previously taken up by family members, clergymen, and teachers—the simple giving of counsel.

As far as sexual dysfunctions were concerned, the problems most frequently mentioned, at eighteen percent each, were impotence and lack of interest in sex. (The latter letters, interestingly, were almost all written by women.) Fifteen percent were written by women who could not reach orgasm, and eleven percent by men who were preejaculators. One of the more disturbing findings was that a full ten percent of the letters concerned women who regularly experienced pain during intercourse.

∞∞∞∞∞∞

On Saturday at eleven-thirty—having showered and changed at home—I drive down to my office on the Upper East Side of Manhattan. I make sure that the windows of the El Dorado are closed, because one of my great pleasures in life is driving along while singing off-key at the top of my lungs.

From noon to 5:00 P.M. I see clients (I don't call them patients because I'm not a medical doctor). At any given time I'm usually seeing somewhere between twelve and fifteen people. That's a good number for me. I know I would not be as good a therapist if it were my full-time occupation. I simply would not be able to sit eight hours a day, from morning till night, and just listen to other people's problems.

People are often surprised that they can get an appointment with Dr. Ruth, but because the kind of therapy I do is short-term by nature (lasting anywhere from one session to three or four months), there is a big turnover and people can usually get an appointment if they are willing to wait a few weeks. Of course they have to be willing to be flexible, to put up with canceled appointments and occasional sessions in the back seat of a limousine. Sometimes the fact that I'm well-known has a beneficial effect on the therapy: people are excited to be with me, so they want to be good and work hard.

I still find psychosexual therapy a satisfying thing to do. Of course, it has its limitations. It will not overcome physiological problems; some men, for example, are physically unable to get an erection. And it also tends to be futile when there is some other psychopathology at work. In other words, if someone who is clinically depressed comes to see me, or if a couple who does not have a basically good relationship comes—not necessarily a Hollywood type of love affair, but warmth and respect—there is nothing I can do to help. I also have my own boundaries. For example, I would not work with a child molester; I would immediately refer him to a psychiatrist. And despite all that I've said about whatever two consenting people do in the privacy of their bedroom, living room, or kitchen floor being all right, I could not treat a sadomasochistic couple. This is because, as a sex therapist, you have to visualize what they do in their bedroom, and that is something I just could not visualize. And sometimes I turn clients down simply because I don't like them.

But given all those caveats, I am able to help an awful lot of people. What particularly pleases me is when my friends—or sometimes even my children—refer people to me. Here you have a type of treatment that didn't even exist twenty years ago, and now it's improving so many people's lives. Best of all, I am able to live out in some small way my childhood dream of being a doctor.

Lately I've seen quite a few young men who have had homosexual experiences but do not want to live a homosexual lifestyle. My agreeing to work with them does *not* mean that I disapprove of homosexuality; it simply means that I will help them with what they want to achieve. And I have good results.

Once I got a call on the radio from a young man who said he was an Orthodox Jew and was in terrible despair because he only got aroused by looking at pictures of men in magazines. He sounded so miserable that I had him hold on so Susan Brown could give him my office number. I knew that his anxiety must have been especially acute, because Orthodox Judaism comes out strictly against homosexuality. One particular prayer used on the Day of Atonement said that a man who sleeps with another man as if with a woman should be killed. This man did come to see me, and after we talked, I found out that he could also get erections by looking at women. I tried to alleviate his anxiety by saying, "Look, you are bisexual. You don't want to live a homosexual lifestyle, so don't. But don't feel guilty about the thoughts that come into your head." I told him that he should keep his mouth shut and not tell a soul about his homosexual thoughts, and I taught him how to think about men in order to get aroused and then switch and think about women. Not long ago, he got married.

Saturday night, Al Kaplan comes over for dinner. He and Freddie and I have a wonderful time sitting around and talking about old times. I *love* good conversation. I learned about the art of conversation in France, where people could sit around the dinner table for three hours and talk. And I'm particular about what kind of talk it is. I don't like an entire evening of gossip, and I don't like constant joke-telling, and I don't like talking about what errands have to be done when—these things get done anyway, so why waste valuable time talking about them? No, I like conversation about ideas, the kind of conversation that can instantaneously switch from humorous to serious and then go back again. If I could have any kind of life from a different time, I would have the kind of salon Madame de Staël had in nineteenth-century France, where all the writers, painters, and statesmen of the day would come to have intellectual discussions. (Then she would choose whom she wanted to go to bed with.) I suppose having a talk show is the next best thing.

After dinner, Miriam calls. She and her husband, Joel, just bought an apartment in a section of New York called Riverdale—close enough so that I can get there by car in fifteen minutes, and my Joel can visit on his bicycle! She's at Columbia, working toward her doctorate in education, specializing in the topic of how teachers can help each other. Once I was a guest lecturer for a class she was giving, and I was moved when she introduced me as "not only Dr. Ruth, not only my mother, but a master teacher."

Tonight she tells me an interesting story about a class she gave this week on teaching sex education. She borrowed a technique I often use—standing in front of a blackboard at the beginning of the hour and letting the students decide what the topics to be discussed will be. I had once told her that when I did that a long time ago at Lehman College, the one topic that was never mentioned was masturbation. Miriam tells me that the same thing happened with her group this week. For some reason this remains a taboo.

At eleven-thirty we turn on *Saturday Night Live*. Lorne Michaels, the producer, has contacted me about possibly hosting the show. I've never seen it, and I figure it's time to see what all the fuss is about. I don't get most of the jokes.

At one o'clock, sitting in *my* living room, with *my* husband and *my* friend, *my* show comes on. Let me say it one more time—what a country.

∞∞∞∞∞

Sunday. Almost as soon as I get up, I do one of my favorite things of the week. I open the Sunday *New York Times* to The Guide section and look under radio listings, in the part under "Other Highlights." There is the listing for *Sexually Speaking* with Dr. Ruth Westheimer. The first time I was listed, at the very beginning of the show, was wonderful for me—there I was in my Bible, *The New York Times*. Now, seeing it in print every week tells me that the whole thing isn't a dream.

Today I have a special treat. There, in the same section, is a listing announcing that Joel and his partner will be performing Saturday night at a nightclub called the Speakeasy. During the afternoon, he and I take a long walk in the neighborhood. We talk about the two-week trip the whole family (including Miriam and her Joel) is about to take to Israel. It's particularly exciting because this will be the first time in years that Joel Einleger has had Passover with his sister, who lives in Israel.

Back at the apartment I work on this book for a while. I have to admit that if I had known how painful it was going to be back when I was asked to write it, I would have said no. I thought it might prove to be cathartic, but I've found that the painful memories aren't any less painful now that I have written about them.

Then it's time to go downtown to Rockefeller Center— first, to eat dinner at the Sea Grill restaurant, then to do my radio show. Actually, I have to do two two-hour shows tonight—one live and the other taped, to be played next week, when I have to be out of town. (Listeners are told when we'll be taping a show, so we do have callers.)

The radio show was the first appearance of "Dr. Ruth," and I still have a warm feeling for it. Even if I have had an upsetting Sunday, I always walk into the studio with a feeling of excited anticipation, and with a determination to concentrate on the calls for the next two hours.

Tonight's two dozen or so calls are a fairly typical selection. There are questions about vaginal odor, a boyfriend who turns out to be married (I play my record of "I'm Gonna

Wash That Man Right Out of My Hair" for that woman—I always say that I can't do the kind of program I do without my values shining clearly through), contraception, premature ejaculation, how to tell friends about one's homosexuality, and various social and emotional problems. There's a call from a Dr. Ruth party at Ithaca College, with a good question about condoms.

There's also an example of something that happens with increasing frequency on the show. A seventeen-year-old girl calls and (speaking softly because she doesn't want her parents to hear) says that she's involved with a forty-five-year-old man. Her friends and parents want her to give him up, but she loves him. What should she do? I try carefully not to follow my first impulse and respond like a mother—she already has a mother. So I try to be compassionate, to listen closely, and then I finally advise her to talk to someone outside the family, someone who is not emotionally involved, like a guidance counselor at school. Later in the show we get three more calls about her problem, including one from a woman who was in the exact same situation and is grateful that her parents made her break up with the man. I love it that my show can be a means to a dialogue among the listeners.

At home after the show I draw myself a bubble bath and relax. I think about how fortunate I am to be able to sit in a bubble bath, and also to have so many fascinating things to do. I think that there's nothing in my life that I would change. Well, maybe a couple of things. I would like Joel's being married before too long, and I would like to have grandchildren. I would like to write at least one scholarly book. I am still only an associate professor at NYU, and I know that to be a full professor I have to publish an academic book. I should have one soon, the book I am now working on with Lou Lieberman.

And one more thing. Dancing shoes. Despite the massages and the pedicures, my feet still hurt after I dance. I think I am going to treat myself to a pair of special, custom-made shoes, so that I can dance all night and my feet will feel as if I just slept for eight hours. Because now that I've started dancing, I don't ever want to stop.

epilogue

1986

About a year ago I went to Frankfurt. It wasn't the first time I had been back; Fred's parents moved there about ten years ago when Fred's father retired and the political situation wasn't good in Portugal. They didn't want to come to this country because they didn't speak the language, so they went back to Germany. Fred's father died shortly after the move, but we've visited his mother there many times.

But for me this trip was different. Writing this autobiography is the end of a chapter in my life, and I knew that even though I might pass through Frankfurt again, I would never again visit my parents' house.

Also, this time I went back home as "Dr. Ruth," the well-known sex therapist; my books had been published in Germany, and my column is printed in newspapers there. I was hailed and interviewed wherever I went. More than once radio interviewers referred to me as "a German who lives in America." I would immediately interrupt: "I am not a German. I am an American of German Jewish descent."

There was one other difference about this trip. For the first time I permitted myself to be sad.

I took a taxi to Wiesenfeld, the home of my grandparents. The trip was only an hour and a half—and I had always thought of Wiesenfeld as a world away. The village looked the same, except that now the streets were paved. I was happy to find that there are still geese there—I took a picture of what must be the great-great-grandchildren of the ones I set free. I knocked on the door of my grandparents' former house and explained who I was. Not surprisingly, the people living there—Germans—had never heard of my family, but they invited me in and let me look around. The house looked the same—except that it was smaller, of course, and there were photographs on all the walls of Jesus and the Pope!

I went to the synagogue in town. It was burned and in disrepair and used only as a storage shed. I went inside and saw that there were some loose tiles on the floor that looked old. I took one with me. I suppose I was breaking German law, but I can live with that.

In Frankfurt I went to the new cemetery, because Fred's father, whom I liked very much, is buried there, and I went to the old cemetery, the one where my grandmother used to go and visit Paul Ehrlich's grave. There is a grave there with an inscription saying that this is for all the victims of the Nazis who didn't have proper burials. I stood before it for several minutes.

I went to the house where I grew up. Brahmsstrasse looked exactly the same, and so did the hospital across the street, and the little park. The amazing thing was that, fifty years later, even bicycles on the street seemed to be parked in the same position. But, of course, so much had changed. I knocked on the door of my house, and it was the same story—no one knew of my family, and there were pictures of Jesus on the wall hung by the current owners, who were Yugoslavian. I recognized the hallway where I used to roller-skate, the place where I used to push a baby carriage back and forth, the room where my grandmother slept, and my little sleeping alcove.

There was one more place I had to go. The railroad station. The station itself was rebuilt some time ago, so it looked nothing like it did when I got on that train to Switzerland nearly fifty years ago. In the rebuilding, the placement of some streets was changed, so as hard as I tried, I couldn't even find the spot where my mother and grandmother had run to, following the train, and stood waving good-bye. It didn't really matter. The image has been clear and bright in my mind for five decades, and I didn't need a reminder. I will carry it with me for the rest of my life.